The Life & Death of
MOZART

MICHAEL LEVEY

The Life & Death of
MOZART

STEIN AND DAY/*Publishers*/New York

First STEIN AND DAY PAPERBACK edition 1972

First published in 1971
Copyright © 1971 Michael Levey
Library of Congress Catalog Card No. 70-163451
All rights reserved
Printed in the United States of America
Stein and Day/*Publishers*/7 East 48 Street, New York, N.Y. 10017
ISBN 0-8128-1530-0

CONTENTS

LIST OF ILLUSTRATIONS

The author and publishers gratefully acknowledge
permission to reproduce the photographs listed above.

for BRIGID

'wir leben durch die Lieb' allein'

TH E greateſt Prodigy that Europe, or that even Human Nature has to boaſt of, is, without Contradiction, the little German Boy WOLFGANG MOZART :

THE PUBLIC ADVERTISER (London), 9 July 1765

'*But thy eternal summer shall not fade*'

Introduction

Mozart is dead. Whatever remains unclear about his life, personality and career, as well as his art, that much is certain. The banal fact, which virtually defines what we mean by the past, has a particular importance in connection with Mozart. Not only is there that always poignant irony of any artist's death to contrast with the continuing life – not, however, guaranteed immortality – of his art, but in Mozart's case there is the prematureness of the death. It came to a most dreadful struggle at the end between the dying man and the still creating musician: 'The last thing he did was to try and mouth the sound of the timpani in his Requiem.' No later over-coloured gloss, this is the testimony of his sister-in-law, an eye-witness at his bedside on the evening of 4 December 1791. More than a quarter of a century after, when she wrote these words about Mozart's last hours, she added, 'I can hear it still'.

A biography of Mozart may well begin by stressing his death rather than his birth, recalling the drab, sad, obscure circumstances at the close of a life which had opened with unparalleled brilliance and fame. Probably no one has ever been as early famous and established, by talent alone, as was the eight-year-old Mozart, who had travelled and composed, played and been applauded in Munich, Vienna, Paris and London. At eight he already had two years' experience as a successful public performer. He had played before the Empress Maria Theresia, had dined with Louis xv and had dedicated his Opus 3 ('Six Sonatas for the Harpsichord') to Queen Charlotte of England. Yet he spent his last years in desperate poverty; he was still performer as well as composer, but his last concerts were financially unsuccessful, and his penultimate opera, *La Clemenza di Tito*, something of an imperial fiasco. In fact, he never regained the enormous success he had enjoyed – in so far as he had enjoyed it – as a child. From the point of view of his career, Mozart's life was really a steady decline. When his widow spoke of the happiest time of his life, she did not pretend it was in the years of being married to her but in a brief earlier period, 'whilst in Munich during which he wrote *Idomeneo* . . .'. That had been in 1780-1, when he was aged twenty-five, before any of his most famous operas were written.

Few people doubted that Mozart was gifted, but when he had ceased to astonish as a prodigy not many of them could be bothered positively to encourage the display of his gifts. Nobody came forward to patronize him firmly – several of the most powerful patrons indeed politely declining. Nor is this because of the social situation for musicians at the period; the careers of Gluck and Haydn – to name only two familiar composers – show none of the struggles which finally overwhelmed even Mozart's vitality. Society might claim that it did not push Mozart into the water; but it found little place for him in its boat, and watched indifferently while he drowned.

Mozart's own intense awareness of death is the strongest reason of all for emphasizing this strand, which begins by glinting through the texture of some of his music and gradually is uncovered as something grave – graven, too, a stone guest at the feast – which is palpably, physically present and, like the stone guest, becomes inescapable. Yet as it is uncovered, it is seen to be less frightening in reality than it had appeared in prospect. 'This true, best friend of mankind,' was Mozart's description of death in a letter of 1787 to his ailing father: a letter written out of profound feelings which accompanied urgent hopes for him to be better soon. Like his son, Leopold Mozart had been initiated as a mason and could understand when Mozart went on to write, '. . . it [death] is the *key* to our true happiness . . . I never lie down in bed without thinking that perhaps I, young as I am, will not survive another day – and yet nobody who knows me could say that in company I was morose or sad.' This also provides a sharp warning to posterity not to claim that Mozart never thought about death just because none of his contemporaries found his spirits anything but remarkably lively. Only since the Romantic period – when hearts were worn on the sleeve, usually attached by heavy black crape – has it seemed unexpected that the artist should gracefully conceal his private woes from the public, or a paradox that in his apparently light-hearted creations there should lurk some sombre notes.

As long as Mozart's century was misunderstood, it was inevitable that Mozart and his music should be misunderstood. Even nowadays, not much justice is done to the facts of Mozart's literateness, intelligence and sardonic wit. It probably still surprises people that his widow should have spoken of his fondness for reading and of his being well acquainted with Shakespeare (in translation). The Pelican selection of his letters (1956) has a preface which tells us that they show 'in many ways an ordinary boy, youth and man . . .'. This is doubtless reaction against romanticized views of genius as extraordinary in every way, but it is quite untrue. Even if no music whatsoever by Mozart survived, his letters would still be one of the most remarkable testimonies written by any artist at any period – the more remarkable, incidentally, because Mozart never set up to be an artist in words. His letters, however, no more show him as 'ordinary' – whatever that may mean in terms of human personality – than do those of Byron or Keats show them to be ordinary. Mozart's letters are actually a good deal closer to Byron's than to Keats's: practical, vivid with reported dialogue and acutely sharp comments on friends and acquaintances, but with nothing much to say about natural scenery. Nor does Mozart generally write regarding his theories about music – any more than does Byron about poetry – but he almost unwittingly reveals the power of his imagination, along with a narrative gift closely related to his absorbing concern with opera.

In opera, passions spin the plot. Men and women are seen drawn into action just as much – and potentially as seriously – as they are in a play or novel, or as in certain types of painting. In the eighteenth century all these art forms did not merely marvellously flourish, but also affected each other: stage plays became operas, operas became as psychologically convincing as novels, while novels and plays encouraged painters like Hogarth to tell stories through a series of pictures – thus getting round the problem of narrative in painting. Less worried than a modern public by whether it was seeing (and reading of) a Spanish barber, a Trojan princess or the Emperor of Peru, the educated eighteenth-century European public, a truly homogeneous, cosmopolitan entity, recognized and enjoyed the dramatic spectacle of human beings engaged in living – and sometimes in dying.

Few, if any, of Mozart's operas fail to touch, in one way or another, on death, and they often do so as reassuringly as in the letter to his father already quoted, '. . . Death, properly understood is the real ultimate object of our life'. In *Idomeneo* a father girds himself to kill his son. In *Die Entführung aus dem Serail* the pair of lovers face death with a duet expressing the heroic exultation of being together at such a moment

3

('O welche Seligkeit'),* much as the lovers in *Die Zauberflöte* unite to face the threat of dangers equivalent to death. It could not be said that Don Giovanni, in the eponymous opera, understands death to be the real goal of life; but he faces it alone with no less courage than pairs of noble lovers display: '*Ho fermo il cor in petto/Non ho timor, verrò.*'† To face death bravely is the test of a heroine as well as a hero. When Fiordiligi in *Così fan tutte* decides to dress up as a man and follow her lover to the battle-field, it is a desperate, serious escape which includes the resolve 'to die if need be'. Even into what might at first hearing seem the unshaded effervescent *Nozze di Figaro*, bubbling brightly and lightly like an illuminated fountain, there obtrudes the sad aria-prayer of the Countess: 'O Cupid, either give me back my lover or at least let me die' – and in no flippant spirit does Mozart score the words '*almen morir*'. *Figaro* might indeed become a tragedy if her prayer remained unanswered; nor, because it is a comedy, does this mean that serious issues have not been involved.

The truth is that Mozart himself believed in the Countess's alternatives, as also in the blessedness of opposing death by love. Against the inevitability of *la mort* nothing stronger exists than *l'amour*. Indeed, the more real the threat, the braver and better – and the more poignant – love. The marvellously moving quartet of lovers, agonized father and unhappy, unloved woman in Act III of *Idomeneo* ('Andrò ramingo e solo')‡ is an expression of feeling so poignant that Mozart himself is recorded as being totally overcome once when singing it along with his own wife, Constanze. '*Solo Amor può terminar*'§ aptly comes at the peaceful close of *Figaro*, after a '*giorno di tormenti*'.|| And in life, whatever judgements are to be made about Constanze Mozart, there can be no doubt that Mozart loved her deeply: 'love me for ever as I love you' is the serious sentence from one of his last letters to her. It is symbolically right that his very last surviving letter, written less than two months before his death, should be to her and that it should end with the hope 'of talking with you myself tomorrow and kissing you with all my heart. Farewell. Ever thine.'

Die Zauberflöte was much in his mind at this period. After one of the first performances he wrote to Constanze about it and quoted from it.

* 'Oh, what bliss.'
† 'My heart is steady in my breast/I feel no fear, I will come.'
‡ 'I shall go, wandering and alone.'
§ 'Love alone can bring an end.'
|| 'Day of torment.'

Earlier, when composing it while she was away from Vienna, he had found it too affecting to play over in the sad, weary hours of her absence. This opera is, among many other things, a consecration of man and woman in marriage, united by love and triumphant over death. It is no accident that Mozart should have thought about himself and Constanze when he thought about *Die Zauberflöte*. Perhaps only when it was finished and actually being performed – and at a time when he was without his wife – could he have realized how totally the duet of Pamina and Papageno crystallized his belief: '*Wir leben durch die Lieb' allein*'.*

Yet such assertion must be seen against actual, untidy, and always diminishing, existence: the world not of perfect art in the theatre, where a triumphal chorus greets the noble man and noble woman fitted for each other ('Du edles Paar')† but that temporal one outside, where Mozart is disconcerted to find that Constanze has sent his two pairs of yellow winter trousers to the laundry. In the months immediately before his death what he was working on was the Requiem, which he never lived to complete. It is easy to believe that this commission (odd, if much less mysterious than was once supposed) may at the very end have seemed to him a sinister omen. The mass for the dead is itself solemnly terrifying enough, nowhere more so than in the sequence *Dies irae*, on which Mozart was still engaged at the time of his actual death. The child of fervent Roman Catholic parents, he could hardly fail to recall masses for the dead which he had attended, and still less fail to respond to the words of that sequence, with their powerful onomatopoeic effect: *Tuba mirum spargens sonum/Per sepulcra regionum/Coget omnes ante thronum*.‡ In many ways, the liturgy of a requiem mass resembles an explicitly Christian *Zauberflöte*: the journey of a soul, narrowly escaping fire and hoping finally after ordeals to be brought into peace and light. In the music, tossing, trembling waves of chorus open the *Dies irae* sequence – with an almost smoky effect conveyed by the strings – and then fall away before the 'Tuba mirum . . .', sung by a bass and accompanied by a solo trombone, high and agile, uncannily brilliant against the depth of voice. Such is the sound which summons 'all before the throne'.

The sequence shifts from that to a vision of all mankind rising at the Day of Judgement, and then to the individual's own agony: a prayer for

---

* 'By love alone we live.'
† 'You noble couple.'
‡ Hark! the trump with thrilling tone
From sepulchral regions lone
Summons all before the throne.

the dead becomes a prayer for the person praying (*Ne me perdas ille die*).*
Mozart, with his intense response to the meaning of words whenever he
was setting them, needed no particularly mysterious event to make him
conscious that his own death might here be involved. If Masonry had
taught him to treat death calmly, as a friend, that was probably something of an intellectual effort, a later structure built over the buried
emotions of a Roman Catholic upbringing, natural fears of mortality
and the crowding sensations of fatigue, poverty, overwork and exacerbated sensibility. 'A sort of emptiness . . . a sort of longing,' was Mozart's
own description of his state of mind at one period during these last
months. He explained it in a letter to Constanze as due to her absence,
but its causes were probably more profound and irreparable.

He never managed to finish the *Dies irae*. Its closing verse of prayer for
mercy and peace was not to be set by him. The soul is left, conscious of
guilt and for ever waiting to be judged. The Last Day remains, as it
began, fearful: *Lacrymosa dies illa.*† It is there that Mozart's autograph
score breaks off.

* 'Nor condemn me on that day.'
† 'That tearful day.'

Part I
The King of Rücken

By the age of eight, Mozart had travelled through many countries, had met many rulers and was himself a king. True, his appeared only a fantasy kingdom, devised partly to while away the long hours of coach journeys, but he still remembered it more than twenty years later and could jokingly claim to have often been there since. He called this kingdom 'Rücken' (Back), a thought-provoking name for which, unfortunately, no one could later remember the reason. Perhaps it was first suggested through the sense – particularly felt by young children – of the landscape seeming to roll backwards while one advances in a vehicle: everything going '*nach dem Rücken*', backwards. Or perhaps everything in Rücken appeared backwards like a mirror image – for that is the sort of device Mozart still enjoyed when grown-up, often announcing or signing himself 'Trazom'.

Rücken had its own geography (conceivably its place names were real ones, spelled backwards), its own laws and its own subjects. It was 'Back' possibly too in a Golden Age sense: a return to a world of youthful perfection. Certainly it was a kingdom of, and for, children. Everyone there was good and happy, under their king. Like the Brontë children's Kingdom of Gondal, there were maps drawn of it – by the servant who travelled with the Mozart family, and perhaps also by Mozart himself, who showed some aptitude for drawing. The maps are lost, but the memory of Rücken lingered on after Mozart's death. His sister, Nannerl, rightly thought it something worth mentioning in her recollections, as an indication of how early his vivid imagination was apparent. She had travelled on most of the same youthful journeys, and was herself not so many years older, but it seems clear that Rücken was entirely Mozart's own personal kingdom. It offered a respite not only from the reality of slow, cramped, travelling conditions but from all the conditions of reality. Reality included a father who was no royal prince – not even a free agent – but an outwardly humble servant and court-musician attached to the Prince-Archbishop of Salzburg. And reality also meant very early realization that the great people who applauded the boy Mozart often cared little for music as such. He was soon demonstrating that he did not want to perform unless his audience was, or was made out to him to be, genuinely music-loving.

A boy-king of a personally created kingdom – all-powerful yet benevolent – might be any child's brief dream of himself. With Mozart, it was more subtle and more significant. To begin with, it was not entirely illusion. He was certainly the little king of his family, recognized by them as royally gifted. And this recognition was soon to be given by a European public. Leopold Mozart was himself too talented a musician to have any doubt but that his son was supremely, incomparably, talented. He loved Mozart to the point where he assumed a maternal as well as paternal role. It seems a positively significant stroke that Mozart once began a letter to him 'Mon Trés chere Pére' and then crossed out the 'e' of 'chere', remarking: 'I nearly slipped into the feminine.' The father – at least at first – did not challenge but fell back affectionately in awe before the spectacle of his son. When he and Mozart (then fourteen) together visited the Papal Court at Rome, he wrote home proudly that the Swiss guards made way for them, assuming Mozart to be a German aristocrat, or a prince even, 'and I was supposed to be his steward'. And once later, when upbraiding Mozart, he wrote quite explicitly that he had always served his son as a servant, *'wie ein diener seinen herrn bedient'*.* As a very young boy, Mozart established a ritual for going to bed which postulates the same relationship: he had to be set up on a chair and then sang out a special phrase of possibly non-sense words (at least as they were written down) to which his father was required to make a special response. Only after this ceremony – like some *coucher du roi* in miniature – would he retire. That the tune was his own variation on the old Dutch national anthem, 'Willem van Nassau', certainly encourages the feeling that associations of royalty and grandeur were connected with this ceremony. And there was something of royal command, and almost of royal lying-in-state, about the boy's pronouncement that his father in old age should be preserved in a glass case and so be protected and honoured.

Although no more than a dubious anecdote, never mentioned in Mozart's lifetime, there is some appropriateness too in the story that as a seven-year-old child at Schönbrunn Mozart had thanked the Archduchess Maria Antonia (later to be Queen of France), by remarking: 'I shall marry you.' He certainly assumed imperial dress, indeed that of Maria Antonia's own brother, when at the same date he was given by the Empress a lilac-coloured court costume, intended originally for the slightly younger Archduke Maximilian. The first portrait ever painted of him was in these clothes, posing like a son of the reigning Habsburg house, with cocked hat and small sword – but with a clavier as well.

* 'As a servant serves his master.'

Painters and engravers always interested Mozart; he liked to collect examples of their work from them, and this image of himself must have had its effect.

Yet it is not in any of these ways that Mozart the sovereign of Rücken is finally most absorbing. 'My mind to me a kingdom is,' he too might have said. His kingdom has significance not as a respite or a refuge but as a positive piece of artistic creation – more remarkable really than his first musical compositions. It reveals concern for inventing and ordering a complete cosmos – beyond, even perhaps *behind*, the ordinary world. The most effective sovereign – indeed the only sort worth bothering about, as Mozart speedily came to know – is the artist. In inventing his own kingdom, Mozart was already revealing that he would create; and perhaps there was already concealed in that concept a spark of resistance to his first role of travelling, prodigious performer, who is a courtier rather than a king, at court merely to entertain.

The scale of the artist's creation is not, *pace* the megalomaniac obsessions of the nineteenth century, in itself important. A small painting by Watteau, like a short piece of music by Mozart, has as much validity *qua* work of art as the largest fresco scheme or the longest symphony. Mozart's sovereignty, however, went further than his very earliest abilities, or opportunities, as a composer. His imagination made a country, with people and place names, which is not only an allegory of all artistic creativity but a positive prophecy of the particular category which fascinated him long before he was adult: the opera. It is probably impossible to say when Mozart first saw an opera, but he had certainly seen at least one in Vienna before his seventh birthday. Leopold Mozart reported of him at the age of eight that he was 'continually' thinking of an opera he wanted to produce. By the age of eleven he had provided the music for an oratorio and a Latin school play. Within the space of the next five years he began an Italian opera for Vienna, composed a one-act German opera for private performance and saw successfully, publicly, performed at Milan his first commissioned *opera seria*.

Benevolent, and sometimes not so benevolent, princes, subject people, exotic locations, peculiar laws and customs: the kingdom of opera, like that of Rücken, offered scope to the imagination. What was needed was no dreamy submission to it, nor writing of merely beautiful music to accompany its often absurd situations, but an artist-autocrat who would so dominate and build on it that it would grow rich in uniquely varied monuments of great art. Mozart's reign was not, in terms of human existence, to be long: in terms of achievement, however, it remains unparalleled.

The boy who dictated the names of the towns and villages of Rücken, who required a map of his kingdom to be drawn, was travelling towards a great inheritance. He was right to think himself a king. Those days of crossing Europe must have returned vividly to his mind when twenty-two years later he was in correspondence with the family's one-time servant, Sebastian Winter, who had become *valet de chambre* to the music-loving Prince von Fürstenberg. Winter had written to ask for some compositions which the Prince's orchestra could play, and in replying Mozart recalled early pleasant memories of his friendly reception at the Prince's court. He also longed to see Winter again, 'dearest friend – companion of my youth': words which led him to mention the imaginary kingdom where they had since never met. Rather than Winter coming to Vienna, Mozart spoke of preferring to go back to the court of Prince von Fürstenberg, to savour the memories of childhood; but there was to be no return.

In some ways, Mozart's career was a very long one, and must have seemed so in retrospect even while he was writing to Winter. To what an extent his thoughts were turning at this time to the past is suggested by the fact that within six months of his letter to Winter, he was telling his father of a proposed journey to London. English friends in Vienna encouraged him: he might write an opera for the King's Theatre or give subscription concerts. He seems to have been considering a long stay, perhaps even settling in England. All these projects, too, came to nothing. Once again, there was to be no return to a place which in his childhood had warmly welcomed – in the words of a contemporary London newspaper – 'the celebrated and astonishing Master Mozart'.

The prodigy aspect of Mozart is bound now to seem on a level with enjoying the feats of performing animals. But the prodigious child, the 'young Roscius', was partly an eighteenth-century phenomenon, and so was investigation into the properties of genius. Something of both is seen in, for example, John Kirby's *Life of Automathes* (first published 1745), the story of an infant who grows up alone on an island: not altogether an original idea 'but the book is not devoid of entertainment or instruction', in the words of Kirby's one-time pupil, Gibbon. Mozart actually owned a copy of this book in the 1761 edition, which had probably been bought by his father in London. Childhood and genius were indeed increasingly to be seen as evidence of sheer natural power – natural in the sense of being instinctive, untrammelled, almost uncontrolled. If that had been felt earlier, it had been with the stipulation that both would benefit from being controlled. Genius had been defined by Voltaire as *la raison sublime*, a definition which would have been widely accepted in the first half of the century.

But Mozart belongs to the second half. In 1757, the year after his birth, Diderot was eloquently to define 'genius' at length for the seventh volume of the *Encyclopedia*. Every sentence proclaims and prophesies new feelings, new freedom and new trust in the sheer convulsive energy of nature: '*Dans les arts, dans les sciences, dans les affaires, le* génie *semble changer la nature des choses; son caractère se répand sur tout ce qu'il touche, et ses lumières, s'élançant au-delà du passé et du présent, éclairent l'avenir: il devance son siècle qui ne peut le suivre*'.* Mozart was not to be the type of artist whose work is so revolutionary that it totally disconcerts, as well as outstrips, its century, though 'difficulties' in his instrumental music were sometimes mentioned. But he himself responded to the fact that the century itself had changed, and was changing.

A division was bound to exist between Rousseau's and Diderot's generation and that of Voltaire, virtually adult when they were born. In government of the Habsburg empire, the disagreement between Maria Theresia and her son Joseph stemmed largely from a similar sort of break; and the Empress sighed that she came from the old century. When the generations were united by artistic as well as family links, the distinctions became only the more apparent. Talented son of a genius, Domenico Tiepolo depicted a more 'natural' world than had his father: earthier, more humorous, in operatic terms *buffa* rather than *seria*. Mozart was a genius begotten by talent. He was radical and reckless in those affairs of life where his father was careful, conservative and ultimately frightened. And in music, he was in effect both Giambattista and Domenico Tiepolo; he fused *seria* and *buffa* finally in *Die Zauberflöte*, an opera his father could scarcely have foreseen and never lived to see. Mozart was born destined to disturb his father; each step which revealed more of his gifts separated them further, emotionally, musically, and geographically. Sadly, inevitably, at the very end, Leopold Mozart felt estranged; he was pessimistic about his son's future, and in his last sur-

---

* 'In the arts, in the sciences, in affairs, *genius* seems to alter the nature of things; its character spreads over everything it touches, and its brilliance – shooting beyond the past and the present – illuminates the future: it outstrips its century which cannot follow it.'

viving letter of 10 May 1787, to Nannerl, notes gloomily that Mozart has moved house once again in Vienna, without a word of explanation but 'I can unfortunately guess why'.

Once it had all promised to be very different. Although Leopold Mozart could never be accused of undue optimism, and not often of extreme emotion, it had been an extraordinarily moving occasion when he had returned home with a musician friend to find the four-year-old Mozart writing a clavier concerto. The manuscript was so covered with ink blots and smudges that at first it seemed to both men mere nonsense. Eventually they realized that it was indeed correctly written, yet of such difficulty that possibly no one could play it. Mozart explained that it was complex because it was a concerto, and he settled to playing it – well enough to prove his point. Leopold Mozart had wept for joy and wonder. The other eye-witness, Andreas Schachtner, court-trumpeter to the Archbishop of Salzburg, was to record the story in detail within six months of Mozart's death.

Such proofs of talent in his son created purpose in the uneventful life of the court-violinist Leopold Mozart, no native of Salzburg but living there since 1737. Though never an optimist, he was able, literate, ambitious, and somewhat prematurely soured. He probably thought himself deserving of some distinction which had never come – until his seventh and last child, christened Joannes Chrisostomus Wolfgang Gottlieb, was born on 27 January 1756. During his wife's pregnancy, Leopold Mozart had himself been involved in the long and tedious labour pains of producing a pedagogic treatise on violin-playing: *Versuch einer gründlichen Violinschule*, published six months after Mozart's birth. It was intended as a major work, but probably to be by no means its author's last. That it became so is due to the arrival of a child who was soon to absorb all the pedagogic gifts of Leopold Mozart for the rest of his life. His letters to his publisher, Lotter, whose wife was also pregnant, mingle proof corrections, as well as acid observations on printing errors, with exchanges of prenatal news and wishes. Frau Lotter was safely delivered of a boy at the end of 1755. The Mozart family had only one daughter surviving from six children before Mozart's birth, and the mother was thirty-six. She was certainly weak after his birth; years later Leopold Mozart said she had then nearly died, but he was at the time emotionally overwrought and anxious to make Mozart himself feel guilty.

The complicated situation of Mozart and his father began so early, and loomed so large for them both, that the mother was virtually eliminated once she had brought him into the world. Her character remains totally faint, if probably equable and agreeable. Her letters are without flavour, apart from tinges of piety and domestic retiringness, and give no hint of any interest in music. She was handsome, high-coloured (unhealthily high-coloured for her age, Leopold Mozart rather typically commented, after her death) and of better class than her husband. The daughter of the Deputy Prefect of St Gilgen, near Salzburg, Maria Anna (actually baptized Anna Maria) Pertl was a year younger than Leopold Mozart, whom she married in 1747, when she was twenty-seven. Hers seems to have been the sort of personality scarcely noticed until it is absent. She was probably content to act as foil to her husband, whose meticulous delight in detail – and in what can only be described as fussing – extended to household arrangements, linen and packing, as well as to professional affairs. When she died in Paris, far away from the familiar circle of her family and friends, Leopold Mozart's grief expressed itself in a poignantly simple sentence on their thirty-one years of life together: 'It is inconceivably painful when death breaks a truly blissful marriage.'

Their daughter, born in 1751 and christened Maria Anna Walburga Ignatia, always called Nannerl, seems to have inherited much of her mother's self-effacing temperament. Though an efficient child performer on the clavier, and later a competent teacher too, she was early overshadowed by her brother. By his standards she was not even a particularly precocious player. There seems to have been no idea of her performing in public during the nine years or so of her life before Mozart was ready to appear; nor did she ever play again at a public concert once their childhood was over. Seeming oddly to go back on her mother's traces, she married at thirty-three the widowed Deputy Prefect of St Gilgen, the successor in office of her grandfather. Even less than her mother's do her few letters and dry childhood notes of places and objects seen present a personality. The most positive thing to be detected, and then it is hard to catch more than the faintest signs of it, is reserve – if not hostility – towards Mozart's wife. In a story so full of irony as Mozart's, it is one further irony that these two women, both widowed, should have finished their lives settled close to each other at Salzburg.

There is nothing to suggest that Nannerl ever felt any resentment, even as a child, at the applause and attention her brother received, beginning of course at home. It is remarkably apt that though Leopold Mozart inscribed a notebook on the cover *'Pour le Clavecin, ce Livre* *appartient à Mademoiselle Marie-Anne Mozart 1759*',* he used the inside to record pieces of music learnt or composed by Mozart in the immediately subsequent years.

Nannerl was in many senses the best pupil of her father. *Her* marriage did not disappoint him. He happily looked after *her* children. Up to his death he wrote regularly to her. And she was his best pupil in other ways, for he taught her the importance of recording facts about Mozart and of preserving documents scrupulously. She must have known that he had intended to write his son's life, and herself compiled a memoir of a sort. She kept the old clavier on which they had both played. Over her bed there hung the group portrait of the family where brother and sister are shown engaged in a duet on what seems this very instrument (its sharps were white, its natural keys black). A few months before her death in 1829 she played once again the minuet from *Don Giovanni* and the deliberately tinkling, enchanted chorus 'Das klinget so herrlich' from *Die Zauberflöte*. In these very choices, one seems to detect an eternal, obedient small girl, true daughter of the mid-eighteenth century, still practising her music up on the third floor of a house in provincial Salzburg.

2

It was natural that Leopold Mozart should teach his daughter to play the clavier – a safe-seeming though actually confused, and confusing, term, which could well have meant harpsichord or clavichord as far as Nannerl's first lessons were concerned; nevertheless, since her father wrote 'pour le Clavecin' on her book in 1759, he presumably indicated the harpsichord. The Mozart family later owned more than one keyboard instrument of the generic clavier type, a type doomed during Mozart's lifetime to be replaced by the new, dynamic instrument, the fortepiano. Certainly by 1769 they possessed a clavichord, because Leopold Mozart absentmindedly took the key of it away with him when he and Mozart were travelling that year to Italy.

The clavichord had been strongly recommended for teaching by Carl Philipp Emanuel Bach (author of an important *Versuch über die wahre Art das Clavier zu spielen* [Pt 1:1753] which possibly prompted Leopold Mozart's *Versuch* for the violin): it was most suitable for learning to give good performances, and the good player of it would do equally well on the harpsichord, but not vice-versa. The clavichord, in fact, possessed

* 'For the Harpsichord, this Book belongs to Mademoiselle Marie-Anne Mozart 1759.'

dynamic effects of its own; at its best it seemed really to sing, and could be at once soft and sonorous. Leopold Mozart mentions one that had been described to him as possessing high notes resembling a violin played quietly, as well as bass notes like trombones. Under Mozart's own mature touch, the family clavichord probably responded with equally subtle range.

When Leopold Mozart first began to teach Nannerl music it must have been simply as a natural aspect of her education and his constant urge to instruct. He did not begin when she was extremely young, possibly because he still thought he would have sons whom he could more profitably teach. The other children – boys and girls – died with tragic regularity: none survived even for a year. His own career showed little sign of advancing. Not until 1763 was he made Vice-*Kapellmeister* at the Archbishop's court, and he never rose higher in the remaining twenty-four years of his life and service there. 'Persecuted . . . not as much favoured [here] by a long way as in other, larger places in Europe,' noted the Abbot of St Peter's monastery at Salzburg, making an entry in his diary on the day of Leopold Mozart's death in 1787.

The Abbot had good reason to know the facts intimately, because he was the son of the Mozarts' old landlord, Lorenz Hagenauer, and had been a boyhood friend of Mozart's. On the day young Hagenauer celebrated his first mass as a priest, the thirteen-year old composer had not only written the music for it (the 'Dominicus Mass') but played brilliantly at the monastery organ after dinner. On this occasion, Nannerl and Leopold Mozart had also performed, no doubt well but no doubt contented to be subsidiary to the combined virtuosity of Mozart as composer and performer. This precocity was itself something perhaps the more respected by his father as it seems to have been in contradistinction to his own early years. As a boy he had sung in the choir of a church at Augsburg, and later at least had learnt to play the organ, but there seems to have been no family encouragement for him to become a musician. When he first went to Salzburg it was with the idea of becoming a priest. He either could not – or, more probably, would not – proceed with the necessary studies and was eventually sent down from the University without a degree. Although that may have been his own wish, it probably left its scar on him: some lingering sense of rejection perhaps made him touchy, conscious of being better educated than most of the people he had to mix with, and yet with no evidence to prove his superiority.

He had been born at Augsburg, an important 'free' city of the German empire, in 1719. His birth was actually on the morning of 14 November, but he was baptized Leopold after the saint of the previous day – St Leopold, prince and patron of Austria – which turned out to be a remarkably prophetic touch. It is the more remarkable since name days and saints' days were to be almost superstitiously important to him (he wrote cuttingly once to his wife and daughter when he thought they had failed to send congratulations for St Leopold's day) and he was to be much concerned with prayers and votive masses being addressed to favourite saints at favourite shrines.

The Mozart family had previously no connections with Austria. They came from the country round Augsburg and in 1643 David Mozart – Mozart's great-grandfather, a mason by profession – had been granted civic rights at Augsburg. Such civic rights were important and prized. When Leopold Mozart decided to marry at Salzburg, he first prudently referred for permission to the City Council of Augsburg and was allowed to marry and live 'abroad', without losing his rights of citizenship there. Hence his children were, technically, citizens of Augsburg by birth. Johann Georg Mozart, Leopold's father, was a bookbinder, a widower who had married for the second time with disconcerting rapidity. His first wife died on 18 March 1718; on 1 May he married Anna Maria Sulzer, the daughter of a weaver. Apart from Leopold, there were to be four other boys, two of whom grew up to adopt their father's profession of bookbinder, both too, remaining, at Augsburg.

If today Salzburg is the more celebrated city, that is entirely due to Leopold Mozart leaving his birthplace. The traditions alone of Augsburg established it in Europe as an ancient, jealous and famous city, ruled by rich and aristocratic merchant families like the Fugger. It was a Venice of the North, without the advantage of a splendid natural setting, yet splendid in appearance and with many Venetian links. Its imperial connections were long, and as distinguished as its often related artistic ones. The Emperor Charles v had summoned Titian to paint him there. And there earlier the Emperor Maximilian had sat to Dürer during the Diet of Augsburg. The city's very name recalled its Roman imperial origin: *Augusta Vindelicorum*, conquered under Augustus by Drusus. Nor was it a city splendid through merely past associations. In the seventeenth century a series of fine new buildings added modern civic grandeur, summed up in the grand classical town hall built by Elias Holl. He himself was descended from a long line of Augsburg masons, and it may well have been the opportunities for employment on new buildings which had in the first instance attracted David Mozart to Augsburg.

Augsburg had also been famous since the Renaissance for printing and publishing books. A bookbinder was therefore likely to find plenty of scope for his craft, and Leopold Mozart's father seems to have grown quite prosperous by the time of his death in 1736. Clearly, however, his eldest son did not wish to follow his father's career, itself more genteel and closer to literacy than that of the grandfather. Leopold's godfather was a canon at Augsburg and probably was involved in sending him in 1737 to the University of Salzburg, in the belief that he would study there for the priesthood. The facts about Leopold Mozart at this period are by no means totally apparent. Even the selection of Salzburg remains unexplained. To some extent it may have seemed not such a great change, any more than a vast journey, from Swabia to Austria.

Yet in exchanging – for life as it proved – Augsburg for Salzburg, Leopold Mozart was in fact entering a narrower, less bourgeois environment, agreeable perhaps but less active, at once deeply feudal and violently Roman Catholic. Augsburg was a well-known republic, of mixed Roman Catholic and Protestant population, and with Reformation associations. Salzburg was an obscure, petty, notoriously anti-Protestant kingdom ruled by a Prince-Archbishop – one of three hundred rulers of such kingdoms between the Alps and the Baltic which made up an invisible and disintegrating Empire. Salzburg had played no part in European politics or culture; within Austria alone it had none of the imperial associations of, for instance, Innsbruck. It was dominated by the fixed points of the cathedral and the *Residenz*-fortress literally dominating on its hill. More picturesque than Augsburg, it too had been improved in the seventeenth century, with a notably handsome baroque cathedral. The court of a ruler who was His Most Reverend Highness reached out to affect all the citizens: it shaped the university entertainments, ordained the particular feast days which would be most splendidly celebrated and, in being both Church and State, offered virtually the sole patronage available to artists of any kind. The buildings, the sculpture, the music, at Salzburg all depended on the personality of the Prince; and his disfavour could obviously be a no less powerful factor. In capital cities like Vienna and Paris there could and did exist cultured and wealthy circles independent of the ruler. Salzburg was too small to accommodate more than one effective patron. Leopold

Mozart was to experience the disadvantages of living there; yet he seems to have had, typically, no very high opinion of his native city, either. Discontentedly superior, he might claim that neither was the proper setting for a man of talent. He may have been right, but his attitude is unlikely to have made him very popular.

Presumably he had never wanted to become a priest. 'How he fooled the clergy,' was the comment of one of his fellow students to Mozart, nearly thirty years later. And this student recalled amazingly bravura playing by Leopold Mozart on the organ – 'something totally new to me', Mozart remarked, probably surprised to learn that his violinist father had once played that instrument. In 1738 Leopold had been publicly commended at the University – not for his music but for his knowledge of jurisprudence and logic. The next year he was sent down, strangely – it would seem – rebuked for lack of application. This sounds quite uncharacteristic of the man, and was more likely the result of a new application: to music. He found his first patron in another most illustrious and reverend person, the Canon Count della Torre, Valsassina e Tassis, as he described him in Italian on the dedication page of his first published work, six violin sonatas *'per Chiesa e da Camera'*.* He entered the Count's service as valet and musician in 1740, publishing the sonatas the same year under his own auspices at Salzburg. The law student abruptly proclaims himself a professionally-employed musician, a composer and a publisher. It has all the air of a riposte to any supposed lack of application. Three years later he became a court musician – fourth violinist – to the Archbishop, Baron Firmian, whose first name also happened to be Leopold. A series of Prince-Archbishops succeeded each other in the next decade, and in 1753 Siegmund Christoph von Schrattenbach became the ruler. His eighteen-year reign was to cover Mozart's youth and early fame; he proved a positive, kindly patron to the family, though even he was to show some displeasure at his servant Leopold Mozart's tendency to overstay leaves of absence from Salzburg.

Meanwhile, Leopold had met and, after a cautious courtship, married Maria Anna Pertl. They were to be called the handsomest couple in Salzburg. Perhaps they matched neatly in height, as in most other things, for he was certainly not tall – shorter indeed than Mozart, who was well below average height for the time. They lived on the third floor of a house in the Getreidegasse belonging to a prosperous grocer, Lorenz Hagenauer, who became their friend as well as landlord. Hung

* 'For Church and Private House.'

today with portraits and relics of Mozart, these few plain rooms are perhaps more strongly personal in their furnishing than they ever were when the family occupied them. Here their children were born – and died. The godparents chosen were always the same couple, a merchant Amadeus Pergmayr and his wife Maria Cordula, and their names were included in those of the second child, a daughter, and the fifth, a son. For the seventh and last child, Mozart, Pergmayr again stood godfather, and hence Amadeus (Gottlieb) among his names. Wolfgang – a name not previously used by his parents – was his maternal grandfather's name, and he was called John Chrysostom after the saint on whose day he was born.

Two weeks earlier Leopold Mozart, not as father nor as teacher, but as composer, had been represented at a concert in Augsburg by his 'Musical Sledge-ride', an at first unexpectedly sparkling and light-hearted piece of programme music. Nicely gauged to entertain any audience, its lively dance rhythms and mock-military airs represent patently social music-making. It mirrors the very society it entertains at the very same winter season: with its interspersed descriptive passages of tinkling sledges and sweating horses which carry a merry-making party to a ball where the minuet is followed by cheerful country dances. As it happened, this also preluded his farewell to composition. At Salzburg he had already written and had performed two solemn Lenten cantatas as well as the music for a Latin school play, *Antiquitas personata*. He also produced popular hunting and military suites, a peasants' wedding symphony and pseudo-exotic Turkish pieces – the very popular quality of which led to his receiving an anonymous letter begging him not to write any more such work, so as to avoid bringing on himself any further disgrace and contempt. The 'Musical Sledge-ride' was among the pieces singled out in this letter from a 'friend', perhaps a fellow-musician at the Salzburg court or an enemy at Augsburg disturbed by the comic, undignified nature of music which introduced sleighbells and even whips into its instrumentation.

Yet it is exactly in its sometimes rather simple-minded humour and lively charm that this music is personal to the man – more personal than graver, formal essays. Rudimentary humour was indeed typical of the family, all four of whom found words like 'arse' and 'piss' irresistibly funny when writing to each other. Mozart had only to describe how *Die Duchesse arschbömerl* and other grotesquely-named aristocrats attended a concert of his at Augsburg, for his father to reply saying how much he looked forward to hearing more of her adventures. Funny sounds, whether in words or music, appealed to them both. Leopold Mozart's suite for toy instruments – with bird noises, drums and whistles – shows the appeal at its most obvious; its rustic effects and jokes are musical exploitation of the toys then made by peasants at Berchtesgaden, near Salzburg. Mozart, too, was to produce a 'Musical Joke', as well as setting some crudely comic texts, but his final use of such devices is in Papageno and the magic glockenspiel of *Die Zauberflöte*.

Leopold Mozart's humour had its satirical touches, and the topical, as well as rustic, quality of some of his music could be compared with Bach's Coffee Cantata, or that Bach wrote for a libretto in Saxon peasant dialect, celebrating the new landowner of a village. But Leopold's is perhaps rather fussy music; as a joke it has a tendency to go on a little too long, and for all the charm of the idiom it is basically uninventive. Perhaps too there is some element of superiority in its attitude – a typically Leopoldian mixture of pride and susceptibility; he wrote music which was intended to please, but possibly despised those whom it pleased. Although he complained about Salzburg and Augsburg, he himself never lived elsewhere. Nor did he find other cities when he visited them much better: at Vienna people cared for nothing serious; in Paris all the women wore too much rouge. Almost out loud, he wondered how his family would ever get on without him; before his children were of an age to learn their failings, he was explaining to his publisher at Augsburg that his mother had remarkably little common-sense. It would unfortunately have to be admitted as a fact, he added, even if she were a thousand times his mother.

Nor was he altogether understanding about the extreme sensitivity and sensibility of his brilliant son. Considering the uncanny subtlety of Mozart's ear, early demonstrated, it was an act of crass stupidity to try and cure his dislike of the trumpet by having one blown directly at him; the boy went so white it was thought he would collapse. Other authenticated anecdotes from Mozart's childhood confirm the impression of a loving father who did not in reality know how to express that love. It happened, or it came as a result, that Mozart grew into a child who repeatedly asked those around him if they truly loved him. Even jokingly, even momentarily, to deny this brought tears to his eyes.

Yet Leopold Mozart was in many ways a good father, doubtless an amusing man in the privacy of his home or among a few friends, and certainly intelligent. He would probably have expressed gratitude that he was not born imaginative. Sensibility he probably associated with women, especially with fine ladies. He had a keen eye – which his son inherited, and sharpened – for the foibles and ridiculous aspects of human nature, whether in a monarch or a servant-girl. It was an eye, too, which encouraged him to look at paintings and statues, as well as people, when he began to travel across Europe. A certain naïvety, combined with his never-quenched urge to teach (if not, positively, to preach), helped him in writing about what he saw and what he felt with unusual articulateness; and there again Mozart inherited much from him.

Above all, of course, he was a musician. He provided the ideal environment for a child whose instinct for music seemed second only to breathing – and who would expire mouthing music. Within this environment, the boy Mozart rapidly, almost imperiously, carved out his own realm. Even his games had to be supported by music; his toys were carried from one room to another accompanied by songs and marches. He sang, he played the clavier, and soon the violin as well. The vitality which thus almost frighteningly manifested itself – so that in practising he needed to be restrained much more than encouraged – constantly found other ways of expression which confirmed a natural superiority. His father was irritably superior, tormented by the sense that his efforts had never received their due. Mozart was born equipped with effortless, unfailing ability. Far from struggling to create, he had to struggle to remain calm amid perpetual creative fever. He was not only quick but fiery – the very adjective used by a friend speaking of his early childhood – with a clever tongue which could select the right word to say, as unerringly as he picked out the right note on the clavier. He had a talent for drawing. In arithmetic his absorption would lead him to cover tables, chairs and the walls with figures when he was – in effect – creating in numbers; and he kept a love for mathematical puzzles. This should not be shrugged aside as typical of all great composers; Beethoven's mathematical ability scarcely rose above the sub-normal. Activity was his first principle – whether through singing, playing and composing, or simply rolling round the room. And so it remained. What has often been described as the childlike quality which he retained into adulthood was in fact a retention of energy: pure, unhindered and of almost explosive force.

Salzburg was unlikely to contain it for long. The thought must have occurred in its own way to Leopold Mozart as he noted down in 1761 the pieces learnt by Mozart on the clavier, and annotated the first of his compositions. To display the small virtuoso performer, along with his sister, it would be necessary to travel; and perhaps Leopold was already planning the steps of a travelling exhibition to grow larger and bolder at each stage across the map of Europe. Among his guidebooks was Keyssler's handy, popular *Neueste Reisen* which covered Germany, Bohemia, Hungary, Switzerland, Italy and Lorraine. Yet its scope by no means covered the itinerary which this humbly-placed, untravelled, provincial musician was soon actively projecting for his whole family.

The immediate future concerned him much more than any clear concept of his son's eventual career. He owned no guide books to the musical topography of Europe. Only the first volume of Padre Martini's huge *History of Music* had then been published. Charles Burney's two provocative books on *The Present State of Music* . . . had not yet been conceived; that provincial music-master had however publicly exhibited his ten-year-old daughter in London as a virtuoso of the harpsichord, and she had created something of a sensation.

Leopold Mozart was girding himself for travel in a Europe which was without any one obvious musical capital, and which had recently suffered the loss of its last widely-recognized, great mid-century composer, Handel, though in fact the aged Telemann survived. At Vienna Gluck was a rising star, producing his *Don Juan* ballet in 1761, to be followed the next year by the revolutionary opera *Orfeo*, which Leopold saw soon after its first performance. Though Bach was dead, two of his sons – Carl Philipp Emanuel and Johann Christian – were very much alive and active; the Mozarts knew Carl's music well and were to become friendly with Christian in London. At Paris, Grétry was still a little too young to have started his successful career. Of the two Haydn brothers, the Mozart family at this period were much better acquainted with Michael than with Joseph, for Michael Haydn became a court musician at Salzburg. In Italy Vivaldi and Domenico Scarlatti were dead. Another Italian, Jomelli, then a famous name, was employed at Stuttgart, but was later to meet the Mozarts in his native Naples. Paisiello, also a Neapolitan, was much in demand, especially as an opera composer; Mozart heard a great deal of his music, though for a significant period of Mozart's lifetime Paisiello was living away at the court of St Petersburg. Among other outstanding composers of the day was Hasse, a German who had worked first in Italy, then at Dresden and had only just moved to Vienna; he was to prove a generously enthusiastic admirer of the boy Mozart, and after that Leopold described him respectfully as the Music-Father, '*der Musick-Vatter*'.

Even such a random selection of names suggests the mingled possibilities of influences, affinities and possible rivals; it hints also at the peripatetic careers which most musicians had to face. Some of these men were growing old, like Hasse. Jomelli's work struck Mozart as old-fashioned. Closer in age to him was Gluck's pupil, Salieri, later to seem the most potent of his rivals at Vienna, but who is now recalled chiefly for that association. Despite the public existence of Gluck himself, and the then obscure one of Haydn, posterity – seeing much further than Leopold Mozart conceivably could from Salzburg in 1761 – can realize that the musical sovereignty of Europe was open to the most gifted candidate.

Leopold's own eye for himself was on a place nearer home: the never-to-be-gained *Kapellmeister* post at Salzburg, occupied by Eberlin, a much older and more talented man, who died the following year. The European place has been gained by Mozart, so overwhelmingly that most of the other composers of the time require annotation and explanation to bring them back briefly to life. That would probably not have greatly surprised Leopold Mozart, because he had never had a very high opinion of his fellow-musicians. Mozart had even less patience with, and respect for, them. His attitude has indeed disconcerted some of his finest and most scholarly admirers, without their perhaps reflecting long enough on whether he was not absolutely right; his intensely critical views certainly emphasize the real admiration he felt for the Bach family, for Handel and for Haydn.

In any event, it is part of nearly every artist's essential autocracy to be unable to bear a brother near the throne. And Mozart must often have heard, from his earliest years, that favourite phrase of his father's: '*Aut Ceasar aut nihil.*'

3

'My heart is quite enchanted,' begins Mozart's earliest surviving letter to his mother – the earliest of all his letters bar one – '. . . because I find this journey so cheerful, because it is so warm in the coach and because our coachman is a fine fellow who, whenever the road allows him the smallest opportunity, drives so fast.' That is virtually the end, too, of the letter, which might be a report of Mozart's reactions to travelling – to being in rapid movement – at almost any age. 'I should like to give it a little kiss,' he said of his carriage when it carried him to Frankfurt in the penultimate year of his life. The message to his mother was written at thirteen, as a scribbled postscript to his father's first despatch back to Salzburg as the two of them stopped in December 1769 at Wörgl, the first stage on the most significant so far of Mozart's many journeys: to Italy.

For over a year he and Leopold toured Italy – like a prince and his steward indeed – well received everywhere, meeting composers, seeing Italian opera, and enjoying themselves (never elsewhere was Leopold Mozart to find life so little disagreeable). Mozart was no longer the constantly performing child prodigy, but a highly-honoured creative musician whose talent was more remarkable than his youth. The tour began by Mozart being given the important commission to write an opera for Milan, *Mitridate, Re di Ponto*; its halfway mark was made memorable by the Pope's knighting him with the Order of the Golden Spur; and it culminated in the double triumph of his successful entry into the Accademia Filarmonica at Bologna and of his public reception for *Mitridate*. Mozart was conducting at the clavier for the opera's first performance, wearing a newly-made scarlet suit, trimmed with gold braid and lined with sky-blue satin. Enthusiasm was such that the audience insisted – unusually – on one aria being encored, and cries of '*Evviva il Maestro! Evviva il Maestrino!*'* acclaimed the one-time boy-king of fantasy, now recognized at fourteen as truly a reigning monarch.

It was six years since Leopold Mozart had written from London that Mozart was planning an opera which he wanted to produce. It was eight years since the winter when Mozart had made the coach journey to the first of so many performing engagements. Perhaps he had then already responded to the warmth of the coach interior and delighted in the coachman's speed; nor should the composer of the 'Musical Sledge-ride' himself have been above responding to such things. The first court to which Leopold Mozart took his two children was that closest to Salzburg, the court of the music-loving Elector Maximilian III Joseph at Munich, a city known to Leopold. As a trial flight, this visit of January 1762 remains something of a mystery; no letters describing it exist, though it would have seemed the obvious occasion for the proud father and punctilious correspondent to write back – as he regularly did during

---

* 'Long live the Master! long live the little Master!'

all his other travels – to his friend and landlord, Hagenauer. Nannerl is the source for the usual supposition that the two children then performed in the Elector's presence, but this seems most unlikely, because when the family met Maximilian III Joseph at Munich the following year he greeted Leopold graciously as an old friend and displayed his royal memory by remarking that they had already met – nineteen years before. On this visit the Elector particularly expressed regret that he had not heard the girl as well as the boy – so Leopold Mozart had to delay their departure from Munich. The Elector's regret scarcely makes sense if he had in fact heard both children play only the previous year. Nor, were this in fact so, is it likely that Leopold Mozart's very circumstantial letters would have failed to comment on how the Elector found their playing improved – or at least make some reference to their visit of the year before.

Nannerl's jottings were by no means flawless (she got the date of her parents' wedding wrong by several years), and her own prosaic little notes as a girl visiting all the enchanting buildings in the complex at Nymphenburg date from the second Munich visit, and are clearly the record of someone who had not seen the building before. It therefore seems likely that Leopold took the children to Munich in 1762 but – as was so often later to occur at other courts – found the ruler absent. Perhaps the children played before some courtiers or even before the Elector's brother, Duke Clemens of Bavaria. Whatever the truth, and however Leopold Mozart's apparent silence is to be explained, the visit must have justified his hopes. The spectacle of brilliant performances at the harpsichord by two young children – probably looking even younger than they were, owing to their small stature – had proved attractive enough. On that occasion Mozart did not perhaps demonstrate his quite extraordinary brilliance by improvising at the keyboard, still playing on it perfectly when it was covered with a cloth, and detecting correctly any note of a bell or clock. All these refinements were certainly included in his performances of later the same year when Leopold executed the next step in his campaign and carried his family to Vienna. The visit to Munich had apparently lasted three weeks; that connected with Vienna occupied some three months, and itself was perhaps planned partly as an experiment with a view to longer, yet more ambitious, travels to totally foreign European cities.

Vienna was probably as novel and uncertain a prospect for Leopold Mozart as for the rest of his family. It was known that the Empress and her husband were fond of music – this being an activity Maria Theresia, strangely proto-Victorian in many ways, could approve of. A success for the performing children was likely to have European repercussions; if they were received at court foreign ambassadors would probably take cognizance of their existence. The capital must have represented the true test of Leopold's strategy: 'Aut Vienna aut nihil.' Failure there would be the end of every dream of fame and prosperity, and it is easy to guess the intention for which he wrote asking Hagenauer quickly to have four masses said, on 3 October 1762, the day before the family left Linz for Vienna. At Linz, slightly under half-way on the journey, they had stopped. There, where almost exactly twenty-one years later Mozart was to write at terrific speed a famous symphony in C major ('the Linz'), he gave the first public concert of his life, and was received with applause. It must have appeared the most favourable of omens. It can hardly have mattered that Mozart caught cold in Linz, the first of so many boyhood illnesses – all of which seem to have attacked him when he was under the double strain of travelling and performing. Leopold's letter to Hagenauer is like that of a great general on the eve of battle: calm, business-like, optimistic – with a tone so unlike his usual one that it suggests he was calming and encouraging himself. A real war, too, was dividing Europe – the Seven Years' War, then coming to an end, in which England and Prussia had been united against Austria and France – and Leopold had time to reflect on the fate of the Prussian prisoners whom he saw arriving in batches at Linz. He always followed European affairs, rightly disliked militarism and felt for humanity – whether enemy or not. One of the surprises to him of Vienna – which shows how little he can have known it – was that far from it being full of the latest war news, nobody there spoke of it at all: it was as if there were no war.

His own musical campaign opened well. Several people travelling through Linz to Vienna promised to announce the forthcoming attraction. Like human beacons, other people caught fire and passed on the message: a Count Pálffy happened to arrive in Linz in time to attend Mozart's concert; Count Pálffy spoke of it to the Archduke Joseph (the future Emperor), and the Archduke told his mother, the Empress. Thus, just as Leopold must often have dreamed, on arrival in Vienna the family was summoned to the imperial summer palace of Schönbrunn. They spent three hours with Maria Theresia and her family, mingling together in a friendly bourgeois party, while Mozart played and kissed the Empress, and the Emperor Francis I insisted – as one parent to another – that Leopold hear his daughter-in-law play the violin. Well might Leopold Mozart's letter reporting this marvellous day end with a flourish of expansive greetings: *'Der ganzen Welt mein Compliment.'**

Compliments, kisses, presents and some money rained – along with a steady patter of invitations to noble houses – on the Mozart family. The prodigy boy, his talented sister – whom he would charmingly applaud – and their benevolent impresario father (the mother already retreating, somewhat functionless in the organization) formed an attractive spectacle for society, more intrigued by the novelty than by the music. And the family really worked for their earnings. Even on the day of the Schönbrunn visit Mozart was again at the keyboard performing at an evening party in Vienna. He had performed in several houses before that visit; following on it, the imperial chancellor, Kaunitz, invited the family to his house and the court requested Leopold to prolong his stay in Vienna, and the French ambassador extended an invitation to Versailles.

Yet the demands and the politeness were largely based on ephemerality, as Leopold Mozart recognized. The family was not seeking employment or a place at court. Maria Theresia owned a composer and music-master, Wagenseil, whose works were among the first Mozart had ever learnt, and her attitude of motherly benevolence would have quickly sharpened into housekeeperly economy if urged to employ an additional musician. When a few years later one of her sons was indeed considering Mozart for his own household, she wrote strongly-worded advice against employing composers and 'useless' people like that. And with the passage of time Mozart and his sister would grow less remarkable – it seemed – as they grew older. Although Leopold wrote boldly of being able to live in Vienna if he wished, he used the possibility as a vague threat in pressing for what he really wanted, a higher post at the Salzburg court.

'Le pauvre petit joue à merveille,'† Count Carl von Zinzendorf noted in his diary for 17 October 1762, mentioning the boy-wonder for the third time in a fortnight, *'c'est un Enfant Spirituel, vif, charmant . . .'‡* Mozart was playing yet again in a Viennese nobleman's palace, delighting in his

---

* 'My compliments to the whole world.'
† 'The poor little boy plays marvellously.'
‡ 'He's a witty child, lively, charming . . .'

own skill, and sparkling in manner, whether playing or conversing. Yet the spectacle obviously struck Zinzendorf, as it was to strike other people, as faintly sad. Some observers wondered if the child would ever reach adult life; and most must have pondered on the future of such a prodigy, should he survive. Mozart's own delighted absorption in performing may have concealed, but in fact increased, the strain put on him. It was perhaps the constant demands made on him as a child which led him as a man to that reluctance to compose until the last possible moment, a sort of 'laziness' which was possibly only an attempt to gain time for the relaxation of creation – a mental relaxation as essential to creating as any romantic fury or passionate pounding at the piano.

The strain of daily performances in Vienna showed abruptly on the evening of a second visit to Schönbrunn. Mozart broke out in a rash which Leopold and the doctor thought was scarlet fever, a common but dangerous illness for children in the city at the time. With the aid of votive masses and medicinal powders, he recovered quite quickly; and as an act of gratitude immediately gave a concert at the doctor's house. Success was beginning to affect Leopold, too; he was anxious to accept invitations for the family to go to Hungary, but he had also to obtain permission from the Prince-Archbishop to extend his leave of absence from Salzburg, and when finally they reached Hungary he was attacked by unusually bad toothache: '*Ich sage:* mir ungewöhnliche zähnschmerzen,'* he wrote, emphasizing the words.

The delays in returning to Salzburg reflect Leopold Mozart's uncertainty, and perhaps a sudden bewilderment in the midst of the storm of popularity he had conjured up but which threatened to become overwhelming. Trying to compare Salzburg and Vienna confused him, he admitted, even before his psychosomatic bout of toothache. Yet, barely back in Salzburg a month of the new year 1763, after what he described as a comfortable trip home in a newly-bought carriage, Leopold was waiting for further news about the proposed visit to Paris. And despite the comfortable journey in winter weather, Mozart spent the first week of the return to Salzburg in bed, painfully ill with what seems to have been rheumatism. It was the first attack of a recurrent illness, one which probably killed him.

When on 9 June 1763 the carriage and the family, with the addition of Sebastian Winter, the future chronicler of the kingdom of Rücken, set off for non-German Europe, Leopold Mozart had shelved, rather than

* 'As I say: I have toothache, which is unusual for me.'

solved, the problem of Salzburg versus Vienna – or anywhere else. It is true that he travelled now as the Prince-Archbishop's Vice-*Kapellmeister*, having been promoted on 28 February, Schrattenbach's birthday. That day had been celebrated in other ways too, for Mozart and Nannerl had made their appearance at the Archbishop's birthday concert, when Mozart played the violin as well as the clavier. Salzburg was thus among the later places to hear the children perform; with what was probably considerable shrewdness, Leopold had reserved this surprise for his adopted city to follow on the children's success in Vienna, stories about which were being gradually disseminated and even published. If Salzburg, Leopold wrote back soon after this European tour began, had previously been surprised by Mozart and Nannerl, it would be utterly astounded on their return. Not the least astounding thing about the tour proved to be its duration: only on 30 November 1766 did the Mozart family return to Salzburg. Mozart himself had by then changed a good deal. Salzburg had not.

Although the European tour was undertaken primarily to exhibit – and to earn from – the Mozart children as performers, Leopold must have seen it also in terms of an education for them and for himself. His curiosity and keen artistic appreciation on these travels are sometimes more marked than his concern with costs or concerts. The Seven Years' War was over, to the advantage of that very talented amateur composer Frederick the Great, and Europe was at peace. Before he left Salzburg, Leopold had not entirely decided the extent of the family travels, remaining uncommitted about whether to cross the sea and visit Frederick's ally, England. Yet he eventually dared to do this, which, as he himself wrote from London, no one else at the Salzburg court had ever dared to do – or possibly would ever do again. And in his zeal for improving others as well as himself, he despatched to Salzburg explanations of essential English terms like 'Roasted Beef' and 'Plumb-pudding', and glossed the particular significance of Vauxhall, 'the City' and a strange native complaint, a 'cold'. The novelty of all their distant adventures was to be summed up unexpectedly in Nannerl's terse description of what she saw, for the first time, at Calais: 'How the sea runs away and comes in again.'

More than once, something in the tone of Leopold Mozart's own comments on things seen recalls those of Dürer on his travels through Germany and the Netherlands. Both men have a directness of vision which is not affected by the fame or eminence of what they are looking at; pithily and uninhibitedly, both of them can note down whether it did or did not please them, and similarly mingle in their jottings brief memoranda of sums paid and things to do. No less assiduously than Dürer did Leopold visit Cologne cathedral and, though he does not mention Lochner's famous altarpiece, he notes the exterior of the cathedral as dirty, while the interior was made horrible by the shrieking – not singing – of the service he attended. That Leopold Mozart can seriously be thought of in relation to Dürer is a tribute to his powers of observation, and he showed himself scarcely less concerned than Dürer had been with seeing the work of great painters, in his case from Bouts to Rubens. Leopold, too, made notes of painters met and the furnishing of princely apartments, and even included in a letter to Hagenauer a long list of the most famous Netherlandish painters over the centuries.

But it is perhaps his response to buildings which seems most notable, recalling that he was, after all, the grandson and grand-nephew of masons. His great-uncle had been a master mason in a period and country where such men could rise to the architectural achievements of Dominikus Zimmerman, master mason and creator of the church at Die Wies. Although Leopold Mozart never names the greatest architect of the period, Neumann (dead ten years before), he visited and admired some of the finest buildings where he had been involved, including the Residenz at Bruchsal and the Schloss at Brühl, near Cologne. Neumann's marvellous staircase at Brühl he tantalizingly mentions – just – and rooms in Chinese style, lacquer cabinets, mirror rooms, all appealed to him. This sophisticated modern architecture (so different from dirty Cologne cathedral) may – more than merely fancifully – be related to music of the same period, and to none more aptly than to Mozart's own. In some of the architecture, as in some of the music (including Leopold's), there are rustic elements. Mozart, like Neumann, was to be quite free from this, on a level of accomplishment where there exist no disparate elements but simply the fabric itself, planned, witty rather than good-humoured, apparently effortless but intensely, ingeniously and totally convincing as great art. Not until 1790 did Mozart visit Würzburg, where Neumann had lived and built a great deal, but – though he stopped there only for coffee – he saw enough to describe the town as 'fine, magnificent'.

In 1763, as he visited places like Bruchsal and Brühl with his family, it is impossible to say how he responded to what Leopold showed him, but it is hard to believe he remained indifferent. His unquenchable receptivity is likely to have enjoyed the glitter of palace rooms all gilt and looking-glass, grottoes built of shells and pavilions in Indian or Chinese taste (Leopold's own Chinese music comes to mind), demonstrating everywhere art's power to play with space and create illusions. At its best, the virtuosity of such art was like his own. And Mozart had now invented his kingdom of Rücken, where there was perhaps his own royal palace and where certainly he was king. Already he was emerging as more than the child performer, though he gave the usual concert-displays in the journey across Germany, wearing a wig and sword – as the fourteen-year-old Goethe saw and always remembered him playing at Frankfurt. For health s sake and the Salzburg court's reputation, the whole family was travelling 'nobl oder cavaglierment',* as Leopold put it. They associated chiefly with the nobility as they travelled, receiving valuable presents both in Germany and Belgium – including two splendid swords for Mozart. More personal and moving was the parting present from one of the noblemen with whom they had travelled: a book of sacred poems, inscribed from an admirer and friend to the 'little seven-year-old Orpheus'. By the time the Mozart family drove into Paris on 18 November, it must have been hard for any of them to recapture the feelings of uncertainty and inexperience with which they had probably faced Vienna little over a year before.

If they were now totally confident, their anticipation proved fully justified. The Vienna success was to be repeated, beginning with a friendly reception at the French court, but this time on a more public, publicized scale. And the achievement was the greater, for though Vienna might be an imperial capital, Paris had long been recognized as the capital of literate, luxurious and cultured Europe. In 1763 it was in fact suffering to some extent from the effects of the Seven Years' War, though its fashions and its luxury could still astonish in that year such disparate visitors as Gibbon and Smollett, as well as Leopold Mozart. The Peace of Paris had represented a humiliating end to the war for France. The king was growing middle-aged. Madame de Pompadour – who reminded Leopold of a Salzburg acquaintance, with a touch of Maria Theresia, and whom he found still handsome – was tired, ill and soon to die. Two of the greatest literary figures, Voltaire and Rousseau, no longer lived in Paris. Even the Salon exhibition of painting and sculpture that year had seemed rather flat and uninspired. Diderot, one of the writers seen and placed by Gibbon as holding 'the foremost rank

* 'Nobly or aristocratically.'

in merit', had lately pleaded for a revival of the competitions and honours which so encouraged the arts in antiquity. Why had there then been such great musicians? *'C'est que la musique faisait partie de l'éducation générale: on présentait une lyre à tout enfant bien né.'**

Whether or not this bears any relation to historical fact, it was certainly not the custom in mid-eighteenth-century Paris. And yet music was perhaps the most flourishing of the arts – at least the one being most pugnaciously debated. The *'guerre des Bouffons'* had begun, though some of its bitterest battles had yet to be fought. Historically, the origins of this war – itself as muddled and as inconclusive as most political wars – went back to rivalry at the end of the previous century between the French and Italian comedians, the latter already associated with low, mocking, topical comedy – topical to the point of its leading to their banishment from France. The partisans now stood for French versus Italian music, though to a large extent they were debating not music but the century's dilemma about art (in this context, dignified, classical drama) and nature (represented, for the argument, by the *buffa* tradition of certain Italian operas). After Rousseau's *Devin du Village*, successfully played before the king in October 1752, it might seem total victory for the Italianate party. But the conflict continued. It is the same clash as that represented in painting by the aims of Reynolds and the achievements of Gainsborough. At Paris, the war was to concentrate, most notoriously, on the composers Gluck and Piccini, reluctant opponents who were personally friendly to each other. In so far as the whole somewhat contrived and complex dispute involved them, it was neatly disposed of in one sentence by Berlioz's admired literary professor, who had survived from the days of the actual warfare: 'Ah, I also was an ardent lover of Gluck . . . and of Piccini too!'

When the Mozart family arrived in Paris, Gluck had not yet been directly involved. Leopold quickly realized that a state of warfare existed between Italian and French music, pronouncing the whole of the latter to be 'not worth a damn'. He would probably have realized the situation soon enough, but must have been encouraged in his views by the acquaintances he made, above all by his great new friend Grimm. Though German-born, Grimm had lived in Paris for some fifteen years and was secretary to the Duc d'Orléans. His *Correspondance littéraire* disseminated events in Parisian life to rulers in less fortunate places, and as

---

* 'It is because music formed part of general education: every well-born child was presented with a lyre.'

a literary figure he was friendly with Diderot, acquainted with Voltaire and alienated from Rousseau. The Encyclopedists, and especially Rousseau and Grimm, strongly favoured the Italian musicians; both he and Rousseau had written on the subject. More relevantly, he now favoured and helped Leopold Mozart. Grimm provided positive instructions on how to leave notes for people of rank whom Leopold could not see. Grimm arranged for the children to give a public concert. Grimm saw to it that Carmontelle, a gentleman-artist in the Orléans circle, executed one of his typical water-colours of the father and children – an authentic, convincing portrayal, with Nannerl in a very subordinate position; it was immediately engraved. And Grimm was available to draft the dedication of Mozart's first published work, two *Sonates pour le Clavecin*, which appeared in March 1764, dedicated to Madame Victoire de France, second daughter of Louis xv.

Despite the interesting daily contact with Paris and its cultured population (impressively documented in Leopold's notes), despite the successful performances both public and private, despite Leopold's delight at seeing Mozart dressed all in black with a French hat – and his worry over a brief illness of Mozart's, followed by indignant rejection of the fashionable French idea of innoculating such a child against small-pox – despite all these things, the significant, memorable event at Paris was this proof of Mozart the composer, '*agé de sept ans*', as the title page read, though in strict fact Mozart was aged eight. Within a month it was followed by publication of another two sonatas, again with a dedication composed by Grimm, this one to Madame de Tessé, the Dauphine's lady-in-waiting, at the same time announcing the departure from France of her '*très petit serviteur*'.*

Surveying the musical scene, Leopold Mozart had expressed hopes for French taste as it was gradually shaped by the publications of German musicians living in Paris. Some of these had come and presented their published sonatas to the Mozart family – among them Johann Schobert, famous as a harpsichord player, and his slightly older rival performer, Johann Gottfried Eckardt. In more ways than one, the existence of these two men's work has been detected as an influence on Leopold and Mozart, seen as shaping the style of these earliest sonatas, formal, elaborate, inevitably somewhat lacking in personality. Whatever the musical influence, where theirs is likely to mingle with that of other composers known to both Mozarts, the example they offered by publica-

* 'Very small servant.'

tion is more pertinent. Musical publication was still something of a novelty, or at least still not common. Remarkably little of Mozart's mature music was to be published in his lifetime. Leopold had shown considerable initiative when at twenty-one he had published his own trio-sonatas; but he saw to it that his son's work appeared in print at virtually a third of that age – and in Paris, not Salzburg.

The works themselves were entirely serious (without exotic or ono-matapoeic effects) and their form a dialogue between harpsichord and violin: the scene depicted, very nearly, by Carmontelle, for – unlike Schobert's and Eckardt's – Mozart's sonatas originate, though at an entirely professional level, in family music-making. Yet the dominant harpsichord part is his own; the very restricted role of the accompanying violin is Leopold's. It is like Mozart's bedtime ritual with his father, or like many a music-loving eighteenth-century prince, whose valet might accompany him in the necessary, subordinate passages – 'As a servant serves his master', in the words of Leopold already quoted. Only, in the Mozart case, the service was to have also trained the prince, for the father willingly stepped down into the lesser role so that his son's miraculous powers might shine the more brilliantly. 'I can tell you, dearest Frau Hagenauer,' Leopold wrote proudly from Paris, 'that God daily works new wonders through this child.'

The next stage in the miraculous progression was London, represented not merely by fresh court successes and a fresh round of concerts, but publication there of Opus III, six sonatas dedicated to Queen Charlotte, and the creation there of Mozart's first symphonies and a reference to his planning an opera. London was to remain for Mozart a sympathetic, memorable experience: he was to make his first musical friends there and, in effect, to discover himself. As an adult, he positively loathed Paris and Parisian life – even before experiencing the shock of his mother dying there. Already as a highly perceptive child, he perhaps detected the indifference and insolence which underlay, still indeed underlie, French assumptions of *politesse*, that concept of surface varnish which Leopold never questioned. The father's faith in Paris, and his continued reliance on the friend ennobled as Baron Grimm, were not really shaken by Mozart's later experiences – which had been largely thrust on him through Leopold's invoking of a Paris which had never quite existed.

About London, however, Leopold remained ambiguous: the varia-tions of weather were appallingly sudden; coffee was expensive to buy while 'the tea kettle is on the fire all day long'. Finally, he himself was taken quite seriously ill for several weeks; he might almost have died, Nannerl long after recorded, echoing doubtless Leopold's own often-repeated belief. Although England under a young, music-loving Hanoverian king, married to an equally music-loving German queen, with many German musicians active in London and the echoes of Handel still plainly audible, might have seemed to offer the Mozart family an ideal environment, Leopold was more conscious of a godless atmosphere 'where most people have no religion at all'. When he declares he had refused certain proposals and would not bring his children up in such a place, he seems to hint that some suggestion had been made of the family settling in England.

Yet, the godless atmosphere was endured for fifteen months – a notably longer period than had been spent in Catholic Paris, or was to be spent by the family in any other foreign city. Several aspects of London impressed Leopold, beginning with the even more than usually friendly and informal reception at court – and he had grown quite a connoisseur of such receptions. Not only was George III pleased by Mozart's playing of his beloved Handel's work, but when he drove past the family in St James's Park he lowered the carriage window to nod and wave to them all, '*und besonders unsern Master Wolfgang*'.* A few years later in Italy, Leopold was glad to encounter English people with whom he had made friends during the London stay. Public concerts were an established custom, and the first one Leopold organized was a tremendous success; considering how often he advertised and displayed his two 'Prodigies of Nature', he continued to do fairly well. And before they left in July 1765, after presenting one of Mozart's motets to the British Museum, Leopold had received the thanks of the Trustees for the work 'of your very ingenious Son'. Perhaps the most touching record of the London stay was Leopold's noting down a passage from Shakespeare, in the original:

> ... The man that hath no Musick in himself
> nor ist not mov'd with concord of Sweet Sounds,
> Is fit for treasons, Stratagems, and Spoils ...

Even the slip into German while copying adds its effect.

Mozart, too, may then have discovered Shakespeare, but more immediately valuable – personally as well as musically – was the discovery of a friend in Johann Christian Bach, Bach's youngest son. He

---

* 'And particularly our Master Wolfgang.'

himself had arrived in England only two years before, but was to settle there virtually for the rest of his life. As fertile, fluent composer, as the Queen's music-master and as a most brilliant harpsichord performer – trained under his father and under his much older brother Carl Philipp (the author of the *Versuch* on the clavier) – Bach might have offered example and affinities enough. His was an inherited talent; he too had early been trained within his family – but with a genius for a father. He had an attractive, kindly, amusing and popular personality – vividly suggested by his friend Gainsborough's portrait of him – and he was delighted by the boy Mozart. Grimm mentions one occasion when he hid Mozart between his knees and they took it in turn to play a sonata, so smoothly that it appeared that there was only one performer.

In this merging of identity there is some symbolic aptness. If Bach found Mozart delightfully gifted, the boy on his side probably experienced strong attraction towards the man, as well as towards the musician. Bach was not only younger, obviously more talented and more carefree than Leopold Mozart. He had been in Italy, could claim to be a friend of the widely-respected Padre Martini – later to befriend Mozart – and had composed operas for Milan and Naples; and new operas of his were to be performed in London while the Mozart family was there. For Mozart attraction meant emulation. It was in London that he wrote his earliest symphonies. They have long been recognized as having been written under Bach's influence. Yet the slow movement of the very first (K.16) is already unexpectedly personal and romantically expressive.

This symphony is probably the first individualized work by Mozart, abruptly oblivious – musically – of his father. At the period a symphony was far from having epic character or dimensions, being normally a three-part overture, often so called, and originally played in the theatre. Bach no doubt showed Mozart the way towards expression of personality in music, and from him derive the almost exaggerated variations of tempo and volume in this symphony, where the last movement boldly drives and swoops to its conclusion. But the andante is something quite personal and starkly simple. Weaving between its hushed yet urgent strings, with their steady, chugging rhythm, is a melancholy thread of wood-wind, giving the whole movement an unconventional, extraordinarily intense pathos. Something strangely muted and slow is apparent too in the first movement, despite its being marked 'molto allegro'. At the very beginning of Mozart's career stands this symphony – like a warning against any equating of his music with elegant, gracefully-formed but not particularly profound works of art. Individual more than imitative, almost passionate in its concern with expression, it might well be thought, in terms of conventional ideas about composers, the first symphony not of Mozart but of Beethoven.

If Mozart's symphonies at this London period were encouraged into existence by Bach, it is likely that Bach's operas, or his talk of opera in Italy, encouraged Mozart to think of emulating him also in that category. A totally new facet of Mozart's ability was revealed (much more interesting than Leopold-style demonstrations of covering the keyboard or detecting notes of clocks) when he improvised for Daines Barrington, a lawyer and antiquary who came to test his powers, music to interpret the contrasting moods of the words *affetto* and *perfido*. He was influenced too by the style of music the fashionable, newly-arrived Italian singer, Manzuoli, might choose. Manzuoli also had become Mozart's friend – as Barrington knew – but, though he appeared in Bach's operas, was something of an antagonist to Bach: for all Bach's Italianate qualities, he seemed to stand for German music, and when one of his operas failed it was a matter, Burney wrote 'of great triumph to the Italians'. That Mozart could be friends with both men is also symbolically apt. He was born to fuse the two worlds they represented: Italy and Germany, the vocal and the instrumental. How well he already responded to the concept of the aria – already with that touch of satire about its typically inflated sentiments which he always kept – is revealed by Barrington's words: '[He] immediately began five or six lines of a jargon recitative.' The boy of eight is recognizably father of the man, who not only understood the importance of the recitative element but would compose music and words for a mock heroic aria: 'Caro mio, Druck und Schluck.'

Opera, indeed vocal music of any type, was a branch of the art in which Leopold Mozart could claim no expertise. Even in singing a duet with Mozart, Barrington noted, he was 'once or twice out . . . on which occasions the son looked back with some anger pointing out to him his mistakes . . .'. The roles of pupil and teacher were being reversed, while Barrington watched. Leopold's long illness in London was his first physical withdrawal from his son, who was inevitably left to his own devices; it was during this illness that Mozart is traditionally said to have composed his first symphony – composing because he could not disturb his father by practising. Certainly he was not rebelling, at least consciously, against Leopold, but his own creative personality was unfolding and dispensing with the father as it did so. No wonder that after his illness Leopold claimed, doubtless with an air of obscure reproach all round, that he might have died. If he had, it is likely enough that Bach would have proved a second father to Mozart, as perhaps he had indeed come to seem. Even musically, fathers make a pertinent appearance in Mozart's thought at this period; the first aria he ever wrote was a tenor one for the revengeful father, Massimo, in Metastasio's *Ezio*, produced with music by various hands (including Bach's) at the King's Theatre on 24 November 1764. Massimo's daughter, Fulvia, goes to denounce him for plotting to kill the Roman Emperor; but left alone Massimo sings a reminder to her to reflect on what her action means:

> *Ma pensa in quel momento*
> *Ch'io ti donai la vita*
> *Che tu la togli a me.**

It is scarcely exaggerating to hear the tones of Leopold Mozart also behind such a reminder to one's child.

By contrast, Bach's experiences, Bach's music – vocal as much as instrumental – and, above all, Bach's lively, easy-going, ever-kindly personality must have made him a hero to Leopold's son. They met again, in Paris, just after Mozart's mother's death in 1778, when Bach came to write an opera (*Amadis des Gaules*, destined to be successful only in uniting Gluckists and Piccinists in condemnation). Bach showed himself still friendly, while Mozart confessed simply: 'I love him with all my heart.' To the end, Bach retained that nature which awoke affection and sympathy. When he was dying, sadly sunk in fortune and reputation, he showed his interest in a young engaged couple who visited him, one of whom later recalled 'his enchanting smile'. Mozart too remembered him. Writing from Vienna to his father in April 1782, he refers to the news of the death of 'English Bach', and adds, '*Schade für die Musikalische Welt!*'†

In fact, the musical world showed little sense of its loss, and Mozart's reaction – so generous when compared with what his usual attitudes were, or are commonly supposed to have been – suggests how deeply his emotions, and memories too, were stirred.

Even apart from Bach, the mixture represented by England was rich in many ways. The musical scene included several gifted native composers

---

* 'But at that moment consider
  That I gave thee life
  Which thou art taking from me.'
† 'What a pity for the musical world.'

– such as Boyce and Avison, as well as Arne – whose work is now rightly being appreciated again. Handel's music, though often brutally fragmented, was still popular; it was played at some of the concerts where Mozart himself performed. Singers like Manzuoli and Tenducci drew the whole town to the opera, which included – during Mozart's stay – one version of Metastasio's *Il Re Pastore* (the libretto he was to set ten years later). A rather different sort of opera, a 'comic opera' in English, was put on at Covent Garden in 1765, *The Maid of the Mill*, to which Bach contributed some songs. Leopold Mozart's travel notes show his typical width of acquaintance: many musicians, several foreign ambassadors, the painter Zoffany, a sprinkling of the English aristocracy, one of whom provided the Mozart family with the opportunity for their final English experience, racing at Canterbury. Nannerl had jotted down some remarkable phenomena seen in London: an animal like a donkey with coffee-brown and white stripes 'as regular as if painted', the waterworks and a camel, a rattlesnake, 'enchange, Lincolsin fielsgarten . . .' (that is, the Royal Exchange and Lincolns' Inn Fields). And so, at Canterbury, on the eve of departure, she made one last, somewhat baffled entry: 'The horserace.' A much longer, more fascinated description was given by Haydn when in 1792 he went to see the races at Ascot.

On 1 August 1765, the Mozart family landed at Calais, safely back on the continent of Europe. Some ninety years afterwards, Herzen, having lived in both England and France, was to sum up and contrast the two nationalities: the solitary, liberty-loving, shop-keeping, rather rude Englishman and the interfering, yet underneath passive, ever-instructing, more superficially polite Frenchman. By these standards Leopold Mozart was by nature a Frenchman, his son an Englishman – as indeed he was to recognize himself: '*ich ein ErzEngelländer bin*,'* he wrote when the English won a naval battle over the French.

Back on the terra firma of a Europe he instinctively understood better, Leopold planned a return to Salzburg by the longest possible route, in a journey which eventually occupied over a year. At London, the Russian, Danish and Dutch ambassadors had each proposed visits to their countries. Leopold chose Holland; there, at the court of the young Prince of Orange, Mozart had his usual success as a performer. At The Hague, as in Paris and London, a royally-dedicated work was published (opus 4: Six Sonatas for Harpsichord and Violin), this one destined for the

* 'I am an arch-Englishman.'

Prince's sister. Yet the very real strain the children were under became abruptly apparent again when Nannerl fell dangerously ill of typhoid during the winter of 1765. She was still convalescent when Mozart caught the illness, growing frighteningly weak. As soon as he had recovered, the tour resumed; Leopold was soon wondering about taking in Turin and, having put that project aside, being attracted to the idea of Venice. This was the time, he explained to Hagenauer, to show the children off, while they still remained young enough to excite admiration.

Although Italy was deleted from the itinerary, the return to Salzburg was unhurried and erratic enough. Even Leopold began to forget when and where he had last written home from, as the family moved in the spring of 1766 from Holland to Belgium, paused at Paris – again performing at Versailles – and then astonished in succession Dijon, Lyons and Geneva. It was autumn when Voltaire missed seeing *le petit Mazar* [*sic*] at Geneva, because of illness, but at Zurich the poet-publisher Gessner, and his physicist brother, made the family's stay very agreeable; Gessner presented them with his own complete works, flatteringly inscribed, and Mozart still owned two of the four volumes at his death. They had previously stopped at Lausanne, where a long laudatory article on 'Mozart' was published; and then hastened to Donaueschingen, to the court of the Prince von Fürstenberg, who had in his employment the family's one-time servant, Winter. Next Messkirch, Ulm, Dillingen and Augsburg were speedily visited; they had reached Munich by early November, and it is not surprising that here, between concerts, Mozart was once again taken ill, with rheumatic pains so severe that he could not stand.

As the family approached Salzburg, Leopold's doubts and worries sharpened. It must have been apparent that absence had not settled anything. Even the need for new accommodation – to provide more space for the family – presented its own problem, small, however, compared with that of employment at court. Perhaps the family would have to set out travelling yet once more, he thought – or, rather, threatened.

The return to Salzburg was, at least on the surface, a triumph. The family came back established as a European phenomenon, widely written about, patronized, portrayed, and discussed. There was an array of rich presents and mementoes for Salzburg to gaze at: from the snuff box given by Louis xv, filled with money by the king himself, to the purchases made cheaply while travelling by Leopold. Local composers like Michael Haydn had now to admit that Mozart's clavier technique outshone theirs. In the cathedral or at court, Mozart was encouraged to contribute some music; and yet, as a local diarist wrote on Mozart's return, 'one could only wish that this boy were able to compose more'. The boy must have felt the same.

His extraordinary early career as performer was virtually over. On his eleventh birthday in 1767, he could look back on so many countries visited, so many people met, so much music heard, his own unfailing demonstrations – whatever the conditions, the audience or his own health – of virtuosity at the keyboard, and of creative ability which asked only to be utilized further. Nannerl appeared grown up; Mozart appeared little changed, but for them both the truth was exactly the reverse. Meanwhile, Mozart was living quietly with his family in Salzburg, amusing himself with a few friends and waiting, waiting for the opportunity to begin a new career.

4

Waiting was not an experience Leopold Mozart ever endured without protest. Time was always too short in his eyes: he was getting older; his children would soon no longer astonish by their youth. Above all, he was impatient by nature. *'Mit starken schritten forteilen'** was his pro- gramme for Mozart, who should be hurrying along the broad road of success, were it not – as it soon appeared – for envious, evil creatures.

Between the end of the family's European tour in November 1766 and the departure of Mozart and his father for Italy in December 1769, there intervened a three-year period during which the broad road of success proved hard to find. It was a new road, along which Mozart was meant to travel now as composer, not performer, though still at his father's side. The series of events which hindered his progress might suggest that to Leopold's favourite challenge *'Aut Caesar aut nihil'*, the reply was likely to be *'nihil'*. In the autumn of 1767, on the news of the forthcoming marriage of the Archduchess Josepha to Ferdinand, King of Naples, the Mozart family travelled to Vienna in the hope of con- tributing a musical share to the festivities. An epidemic of smallpox had already broken out in the city. The Empress – like Leopold, a strong opponent of innoculation – caught it but recovered; her daughter-in- law died from it, followed a few months later by her daughter, the

* 'To hurry onwards with firm strides.'

affianced Archduchess. Public mourning had hardly begun before Mozart himself caught smallpox, the last but the most serious of his childhood illnesses. Nannerl too caught it, but had a milder bout. When they had both recovered – Leopold had quickly moved them out of Vienna – they returned to experience a year of the involved, infuriating negotiations round the commission for Mozart to write an Italian opera. The widowed Maria Theresia no longer took her previous interest in music and it was her eldest son and co-regent, the Emperor Joseph II, who hoped to see an opera of Mozart's performed in Vienna – a wish actively frustrated by Affligio, the manager of the two chief theatres there.

Not until January 1769 did the family arrive back in Salzburg, after the least miraculous months since Mozart's abilities had first been revealed. It is true that the opera intended for Vienna, *La Finta Semplice*, was given before the Prince-Archbishop later in the year, but that was inevitably a single and private performance. By September Leopold was making plans and consulting friends about the journey to Italy. Only through travel, it seemed, could the road to success be discovered.

Yet the outward events, and non-events, of the period between the two major tours give a misleading impression of time wasted. It is perhaps for this reason that most scholars and popularizers have united to dismiss Mozart's work at this period as not worth discussion. Looking, as Leopold doubtless partly did, from the point of view of Mozart's career, there was no public advance. No fresh astonishment had been wrung from a fresh audience, and Vienna had failed to show its previous enthusiastic interest. But there was another aspect of this period, and Leopold recognized it – even while also consoling himself by evoking past achievements – in drawing up at Vienna a list of 'all that this twelve-year-old boy has composed since his seventh year'.

Many adult composers might at any period envy the activity and variety recorded by this list. In his twenties, Haydn – once a highly talented boy-singer – had been living obscurely and miserably, burdened by teaching. Gluck had composed nothing for public performance until the age of twenty-seven. Even Weber, whose father consciously tried to force him into the role of Mozartian *Wunderkind*, and sent him to study at Salzburg, was to compose only one extremely short and slight work by the age of twelve. Leopold Mozart's list becomes an impressively rising graph: tracing the growing mastery of Mozart, from those earliest sonatas published in Paris to the *opera buffa*, *La Finta Semplice*, then just composed and amounting – Leopold carefully notes – to 558 pages. Between these two points lie symphonies, Italian arias, divertimenti, marches, two masses as well as other church music, an oratorio, music for a Latin play, and the *Singspiel* of *Bastien und Bastienne*. For a substantial amount of this music, the instigation came from the Salzburg court, where Archbishop Schrattenbach had clearly given a sympathetic welcome to his vice-*kapellmeister*, and his son, on their return.

Whatever Leopold had feared about his reception, there seems little he could complain of. The family had scarcely settled again when the anniversary of the Archbishop's consecration day was celebrated at court: by an Italian comedy, a musical intermezzo and a so-called 'licenza', a tenor aria composed by Mozart ('Or che il dover'; K.36), which was much admired and closed the proceedings. This aria has been rather dismissively described as 'provincial . . . and bravura', but as a commission it was a compliment and is itself a complimentary address to the Archbishop, an occasion for showy rather than profound feelings. And 'provincial' seems harsh, if not inapt, for any product of the much-travelled, cosmopolitan, not yet ten-year-old composer, whom Barrington had already found capable of extemporary production of an aria showing 'most extraordinary readiness of invention'.

Mozart's concert arias – probably still the least appreciated of all his music – are perfectly serious works of art, at worst virtuoso compressions of drama for an age of virtuosity, suited to different singers and different occasions, highly-wrought for all their miniature scale. If the very early K.36 proves no more than competent when performed (when indeed?) the late arias (K.505 and K.528), written for Nancy Storace and Josepha Duschek, are the triumphant justification of Mozart's steady interest in the category, intensely personal – almost private – and deeply poignant. They touch on emotions which could perhaps scarcely be aroused by the celebration of an elderly Archbishop's anniversary.

With this 'licenza', however, Mozart had been given one sort of opportunity to match voice and music, and he probably took it gratefully. The following year his opportunities were considerably greater: the dream of writing an opera was partially realized when he contributed substantially to the Lenten oratorio, *The Obligation of the First Commandment* (*Die Schuldigkeit des ersten Gebotes*, K.35) and provided the music for a Latin play *Apollo et Hyacinthus* (K.38), both Salzburg University productions. Both 'may be dismissed at once', according to the late E. J. Dent (*Mozart's Operas*), and his advice was for long widely followed. Fortunately, it is judgments like these that in recent years have at last been dismissed in the light of some re-appraisal of the facts and even an English stage performance of *Die Schuldigkeit* . . . (at the Camden Festival in 1968).

Admittedly, a painfully jokey production of what can never have been intended for actual staging increases the difficulty of estimating Mozart's first operatic experiment – for that is what it is. As a Lenten oratorio, the story of a lukewarm Christian, allured by Worldliness but strengthened by Justice and helped by Mercy, was comprehensible, suitable and – it seems necessary to explain – not comic. Mood, not character, was what Mozart had to convey; and in an age of Tiepolo's effortless painted allegories and of the elegant sculpted angels of Bavarian or Austrian church interiors, the fact that the singers represented personifications implied neither absurdity nor insincerity. The text was straightforwardly didactic, and in Mozart's native language. Its author, Ignaz Anton von Weiser, was a prosperous Salzburg merchant, later to be burgomaster, and already an acquaintance of the Mozart family's; his text was at least a fresh one, probably seeming then less artificial than, say, some often-set Metastasian verses, and ethical rather than religious.

Mozart's music is largely concerned with depicting the Virtues which should stir a Christian soul – not typical Roman Catholic church music, but closer to *opera seria*. Johann Christian Bach has inevitably been claimed as an influence on the delicate orchestral colouring of *Die Schuldigkeit*, but the solemn tenor aria with trombone obligato suggests the influence of Maria Theresia's court composer Wagenseil, whose work was among the first Mozart had ever studied. His Trombone Concerto was probably the earliest piece of music to feature the instrument so prominently. It would be nice to feel that Mozart, so quick to assimilate, already knew this striking demonstration of the trombone's capabilities. What may be called still tentative about the use of the trombone in *Die Schuldigkeit* becomes totally accomplished in *Idomeneo*, not to speak of Mozart's later works.

Of the three parts to the oratorio, the remaining two (now lost) provided by Michael Haydn and the composer-cum-court organist, Adlgasser, each was performed on a different day in March 1767. It is perhaps a sign of the success of Mozart's contribution that his was repeated by itself a few weeks later. In May came a different sort of drama – livelier and yet more learned – represented by the Latin 'comedy' *Apollo et Hyacinthus*, which was performed by students at the university, with a boy soprano taking the one girl's role. It has probably never been staged since and about it has gathered a heavy critical silence. Yet musically it represents at least one development, for it contains Mozart's first duet, with a melody which has actually been praised – at least as it reappears in his Symphony No. 6 (K.43) of the same year.

Although the hand of the play's author, Father Rufinus Widl, is heavy as he pulls at the silver filigree of Ovid's verse to make a story with little about Hyacinth and a good deal about Apollo's love for a king's daughter, Melia, he provided – in however crabbed a fashion – a sort of *Acis and Galatea*. It was not a comedy in any modern sense, but a series of interludes with a happy ending. Although possibly, probably rather, Mozart had to have parts of the Latin text explained to him, the feelings of the characters are at once varied, direct and thoroughly understandable. The plot is really a love story into which Hyacinthus (mortally wounded off-stage by Zephyrus) obtrudes only to die. Apollo appears, changes him into a flower and then betrothes himself to Melia who has previously refused him. The precocity of Mozart's response to emotions of love was to be confirmed within a year or so by his setting of *La Finta Semplice* and *Bastien und Bastienne*; it would be easy, but mistaken, to claim that Mozart would find the modern peasant-pastoral world of the latter much more sympathetic than Sparta in mythological times. In many ways, *Apollo et Hyacinthus* was more interesting and more of a challenge to his imagination: it was a sort of masque-cum-*opera seria*, certainly an advance in structure on the simple, scarcely plotted *Die Schuldigkeit*, and useful training – if nothing else – for the future composer of several *opere serie*.

And there remained, finally, one traditional opportunity for music-drama, combined frequently with spectacle, in setting the liturgy, especially the mass. Indeed, the mass itself is a dialogue and a drama, one Mozart had been familiar with from his earliest years. At Salzburg, the celebrant in the cathedral would often be the ruler himself, become the centre of a religious not court ritual, at the most solemn moment of which he too had to bow his head, humbled briefly before a divine Ruler. The whole shifting annual pageant of Roman Catholic ritual – from the visually, and musically, severe services in Lent to the colour and splendour of great feast days – has continually exercised its spell over artists. From the Council of Trent onwards, the Church had deliberately utilized theatrical effects in casting that spell and it would be surprising if Mozart had not responded to them. He must certainly have speedily realized the dramatic alternations between spoken and sung in most services, with the celebrant set against the choir. Modern concert performances of masses inevitably lose the recitative element, such as the '*sine fine dicentes*' declaimed by the priest, which leads straight into the burst of the 'Sanctus'. (That those actual words had stuck certainly in Leopold Mozart's mind is shown by his sudden, perhaps barely conscious, quotation of them in a letter.) Although his Passion Cantata (K.42) had probably been performed in Salzburg Cathedral, Mozart's first mass was written for Vienna in 1768. He was to compose another fourteen; and, as if in preparation, was at this period also copying down portions of mass settings by local men like Adlgasser (some later mistaken for his own work).

It was not therefore after any bout of idleness that Mozart was borne off to Vienna by his father in the autumn of 1767. Nor should Salzburg be thought of in terms only of its musical opportunities. Mozart was growing up – if indeed he was not in effect grown up. He now had his own friends in the city, including girl-friends. None of his letters from this time survive, but they are referred to in Leopold's own correspondence, as is the delighted receipt by Mozart of a verse letter from Rosalie Joly, an almost too patly-named chambermaid in a noble household in Salzburg. Petted by great ladies virtually from his infancy and probably made much of in very similar fashion on his travels by chambermaids and servants, Mozart might seem destined to become something of a king with women. A private letter by the aged '*Musik-Vatter*', Hasse, describes the boy at this date as 'handsome, vivacious, graceful and full of good manners'. To these attractive qualities may be added Mozart's intense sensibility – not necessarily the same as susceptibility. The man who was to write rather cruelly about an ugly female pupil infatuated with him is anticipated by the small child who had wiped his face in public after receiving a kiss from a lady harpsichordist; she, we may guess, seemed either ugly or old, or both. Sensibility was quickened by fame and flattery but then probably doused by the reality, the absurdity, of a boy having serious erotic emotions.

Something teasing and tantalizing thus entered early into Mozart's relations with women: he flirted, and then perhaps drew back before the passion he had aroused; more frequently a woman flirted and he might be truly in love. It seems not too far-fetched to compare it all to a sport, like the air-gun shooting which Mozart also enjoyed at Salzburg. Shooting can turn deadly; and so could the *jeu de l'amour*. Nevertheless, at this period both must have seemed merely delightful recreations: one at least enjoyed by Mozart earlier than by most boys. And exchanging letters with Rosalie Joly was part of his experience. It is constantly found astonishing, even today, that a child of eleven or twelve could produce music to fit the teasing little love story of *Bastien und Bastienne* or the more involved *buffa* plot of *La Finta Semplice*. But Mozart was not some isolated schoolboy genius, creating *ex nihilo*; he was socially, emotionally, sexually, aware, and equipped too with a sharp sense of humour. Ninetta, that pert, domineering chambermaid of *La Finta Semplice*, is basically a stereotype. But (without wishing to malign Rosalie Joly herself) who shall say that Mozart's precociously wide knowledge of chambermaids played no part in Ninetta's musical creation?

Although the sixteen months at Vienna were to culminate in Mozart's *Missa Solemnis* (now established definitely as K.139) performed at an orphanage church and conducted by the composer in the presence of the Imperial family, the significant achievement of this long stay was in composing the two operas. However strongly they may be criticized, they are patently an advance – in form alone – on the Salzburg dramas. The Emperor proposed that Mozart should write an opera for the theatre at Vienna. Leopold soon realized that *opera seria* was not required: only *buffa* singers were available and the Viennese public wanted to see only foolish shows with dances, devils, magic: '*Närrisches zeug, tanzen, teufel, gespenster, Zaubereyen, Hanswurst ... Hexen und Erscheinungen.*'* (This list of wants was remarkably to be catered for in *Die Zauberflöte*, more than twenty years later.) While Leopold battled with intrigue, detected conspiracies everywhere and finally appealed, in vain, to the Emperor, Mozart had – apparently in total confidence – faced the challenge of setting a three-act opera, based on a Goldoni libretto, with music needed for seven characters.

The story is of a 'feigned innocent', Rosina, who encourages two unpleasant brothers to fall in love with her so that she may bring pressure on them to agree to the love matches of their sister, loved by Rosina's own brother, and of the sister's maid. Although it had been a failure when first produced as an opera at Venice in 1764, *La Finta Semplice* had a plot no more ludicrous than that of many operas; and too much can be made of superciliously finding such plots ridiculous when set down in précis. The basis of *La Finta Semplice* certainly lies in *commedia dell'arte*; its characters are, to some extent, types, though the Hungarian baroness,

* 'Foolish stuff, dancing, devils, ghosts, magic, a clown ... witches and apparitions.'

Rosina, becomes something less conventional. All revolves round her high spirits and her ruses. She stands for a world where women outwit men in wars of the emotions: love triumphs over family obstacles, and triumphs finally over Rosina herself, who marries the bullying elder brother Don Cassandro. The opera ends with a cheerful septet in which all agree that: 'E spirto e bellezza son gran qualità'.* There may be, as Einstein complained, no psychological insight into the people involved (indeed, Rosina has no 'reason' to marry Cassandro) yet humour and perhaps psychological truth in the situation. One might as well criticize an early Shakespeare comedy as inadequate because its characters are not studied in depth. Ingenuity, absurdity, touches of artificiality – and final solutions sweetened by music – are all to be found too in Molière's theatre, the true ancestor of this type of Goldoni play.

However it is approached, *La Finta Semplice* remains a remarkable exercise in virtuosity, for its moods range musically from *buffo* humour, boasting and drunkenness, to the often tender, faintly melancholy soliloquy arias of Rosina, whose music has some touches anticipating mature Mozart. He was given a tremendous opportunity, it must have seemed, in being encouraged to write an Italian opera, destined for the very theatre where the operas of Gluck and Hasse were performed. Not even Leopold Mozart at his proudest can have thought that the German oratorio and the Latin play performed at Salzburg were important in themselves. But *La Finta Semplice* aimed to be in the most sophisticated of all categories of opera; and in many ways not even Mozart could succeed – at that age – in achieving the polished vitality needed, nor vary the humour, nor preserve the pace. Some of the music is spread very thinly and seems rather weary under the apparent liveliness. Despite what might at first be thought, comedy was probably a harder task for Mozart, as for other artists, when he was very young. *La Finta Semplice* is certainly inferior musically to *Mitridate*, written only two years later. Both tasks were dauntingly heavy, but the constant requirement of producing humourous music to words in a foreign language might make anyone flag.

Perhaps *La Finta Semplice* was more valuable ultimately for what it provided as experience than for itself. But its tuneful overture, some of the vivacious comic arias, and especially the heroine's arias in the first and last acts, lift it out of being a mere curiosity or lifeless pastiche. Rosina's opening aria is rather hard and soubrettish, but there is a

* 'Brains and beauty are both fine qualities.'

gentle, romantic quality about the slow music of her second aria, in which the words *'Senti l'eco . . .'** probably suggested the dying fall effect. Real emotion seems to be softening the character's stereotyped shell, and the third act begins with her discovered alone in the garden, singing a quite serious prayer not to be wounded by cupids ('Questo cor non venite a piagar').† This is the most individual and subtle aria in the whole opera. Its opening phrase of sustained appeal on the word *'Amoretti'* quickens as if Rosina felt herself increasingly surrounded by armed, dangerous, winged creatures (*'E volendo d'intorno ferite'‡*); and Mozart already shows his sympathy for the heart that is vulnerable to love, in music which is not only beautiful but expressive.

This aria is in itself enough to make one feel that the opera deserved to be a great success, had it ever reached the stage in Vienna. Leopold's chagrin and his eventual appeal to the Emperor were not misplaced. Even more significant was the admiration of the work expressed by two of the most experienced men of the older generation, Hasse and Metastasio, the latter himself a one-time youthful prodigy.

In all Leopold's complaints and explanations over the fiasco of *La Finta Semplice*, he is silent where one would most like him to be eloquent: about Mozart's own reactions. Yet the silence is perhaps significant. Mozart probably recognized that he had achieved what he set out to do. Competent people, including the singers, thought highly of the result. It had been created, whether or not it was performed. And, almost tragically, Mozart's career was to show that he could not too early teach himself that lesson: satisfaction must come from creating, not from public applause. *La Clemenza di Tito* was – is – a great work of art, as doubtless Mozart knew: knowing that he had carried out his task with no failure whatsoever of inspiration. He must have realized that in *La Finta Semplice* he had the opportunity he had been longing for since the age of eight. He took it, and perhaps that was achievement enough. The creator of it was not likely to be daunted by setting *Bastien und Bastienne*, a minute one-act opera of barely three singing characters (Colas scarcely needs to know how to sing). This commission was the unexpected bonus during the discouraging months in Vienna. It was a trifle (never mentioned by Leopold Mozart in his letters) performed privately at Dr Anton Mesmer's house. Charming and also popular – for performing

---

* 'Listen to the echo.'
† 'Do not come to wound this heart.'
‡ 'And flying around, you wound.'

because it needs few and not highly accomplished singers and little production, and on records because it can be accommodated on two sides – *Bastien und Bastienne* is a remarkably untypical, consciously naive and largely over-praised work.

Derived at two removes from Rousseau's *Le Devin du Village*, it retains something French, or perhaps, more truly, Frenchified, in atmosphere. Its village setting and characters have an insipid artificiality and tedious simplicity; for the first but not last time (for there lay in the future *Il Re Pastore*) Mozart had to deal with a pastoral convention which did not really interest him. There is something childish about *Bastien und Bastienne*, but this must not be thought of as Mozart's natural childishness, because he had already proved himself a mature musician. Indeed, he is more likely to have felt an awkwardness in having to ape being a child: a child-composer writing – one might think – for child-singers, or at least for amateurs, and producing simple little arias, ariettas, with childish rhythms and of unremitting, actually un-childlike, gaiety. The whole project is like a lollipop offered to a boy who had long outgrown sweets and was anxious to show he could do justice to a four-course meal. As for Bastienne, to whom most of the arias are given, and whose name alone was the original title of the libretto, it is difficult not to see her as possessing something of that hard youthfulness of middle-aged French actresses, intolerably playful and eternally vivacious.

At least, however, *Bastien und Bastienne* had been performed. And when in 1769 the Mozart family eventually returned to Salzburg, the Archbishop, whose consecration day anniversary two years before had been the occasion of Mozart's first concert aria, commanded *La Finta Semplice* for his name day. Schrattenbach had proved a patient master while Leopold lingered in Vienna, and before the year was over he gave additional support: granting Leopold and Mozart permission to travel to Italy, he presented them with money for the journey and, before they set out, appointed Mozart his third concert-master. The post was unpaid, but it provided Mozart at thirteen with a title and a position at court. If Leopold looked for omens, there were good ones – at last – for Mozart's journey on the road to success. And socially, too, Mozart made an appearance at Salzburg before the Italian tour; he acted as best man at the wedding of the court-organist, Adlgasser, who was marrying the Ninetta of the first performance of *La Finta Semplice*.

That opera's Italian world, located *'in una terra del Cremonese'*,* was now

* 'On an estate near Cremona.'

to be experienced for the first time in reality. In January 1770 father and son indeed passed through Cremona; they stopped just long enough to hear Hasse's *Clemenza di Tito*, on Metastasio's *seria* libretto which Mozart would set as his last commission. Some of Leopold's travel notes, made in Italian, might almost be read as a cast of characters for an *opera buffa*: '*Sgr. Pasqualini Violino – Vecchio bono . . . le due Sgre Cameriere della Principessa . . . il Frate con occhiali . . . sig. nedi schnid*, inglese di 15 anni . . .'.* Certainly it must have seemed that Italy was in fact almost as enchanted, and as musical, as it appeared in operatic convention. It was impossible for the two worlds not to blend, so regularly did the Mozarts attend the opera, whether they were in Cremona, Milan or Naples, and so hospitable and delightful did everywhere prove. Speaking Italian was at once amusing and part of the experience – and going to the opera was pointedly, professionally necessary, since Mozart had to end the year by returning to Milan with his own *opera seria* of *Mitridate* completed. That it must be a success was equally important.

Not until July was the libretto ready, and in October Mozart was hastily writing the recitatives. Yet even this commission almost disappears beneath the expansive tone of Leopold Mozart's letters. Not only did he chronicle his son's successful performances and appearances, the singers they heard, the bouquets they received, the courtesies they experienced, the visits to private picture collections, the sights seen – from St Rose's body at Viterbo to Vesuvius and Caserta – but also in some detail the increasingly handsome clothes they both had tailored. '*Wir waren schön wie die engeln*,'† Mozart wrote, when they wore their newly-made clothes in Naples. How far Leopold's complaisance stretched was early shown on the tour when he consented to dress up in cloak and domino during the carnival at Milan. He saw himself in the mirror while trying the costume on, he reported, and thought of how in his old age he was taking part in such foolishness. But this, like his typically economical remark that the clothes would always come in useful later for dish-cloths and so on, is scarcely more than apology for enjoying himself. Besides, he could add fondly that masquerade costume suited Mozart outstandingly well.

The Italian tour marks the clear emergence of Mozart – as personality as well as composer. A new view of Leopold Mozart also emerges, since

---

* 'Signor Pasqualini violinist – good old man . . . the Princess's two chamber-maids . . . the Friar with spectacles . . . sig. Nedi Schnid, a fifteen-year-old English boy.'

† 'We were as beautiful as the angels.'

he writes with his son beside him and that son was himself now articulate and to some extent emancipated. Although many of Mozart's letters at this date are either facetious ones to Nannerl or hasty postscripts to his father's, they are never less than vivid and sharply personal. When Leopold referred to the magnificent festival celebrated in S. Petronio at Bologna on the saint's day, Mozart's postscript commented that it had been beautiful but lengthy (*'aber lang'*), and that the trumpeters brought specially from Lucca blew abominably (*'abscheulich'*). Throughout, his comments on music, musicians, and especially singers, are definitely his own, as well as extremely definite. He made too his own friendships – with a young Count Pallavicini, heir to a property near Bologna, and with Thomas Linley, an English boy-virtuoso on the violin, who was exactly his contemporary. Mozart's sole surviving independent letter during this Italian tour is to Linley, who when they parted regretfully in Florence had given him a specially-composed poem of wishes never to come true: 'Ma in mezzo al pianto rivederti io spero.'*

Just like Gluck, as Leopold noted with reasonable pride, Mozart was the recipient of a papal brief creating him a Knight of the Golden Spur: *'Te creamus auratae Militae Equitem.'* A copy of the very wording was despatched by Leopold to the Prince-Archbishop at Salzburg, with a covering letter that is unfortunately lost. Mozart satirically signed his next trilingual postscript to Nannerl, *'j'ai l'honneur d'etre . . . chevalier de Mozart'*,† adding a childishly scatalogical message, as if to put the whole incident in perspective. Unlike Gluck, who in all formal letters signed himself Chevalier (his widow carefully signing herself 'von Gluck'), Mozart rarely again used his knighthood. In fact, his was a higher class than Gluck's – one not awarded to any composer since Orlando di Lasso.

More relevant to musical self-esteem must have been his reception as a member of the Accademia Filarmonica at Bologna on 9 October 1770. The preliminaries required the candidate to compose an antiphon in strict counterpoint; Mozart's 'Quaerite primum regnum Dei' (K.86) was improved a good deal by the kindly, immensely learned Padre Martini (a point on which Leopold remained totally and discreetly silent) before submission. Although this was perhaps a sort of cheating, Padre Martini is unlikely to have done it for a musician he did not esteem. The old-fashioned, academic standards he represented might

* 'But in the midst of weeping I hope to see you again.'
* 'I have the honour to be . . . the Chevalier Mozart.'

not concern Mozart, but the honour of reception was a real one. Among the rules waived on this occasion was that requiring the candidate to be aged no less than twenty. Mozart was received unanimously, with applause, and on the following day there was delivered his certificate: '*Testamur Dominum Wolfgangum Amadeum* . . .' It was the opportunity for Leopold to write again to the Prince-Archbishop, a letter certainly lost, possibly never received.

The one-time composer, the paternal impresario, was dwindling into the role of chronicler; even when he spoke of 'we' and 'our' battles – for, of course, there were inevitable intrigues and tensions as *Mitridate* took shape – it was now apparent that he was the less dominant partner. And perhaps nothing testifies better to Mozart's independence and confidence than that he was still refusing in late November – barely a month before the first performance – to write most of the music for the leading male actor, the castrato Benedetti, because the singer had not yet arrived in Milan: '*Doppelte arbeit, will er nicht haben,*'* Leopold wrote, catching something of the composer's decisiveness. Mozart preferred, as already mentioned, to meet the singer first and then match the arias to his voice, '*um das Kleid recht an den Leib zu messen.*'† So successful was his policy that Benedetti wittily remarked of the big Act II duet that if it did not please he would willingly be castrated again.

This proved unnecessary. As we know, *Mitridate* was a tremendous success. Leopold found himself occupied sending home the Milanese newspapers and explaining that the opera '*wie die Italiener sagen: ist* alle Stelle!'‡ He wrote also to Padre Martini with the good news, wishing him a happy new year. The sudden announcement of Mozart's reception by the Accademia Filarmonica of Verona was merely incidental amid the euphoria of these weeks. '*Ich habe an die halbe Welt zu schreiben,*' § Leopold scribbled frantically to his wife, with really less exaggeration than usual. Mozart's own tone – for all it remained incredibly calm – breathes relief at the opera's continuing success, while almost off-handedly referring to a fresh implication of that success: the opera had to be copied for the court at Lisbon. And, though he did not say so, it was also to be sent to Vienna and Parma.

All the waiting was over; the humiliating collapse of *La Finta Semplice*

---

* 'He does not want to do the work twice.'
† 'so that the costume will fit the body properly.'
‡ '. . . [is praised] as the Italians say, *to the stars.*'
§ 'I have to write to half the world.'

buried and forgotten. New Year 1771 had opened with the triumph of the boy-composer, newly-christened by the Italians 'il signor Cavaliere Filarmonico' – his age unimportant in comparison with his talents and fame. The knighted, distinguished, successful composer travelled for a few weeks in northern Italy with his father, partly in relaxation. There was no haste to return to Salzburg. From Venice Leopold was able to boast of their overwhelmingly friendly reception by all the noble families, itemizing the Cornaro, the Grimani, and the Mocenigo. Some observers questioned whether in fact the attention at Venice was as great as Leopold felt it should be: what was also noticed was his tendency to be piqued by such matters, while Mozart in contrast seemed unconcerned. And what he reported from Venice was about playing *attaca*: a typical-sounding Venetian game of being thrown on the ground and having one's bottom smacked. Seven women in a friendly, German, quite unaristocratic household had tried it on Mozart 'and yet they weren't able to bring me to the ground'.

When both noble hospitality and simple games were concluded, the opera performances over, with Mozart and his father turning towards home as Easter approached, there appeared the promise of a new, exciting distinction and opportunity for Mozart. A letter was coming to Salzburg from Vienna: 'It will amaze you but do immortal honour to our son,' Leopold tantalizingly told his wife. It was indeed the highest – and best – compliment to pay the composer. He was commissioned, in Maria Theresia's name, to write a *festa teatrale* for the marriage of her third son, the Archduke Ferdinand, to be celebrated at Milan in the autumn of 1771. Between the recent accomplishment of *Mitridate*, and the glowing future suggested by this imperial commission, Mozart is not likely to have minded the unexpectedly icy weather which he and Leopold encountered as they returned to Austria.

The triumphant return from the European tour five years before had marked the virtual end of Mozart's career as child-performer. The return from Italy early in 1771 was that of an abruptly-established, famous composer – established through composing an opera, the very category which he had already been thinking of, aiming at, for half his lifetime. That this should be his career, and that it would probably be a blazingly brilliant and successful one, seemed confirmed by the new commission. Italy had provided the vital experience; Salzburg was merely somewhere quiet for working and relaxing. Leopold Mozart's dreams for his son's future must have been almost feverishly excited in the months before going back to Italy. It is impossible to think Mozart was equally excited; wisely, he probably looked no further than his next tasks – happy enough that they existed. In such an attitude he would prove – not for the last time – more mature than his father.

Part II
'Ich bin ein Musikus'

THE irony of Mozart's future in 1771 is that, in terms of career, he had no future. Ten years later he would find himself dismissed finally from the Prince-Archbishop of Salzburg's service, living precariously in Vienna and placing his hopes of success on the prospect of writing another opera – this time for the new national theatre. He wrote the opera *Die Entführung aus dem Serail*. It was a success, but that did not improve his position. And by then he had become an adult, about to marry, requiring not merely praise but employment. Within another decade he was dead.

It is worth repeating that Mozart was not a consciously revolutionary artist. He never rebelled against any commission he was given. He served the Church and the Habsburg monarchy much better than either institution treated him; but his service was in the realm of the imagination, leaving him independent, or would-be independent, in reality. The stiff or reactionary sentiments of the libretti that he often had to set have worried modern critics much more than they worried the composer. Nor is this to say that he was simply indifferent to what he was setting. Mozart understood instinctively that gods from machines and incredibly clement rulers, for example, are artistic metaphors. The proof that he understood is shown unmistakably by *Die Zauberflöte*, which is *not* a mixture of silly story and sublime music: what the story is trying to express positively prompted the sublimity of the music. One might go further and add that Mozart's clear distinctions between life and art – between a real Archduke and some Metastasian prince-hero – helped him when composing an aria for the latter, leaving him the freer to exercise his imagination. Imagination could be satisfied only through creation; and the only creativity Mozart claimed to practise was in music. There he had long known his powers.

At the age of twenty-one, having left Salzburg in search of a more sympathetic post, offering him more scope, he wrote back to his father to express congratulations on St Leopold's day. In this letter, more openly tender and more serious than usual, there is an almost defiant ring, as well as quite unexpected eloquence, as Mozart explains that his expression of congratulations will be a musical composition. Though writing to Leopold, he is addressing in effect Salzburg – and indeed the world beyond, where he desperately hoped to find a patron able to respond to his declaration: 'I cannot versify; I am no poet. I cannot manage expressions artistically enough to convey light and shade; I am no painter. I cannot even express my feelings and thoughts through signs and mime; I am no dancer. But I can do it with notes; I am a Musician' ('*Ich bin ein Musikus*' – and Mozart uses a capital letter for this profession alone among those he names).

Mozart's knowledge of his own creativity had received public confirmation with the first – and, as it has proved, virtually the last – performances of *Mitridate*. Unfortunately for the modern denigrators of *opera seria*, the story and the libretto of this opera are not at all absurd. Something in *La Finta Semplice*'s story might be vaguely traced back to Molière; *Mitridate* is firmly based on a more sublime and more poetic French source, Racine's tragedy of the same name. So far, incidentally, from being a hack translation, this was the work of Parini, one of the few indisputably great Italian poets of the century.

But for the very conventions of *opera seria*, indebtedness goes beyond one specific literary source. Those virtuoso displays of the voice – arias, and sometimes coloratura arias for which, it has been said disapprovingly, listeners would be waiting – derived from the tirades of French seventeenth-century tragedy, which had been indeed one of its glories and for which its audiences also had waited. A glance at Racine's tragedy shows that here, as elsewhere, his characters explode in the heat of events and the play has hardly opened before the nature of this particular emotional furnace is revealed to us: two half-brothers, the sons of Mithridates, love the very woman the king has chosen for his own wife. A rumour of Mithridates' death – announced in the first couplet of the play – fires the situation. The honourable son flares up to explain his state of mind: in effect a soliloquy, though by convention addressed to a confidant. In a speech of eighty-six lines, he reveals what he himself calls 'secrets'. Like such speeches, the arias of an *opera seria* take us behind the action of the plot; far from holding it up – another typical criticism – they serve to emphasize that each person involved in the plot has his own passionate, often complex emotions (emotions, admittedly, rather than 'character' in any realistic sense):

> *Je l'aime, et ne veux plus m'en taire,*
> *Puis qu'enfin pour rival je n'ai plus que mon frère.**

* 'I love her and no longer wish to keep silence about it,
Since at last as a rival I have no one but my brother.'

This itself is dramatic irony, since Mithridates is, in fact, still alive. Yet the rumour of his death finally proves prophetically true. The play ends with the dying heroic king, '*Ennemi des Romains et de la tyrannie*',* carried on to the stage to hand over to his faithful son both his crown and his intended queen.

Abdication here is forced on Mithridates by circumstance, but the situation of abdication and heroic surrender – of impulse controlled by a sense of duty – is a common one of *opera seria*. It is especially a favourite one for stage works destined to be performed before royal persons (and can already be found crystallized in *The Tempest*, written for a royal occasion): while intended to flatter, such situations contain a strong dose of hard truth and – in the inevitable replacement of fathers by sons – something with applications far beyond royalty. Mozart was not the son of the king of Pontus; nor had Leopold Mozart any wish to marry the women Mozart fell in love with, but he felt an equally strong emotion, a jealous prejudice, when Mozart attempted to marry. At that point, some sort of abdication was indeed forced on him; the last pretence of tutorship to his son had then to be surrendered.

The usual modern reaction to *Mitridate* (never performed, it would appear, in the past two centuries) is to assume that it was beyond Mozart's capacity – at fourteen – to understand the situations, passions and significance of the libretto. This is at least a welcome change from the alternative presumption of there being no significance or situation in what he had to provide music for. There is no reason, incidentally, why someone who was certainly to read Molière could not already have looked at Racine. The only objection is that, then as now, Racine would scarcely be easily available in Italy, though Alfieri had seen French tragedies performed by a French company at Turin only a few years earlier. And it is worth noting that the actual librettist, not the translator, of *Mitridate* frankly referred the reader further to his source: '*Veggasi la tragedia del francese Racine*.'† And if the passions of the story and the rivalry of father and sons really meant nothing to Mozart in 1770, it cannot be denied that ten years later the royal father-son situation of *Idomeneo* moved him profoundly.

The letters which Mozart wrote to his sister from Italy during 1770 do not by any means support the idea of a boy indifferent to what libretto he will receive. He himself had suggested one of Metastasio's

* 'Enemy of the Romans and of tyranny.'
† 'See the tragedy of the French writer Racine.'

63

(possibly *Artaserse*, for which he had just composed some arias, after being given a complete set of Metastasio's work) and there is no evidence that *Mitridate* alarmed or baffled him. His letters are full of reference to the operas he saw during the year – and they are intensely practical references, concerning the style of the music no less than the quality of the singers. It would never be guessed that they were made by anyone other than an experienced '*Musikus*'; and instead of approaching *Mitridate* with prejudice against its conventions, and awareness that it is by a boy, it might be better to consider it on its merits, as the work of a composer with several operas already behind him, an instinct for the theatre and a natural understanding of the voice. Since in several instances Mozart produced several versions of an aria and these versions survive – doubtless to please the singers rather than himself – he was obviously making every effort to fit his music to the individual voices (just as we know he later did in *Idomeneo*).

No one at present is in a position to appreciate, still less to criticize, the full impact of *Mitridate* when staged – nor to realize the original effect when its staging, its scenery at least, was by one of the distinguished Galliari family. Their style represented an elevated, generalized, theatrically classical, though not antiquarian, idiom which is the ideal framework and parallel to *opera seria*. Not surprisingly, their décor was much in demand. Huge and yet light palace façades rose under their hands – one member of the family actually building what the others designed – and rooms and gardens in excitingly steep perspectives. Fabrizio Galliari had designed the scenery for an earlier setting of *Mitridate*, at Turin, and perhaps the same décor was used at Milan. He was certainly to be responsible for the scenery of Mozart's next two operas: *Ascanio in Alba* and *Lucio Silla*. And the scenery for Mozart's version of *Mitridate* was singled out for praise in at least one Milanese newspaper.

The principles understood by the Galliari in scenography and by Metastasio in writing libretti were instinctively understood in music by Mozart. A Galliari garden is grand, effective, but scarcely localized in any real country; it has indeed no 'character', serving equally well as something now in ancient Rome and now in Macedonian Nymphaea (the exotic scene of *Mitridate*). But it has theatrical effectiveness. This very quality in music, well described by Leopold Mozart as 'the *chiaro ed oscuro* necessary for the theatre', was possessed by Mozart and revealed with dramatic vividness in *Mitridate*.

The problems presented by a Tamburlaine-like figure such as Mithridates had already been experienced by Racine; his *Mitridate* is a somewhat stilted and meanly monstrous character, more oriental tyrant than hero, condemning his son and his intended wife to death not for any disloyalty but for their love. Racine's play is altogether a 'difficult' one. It is rarely performed. For the purposes of the opera, its grim ending (*'Et par tout l'univers cherchons-lui des vengeurs'*)* is softened by both Mitridate's sons being united to suitable women, and the opera closes with a brief, conventional quintet.

Probably recognizing the problem, Mozart preferred as far as possible to emphasize the tender and especially the pathetic aspects of the story: the pair of lovers overshadowed by the threat of death join in a duet (anticipating Belmonte and Constanze in *Entführung*), 'Se viver non degg'io',† which enchanted the two leading singers. It is the only duet in the opera: its place at the end of the second act is dramatic (as well as a *seria* convention), since this is the blackest moment of the story. For the lovers no further action seems possible; they declare their love and prepare to die. Aspasia (Racine's Monime renamed), who opens the opera, has a second aria, 'Nel sen mi palpita dolente il core',‡ which is almost hectically dramatic, agitated and yet most movingly sad. The news of Mitridate's return prompts a burst of grief which is also a revelation of the intensity of her feelings for Sifare: 'Your danger is the cause of my pain.' The music here touches emotions to a degree which simply makes inconsistent – if not absurd – the critical assumptions that Mozart could not deal with the opera's theme. It is significant that Mozart's Mitridate also takes on a certain aspect of pathos, at his very first appearance; his first aria reveals, in almost romantic terms, a weary warrior and monarch (distinctly different from the admittedly tired but still imperious king of the play). What Mozart was in fact doing was reinterpreting an exotically harsh play, where the heroine is unexpectedly tepid for Racine and none of the characters is sympathetic, so as to bring out the reasonable and human elements – love, fidelity, ultimate happiness – in a way to appeal to not only his audience but to himself.

It is no criticism of Racine, but still less is it one of Mozart, to point out that elements of stoic heroism and duty in Racine's bitter tragedies were

---

* 'And throughout the universe let us seek his avengers.'
† 'If I am not to live.'
‡ 'My heart beats sorrowfully in my breast.'

likely to seem unnecessarily extreme to a mid-eighteenth-century world. Mozart himself would probably have responded, for example, to a Bérénice and a Titus who were less self-lacerating in their heroism, whose lives could have been better spent than in serving merely as barren illustrations '*De l'amour la plus tendre et la plus malheureuse*'.* At no age, one may guess, would this sort of situation have found much response in him. He put his trust in love – not facilely, but as something to which human beings finally win through after often profound troubles. Perhaps he believed it too precious an emotion to be surrendered – even for the Roman Empire.

Musically, the advance of *Mitridate* on anything Mozart had written before is remarkable, but what matters is not so much its advance as its achievement. It deserves a place close to *Idomeneo* and *La Clemenza di Tito*. Now that those two operas are gradually being appreciated at something near their true merits, it might be possible again to understand and enjoy the grandeur and pathos of *Mitridate*. If youthfulness shows in its execution, it is in the wonderfully copious, varied outpouring of music which requires – but also justifies – extreme virtuosity in its singers. Great passions are aroused and set blowing through a doomed, half-oriental, antique world, shaking and nearly destroying people whose intense responses need intense expression. Love is a frail torch amid revenge, lust and the threat of a great kingdom falling, but it burns the more brightly against such a background. And thus '*chiaro*' and '*oscuro*' contrast effectively with each other.

In the music for the half-brothers, Sifare and Farnace, Mozart had opportunities for contrasting characters in a particular way which never occurred again. Consciously or not, they seem to express different aspects of their father, Mitridate, to whom both are reconciled at the end of the opera. As the hero, Sifare combines high declamatory passages with an undercurrent of tenderness which overflows in his agonized second act scena ('O momento fatale, che mi fa de' viventi il più felice e il più misero ancor')† when he parts from Aspasia; a *recitativo accompagnato* of real feeling leads into the actual aria of farewell, the sweet melancholy of which is accentuated by use of a solo horn. Incidentally, this aria is followed by one for Aspasia which even more vividly conveys her eddying moods under the double burden of love for Sifare and obligation to Mitridate. The other brother, the wicked Farnace, has arias as

* 'Of the most tender and most unhappy love.'
† 'O fatal moment, which makes me the happiest of men and yet the most miserable.'

brilliant as Sifare's but more baleful; his violently excited defiance at the news of his father's return ('. . . *questo cor nīn cederà*') has something of the dark joy of the Count's 'revenge' aria in *Figaro*.

Throughout the opera power is made a positive factor. The first act closes with Mitridate, no longer weary, calling for vengeance in a martially brilliant aria, accompanied by trumpets, which re-asserts his authority. Though his kingdom may be threatened, he still has power over his sons and Aspasia; and the opera, unlike the play, culminates with all the main characters (including the abruptly-repentant, newly-patriotic Farnace) clustered about Mitridate, who is still commanding though dying, and who dies in triumphant happiness: '*moro felice appieno*'.*

Mozart's next important task was the music for the imperial wedding *festa*; some critics have commiserated with the task and passed perfunctorily over the result, *Ascanio in Alba*. Neither response is justified. *Ascanio* was only the more honourable and imperial of two major commissions which drew Mozart back to Italy and which must have made the few months at Salzburg in 1771 seem even shorter than they were. In August he and his father were returning, via Verona, to Milan, where the marriage was to be celebrated. Parini had written the libretto of this *festa teatrale*, a pastoral masque-like entertainment with patent allusions to the royal pair in the audience, rather similar to the effect of, say, Milton's *Arcades* for the Countess of Derby, where 'some Noble personages' appear 'in pastoral habit', praising her as 'a rural Queen'. *Arcades*, slight though it may be, is a warning against dismissing this kind of literature as by its nature tedious or insipid – even when lacking the buoyant support of Mozart's music.

For such an entertainment the '*chiaro ed oscuro*' of the theatre was necessarily replaced by steady clarity: in the literary form and to some extent in the music too. Venus, with a chorus of genii and country people, frames what story there is: Ascanius, Venus' grandson, is to marry the nymph Silvia, who has fallen in love with an image of him, not knowing his identity. Silvia realizes she is pledged to marry Ascanius and so, despite her first impulse of love, flees the young stranger whom Venus has forbidden to reveal himself at first. A shadow almost too dark for a *festa* (but typically Mozartean) falls over Silvia's music as on seeing him she struggles in a long urgent and agitated recitative – its phrasing out of context virtually suggesting Bellini's distracted Elvira – leading into the hauntingly sad aria, 'Infelici affetti miei'. Only after this does Ascanius

* 'I die completely happy.'

explain that her heart prompted her truly: she need not struggle against love, for her destined husband and the stranger of whom she dreamt are the same. 'How much we owe you,' he goes on to sing, rather sweepingly, to his divine grandmother, who makes one final appearance and departs amid a chorus assuring her: 'La tua stirpe propaghisi eterna.'*

In this somewhat tough goddess testing a future granddaughter-in-law, it is easy to recognize Maria Theresia; she had selected for her young son Ferdinand, a blameless, cultivated but not beautiful wife, Maria Beatrice d'Este, a princess of Modena – hence a reference by Parini to Silvia being descended from Hercules, a name common in the Este family, and hence his tactful omission of any praise of Silvia's beauty when Ascanius first sees her. And, in reality, there had been considerable uncertainty as to whether the Archduke would be grateful for the Empress's arrangement.

Not only did the happy couple applaud *Ascanio in Alba*, 'leaning from their box towards Wolfgang,' wrote Leopold, but the extraordinarily friendly princess had captivated her husband. Perhaps Mozart's music had a nearly equal effect on him. A month or two later the seventeen-year-old Archduke consulted his mother about taking 'the young Salzburger' into his service. As we have seen, she stated that she could see no need for him to employ composers 'or useless people': if, however, he felt strongly ... He did not. The impulse died and no offer of employment was made to Mozart. Yet it is a tribute to *Ascanio* that the Archduke had approached his mother at all. Her usually devastating letters to her children far outclass Leopold Mozart's in trenchant criticism, astonishing admonishments and assurances that it is only affection which prompts the plain speaking – along with an inborn sense of being right on every topic. Well might the Archduke-Ascanio exclaim: 'Oh Madre!'

Parini had chiselled *Ascanio in Alba* into a gracefully antique frieze, delicately stained here and there with pastoral colouring: flocks, green banks, some inevitably courteous shepherds. Some thin, graceful, stately music – the sort of music with which indeed the *festa* opens – would have served well enough to accompany it. Mozart took the frieze and animated it, allowing something of dramatic *oscuro* to pass over it in places and largely remaining musically impervious to Parini's pastoral hints. Handel, in contrast, would surely have made his music paint some of those typically enchanted, enchanting landscapes with almost tuneful

* 'Thy race propagates itself for ever.'

sheep and certainly tunefully warbling shepherds. Parini's shepherd, Faunus, is turned by Mozart into a semi-divine *genius loci* with brilliantly high coloratura arias which it would be an insult to call rustic. The second one suggests nothing so much as the Queen of the Night. What is painted in the two main personages is emotional states. Ascanio experiences '*palpiti soavi*',* and the music makes us feel them with him; as he trills that he has learned to sigh, so the music sighs. Nor are such effects just decorative or mere excuses for the singer to vocalize. Even Faunus's showy second aria is justified; not only is it an effective firework of soaring brightness before the low-pitched encounter of the lovers, but its prominence is justified as a sort of 'licenza' which hails Ascanio, whose physical appearance inspires its bravura. Silvia's beautiful, slow, intensely sad aria is the deepest moment of darkness; it is followed by a ghostly, plaintive chorus of women's voices which is far from the gaiety with which the entertainment opened. Everything seems to pause, listening. An emotional onus lies on Ascanio who – with no less intensity than Silvia – sings a tender adagio aria to win her back to happiness ('Torna, mio bene, ascolta').† Insistent and firm, perhaps even somewhat naive if one accepts that interpretation of Mozart's use here of the key of F major, the aria expresses the resolution point of the whole miniature drama: 'Il tuo fedel son io.'‡ Only after this affirmation on Ascanio's part can the *festa* hasten into the cheerful spontaneity of a lovers' duet and a triumphant final chorus which probably swept out from the stage to include the bride and bridegroom in their box.

Ascanio was successful enough to be repeated; if Leopold Mozart is to be believed, its success quite eclipsed *Ruggiero*, the opera commissioned also for the wedding from the aged Hasse. Less fortunate circumstances surrounded the other Italian commission which Mozart had received: it was for a religious work, *Betulia Liberata*, intended for Padua but apparently never performed there or anywhere in Mozart's lifetime. Although usually described as an oratorio, the text had been written by Metastasio in 1754 as an '*azione sacra*' to all intents an opera, but for concert performance only because it was to be played during Lent (probably on Holy Saturday, like Metastasio's *Giuseppe Riconosciuto* of the previous year). Nowadays it is perhaps easier to think of the eighteenth century in terms of *Ascanio in Alba* rather than remembering that

---

* 'Gentle heart-beats.'
† 'Return, beloved, listen.'
‡ 'Thy faithful lover am I.'

social religious music was equally typical of the period; Metastasio's
'*azione sacra*' had itself been an imperial commission, written for Maria
Theresia's father. Its references to Judith and triumphant Israel extend
outwards – not, however, to a courtly world but to the Virgin and the
Roman Catholic religion. When the converted Achior sings to the holy
heroine ('*santa eroina*') who has returned victorious from the Assyrian
coup, 'Tu sei/La gioia d'Israele . . .',* he uses the words from the *Book of
Judith* which are used in the mass for the feast of the Immaculate Conception of the Virgin.

Possibly this provides a clue to one of the puzzling facts about *Betulia
Liberata*: the proposed period of its performance. The commission had
been given to Mozart just after the success of *Mitridate* and he was
working on the music at Salzburg during the summer months of 1771.
A letter of Leopold's implies that he and Mozart were then intending to
go to Padua to hear it after the archducal marriage festivities were over,
that is in the autumn of 1771. It cannot therefore have been intended for
Lenten performance, but it could have been for an only slightly less
liturgically severe time of year, Advent. In these weeks leading up to
Christmas, Italian theatres seem to have been closed. At the Prince-
Archbishop of Salzburg's court not even concerts were given. The
Immaculate Conception is always celebrated on 8 December, thus
always falling within Advent, and it may even be that *Betulia* was
planned originally for performance on that feast day in 1771. Mozart
and his father were travelling home from Verona when 8 December
came; they had never returned to Padua and no references were ever
made again to an Italian performance of the *azione sacra*.

It would certainly have deserved to succeed, for while it is as effectively executed a commission as *Ascanio*, it is a much more profound
and a more strikingly original work. In scale also it is grander: not a
frieze in the classical manner but an Old Testament temple. Its unrelieved and yet tender solemnity is more truly serious than many an
opera seria; it verges on a particular mood of sublimity which does not
occur again in Mozart's music, any more than does a contralto heroine.
This might seem a slight, if not positively trivial, point to pick on; and
yet it is the contralto Judith herself whose dark voice – matching the
oratorio's shadowy evening setting – spreads a sublime quality of
quietly steady confidence: 'Parto inerme, e non pavento.'† She sings

---

* 'Thou art/The joy of Israel . . .'
† 'I go unarmed and unafraid.'

this aria, prepared for only by the orchestra, without any recitative, and then goes alone at dusk to the hostile Assyrian camp. Night, darkness, shadows amid which it is hard to see (both physically and mentally): Metastasio's libretto is thick with such references, and they have tinged Mozart's music, which aptly uses for the interspersed choral sections accompanying Judith's long final recitative, the *tonus peregrinus* associated with the Sunday evening service of Vespers.

At the same time, the work is an *azione*, not some substitute for a religious rite. Its overture opens with chords of turbulently bravura boldness, suggesting a dark night of confusion with clash of armies and eddying emotions; perhaps significantly, otherwise only *Don Giovanni* has an overture in D minor. Obvious dangers of monotony in the action itself are avoided by matching Judith's inflexible contralto faith with the emotionally wavering, vividly dramatic, soprano of Amital, a noble Israelite woman. It is to her that Mozart gives the two finest arias of the piece, both exploring a wide soprano range, including poignantly low notes for her third aria, of repentance; in this profoundly quiet, slow, almost broken music – the pendant and contrast to her first accusatory aria ('Non hai cor')* – she humbles herself before God with an intensity even Mozart seldom elsewhere achieved. The closing words of the reprise, 'Signor, pietà'† are breathed more movingly in their very simplicity than all Judith's confidence, and perhaps Amital was Mozart's preferred woman in the *azione*; the opportunities he gave her certainly suggest that he had a particular singer in mind for the role.

As well as effectively bringing out Amital as a second, more human heroine, he took every opportunity for painting boldly the horrific, barbaric aspects of Holofernes, not present but described by Achior in a robust Handelian bass aria ('Terribile d'aspetto'),‡ and the 'insane terror' of the Assyrians after his death. This is conveyed in such an agitated aria, accompanied by a storm of strings, that the character Carmi, an Israelite leader (soprano) becomes almost the vessel of the emotions described. Musically, in its combination of aggression and disturbance, there are positive hints of Electra's revenge aria in *Idomeneo*.

Betulia Liberata seems indeed to have several anticipations of that opera: the first chorus, for example, suggesting something of the chorus of afflicted Cretans, and elsewhere are heard perhaps only accidental

---

* 'Thou hast no heart.'
† 'Lord, have mercy.'
‡ 'Terrible to look upon.'

assonances. What is, however, more than accidental is a similarity of mood: the nobility, dignity and exaltation of the music in *Idomeneo* is fully anticipated in *Betulia Liberata* of nine years earlier. And not until *Idomeneo* would Mozart write anything to approach the grandeur of concept and musical thought found in his unperformed *azione sacra*.

2

Although *Betulia* had not been performed, Mozart returned home in December 1771 with two new Italian opera commissions firmly settled. He was to write another opera for Milan the following year and one for Venice in the year after that. Once again it seemed that his future lay outside his own country; and perhaps it would have been a happier one had he realized this and left it for ever. Meanwhile, Leopold took the opportunity to approach the music publisher Breitkopf at Leipzig, suggesting he might care to print some of Mozart's work. Trios, quartets, symphonies – Mozart could produce them all. Breitkopf had only to order what he wanted: '*Alles wird er machen, wenn sie es nur bald melden.*'*

But Breitkopf never replied to this letter. Most of Mozart's instrumental music thus already seemed doomed to be heard only once, or privately, and not become available for public performance unless he was present. What was published was a perhaps maliciously obtuse prophecy, which seemed to close the history of the one-time boy prodigy. From his orchestral compositions it could be judged that 'he is one further instance of early fruit being more extraordinary than excellent'. This verdict on Mozart in Salzburg in 1772 was printed by Dr Burney the following year in his '*Present State of Music in Germany . . .*'; he preceded it by a kindly paragraph on the sovereign of Salzburg who was 'very magnificent in his support of music'. Mozart can hardly have minded about Dr Burney's anonymous correspondent's pompously-expressed views on himself; he might have smiled satirically over the 'sovereign of Saltsburg'. A few years later he would probably have wept with rage to read any reference to the Prince-Archbishop's support of music.

The day after Mozart and Leopold returned to Salzburg, the old Prince-Archbishop had died. Not until 14 March the following year was a new ruler elected, Hieronymus, Count Colloredo; it was he who was eventually to dismiss Mozart irrevocably and ignominiously, after

* 'He will compose everything, you have only to state what you want.'

several violent quarrels, and it is for this act alone that he is now remembered. Yet like so much in Mozart's life, this famous incident reverberates with ironies. For one thing, it was only under Colloredo, and soon after his election, that Mozart began to receive any salary as a court musician. The succession of Colloredo to Schrattenbach was not at all the replacement of a cultivated ruler by a stupid tyrant. Schrattenbach belonged in Maria Theresia's *ancien régime* world, pious, autocratic if kindly, and unenlightened. Colloredo, aged forty when he became ruler, was in the mould rather of Joseph II: reforming, cosmopolitan, a liberal – indeed, an admirer of Voltaire and, just like the Emperor, an admirer too of Frederick the Great. But in both Joseph II and Colloredo personal arrogance and a contempt for other people tarnished the enlightenment image; there was probably more genuine humanity and kindliness in Schrattenbach, as there undoubtedly was in Maria Theresia, than in either of their successors.

Yet Mozart's ultimate rebellion against Colloredo was, when it came, a symptom of something deeper than a clash of personalities. It was basically a rejection of Salzburg and all it stood for, Leopold probably included. Certainly the father-son relationship never recovered. As for Salzburg, working in it had always been a burden, Mozart then confessed; when he played, or his music was performed there, he had found the audience reaction utterly wooden, *'lauter tisch und sesseln.'** Why had he never settled down there? he asked rhetorically, answering, 'because I wasn't happy' (*'weil mein gemüth nicht vergnugt war'*).

Nevertheless, that was probably a view deliberately darkened by time and resentment. In the early months of 1772 Mozart, if not pleased with life there, was creating with typical zest and with a new sense of mastery, especially over the symphony. As Leopold wrote, *'alles wird er machen . . .'*. Behind the very real peaks, in both music and prestige, which the early, commissioned operas represent, lie the foothills of much social music, written for public performance or private occasions.

The infant Mozart had marched from room to room, moved his toys and gone to bed, accompanied by music. Actions seem positively to have suggested music to him. Keats would claim to have loved the principle of beauty in all things, but Mozart might have said he loved in all things the principle of movement. Music and movement combine most

* 'Mere tables and chairs.'

obviously in the dance, and Mozart wrote many dances, in addition to the patent dance-movements of so many of his symphonies. Indeed, the dance as such in all its varied moods – yet always being an expression of attraction between human beings – lies perhaps at the centre of Mozart's creativity. He was to be delighted years later to find that the music from *Le Nozze de Figaro* was arranged at Prague for contredanses and German dances, not joining in only because he was too tired. He was writing German dances (e.g. K.605) in the final year of his life; a last echo, literally, of Leopold can be heard in the 'Sleigh-ride' with its musical bells. As early as 1770, when in Rome, Mozart had written a contredanse (K.123) for fun and performance at Salzburg, and had virtually devised the choreography: 'When the two violins play as leaders, only two people should lead the dance . . .' This is music serving a very clear social purpose, not just listened to but actively participated in. At times like carnival in Salzburg, everybody became a child again – a Mozart-child, one might say – ruled by music, whether in a stately minuet or in the popular country dance and waltz, the latter once a low-class form but rising even in Mozart's lifetime towards the vogue which it was to enjoy in the following century.

In some ways, one may extend the concept of social participation to some other instrumental work by him: quartets and concertos written with a specific performer in mind, whether the King of Prussia on the 'cello or Anton Stadler on the clarinet – the latter inspiring the hauntingly beautiful clarinet concerto (K.622), as well as several other works. Just how Mozart was to think sometimes of soloists is amusingly shown by his writing on the autograph of a horn concerto for the horn soloist Leutgeb: 'took pity . . . on that ass . . .' He probably took pity the more feelingly for being himself a soloist, a virtuoso one, who never ceased to perform; and it is easy to believe that when he encountered a virtuoso like Stadler, on an instrument he loved but did not play, he could create music for him in a mood almost of self-identification.

All the great work of this kind comes later in Mozart's career, and it becomes perhaps more personal than social. But the century demanded some sort of social purpose in all its art – the purpose of pleasing being just as important to society as that of instructing, and as much art being expected therefore in designing a boudoir or mirror cabinet as in designing a throne-room or a church. Musical forms trifling in themselves – pastime-music for helping time pass agreeably – were filled by Mozart with quite untrifling content. The most famous example, which no amount of performance can stale, is '*Eine kleine Nachtmusik*' (K.525), though it is possibly significant that this last, miniature and economically concentrated serenade appears to have had no specific external impulse. It was written during the composition of *Don Giovanni*, an opera with a continual series of night-scenes and more than one use of serenade-cum-entertainment music within its action. Perhaps to Mozart '*Eine kleine Nachtmusik*' represented relief while pausing in the profoundly serious task of writing this major opera. Being Mozart, he would express even relief in music: in something which is certainly not profound, but is diversion music of an electric vitality experienced by most people only, very briefly, on emerging from a brush with death. But death had crept close to Mozart in the year of *Don Giovanni*.

The very names of the types of occasional music – serenades, notturni, divertimenti – mingle suggestions of relaxation in the evening with vague hints of faintly amorous diversions ('*Io so, crudele, come tu ti diverti*',* as Elvira says to Don Giovanni when she finds him carrying off Zerlina to his evening party). Serenades by night in the open air (scored for wind instruments rather than the strings better suited for indoor performance) seem to evoke the most attractive, graceful side of leisured eighteenth-century life. The sound of horns may suggest the unrolling of an enchanted, velvet night in which at first only a bassoon bubbles liquidly, like a fountain gleaming in a shadowy garden, to be followed by some minuet which might be imagined drifting through the darkness from a ballroom.

Several of Mozart's serenades were written for small, special, social occasions – birthday and marriage offerings. One of them (K.375) was to be used again to serenade the composer himself as a surprise, on the evening of his nameday in 1781. He was just undressing for bed when he suddenly heard the first chord of his own serenade, being performed by a group of friendly musicians who had crept quietly into the courtyard of the house where he lodged in Vienna. It is Mozart who relates this incident and perhaps it is the neatest – as well as the most charming – illustration of music put to social use in the eighteenth century. Opening one's window on an autumnal evening in the centre of Vienna and hearing the notes of a Mozart serenade would have been to experience something substantiating the *ancien régime* myth of '*douceur de vivre*'.

Possibly the climate of life in Salzburg too was favourable when, in

* 'I know, you cruel man, how you amuse yourself.'

the early months of 1772, Mozart wrote a group of eight symphonies, of partly serenade-like character, which represent the most serious and sustained non-vocal music he had so far created. With the recent success of *Ascanio* still vivid, and before him the guaranteed prospect of writing the next opera at Milan, he might well exult in the intervening months – and not merely take, but make, the opportunity to produce work of a different character. The new symphonies were perhaps begun to provide Breitkopf with up-to-date examples should he ask for Mozart's music – which we know he did not – or perhaps with a view to animating typical Salzburg audiences of 'tables and chairs'. What they most strongly suggest, however, is that the impetus for their creation was internal and highly personal to the composer. A more critical and careful attention to symphonic form as such is shown by the finales, much more elaborate than in Mozart's earlier symphonies; and balancing much better with the first movements.

Every sort of influence has been detected in them: Italian example, German example, recollections of French music, as well as awareness of Viennese form (e.g. four instead of three movements). They are marked at times by dynamically strong contrasts of tone, echoing Johann Christian Bach; and even to the unlearned ear the later ones in the group contain some remarkable complete movements whose broad steady rhythms ought to be – conceivably are – by Haydn. But it is exactly out of such mingled, almost conflicting influences that Mozart makes something quite individual and often moodily personal. Apart from the earliest symphony, the A Major (K.114), of a group highly varied and composed over a period of some eight months, none perhaps is flawlessly consistent. Yet each contains, increasingly in terms of execution, movements of quite wild and stirring beauty.

The variety of effect between one symphony and another seems intentional, suggesting that perhaps there lingered some hope of seeing them published. The first dates from the very last days of 1771. It is sparkling, light-textured and light-hearted, ending in a fast, brilliant finale with the strings racing to a triumphant conclusion which impels applause. Early in the new year Mozart was possibly ill, but that in itself hardly accounts for the very different character of the next symphony (K.124), heavier – or, at least, more weighty – and rather agitated. A sort of dreaminess comes over the music, to which the adjective 'romantic' truly applies. And perhaps it is not going too far to see in all these symphonies a constant conflict between observation of conventional form and urge towards almost wayward content, so that it is in the slow movements especially – in contrast to some rather perfunctory minuets – that Mozart himself speaks most individually.

Scoring for different instruments produces subtly different effects within the compass of a small chamber orchestra, and the most elaborate of these symphonies, the penultimate one, calls for the largest number of instruments, including trumpets. It was composed in July 1772 and has something courtly and solemn about it. With its opening fanfare touches and unexpected flute obbligato in a very pondered slow movement, its grand minuet and an extraordinarily mature Haydn-like joyful finale, it might positively have been intended for performance at Colloredo's court. Certainly it demonstrates the virtuosity of the young composer whose salary he started to pay the following month. The group closes as it began with a symphony in A major (K.134), the slow movement of which is almost singingly sad, a complete *scena* for the pleadingly eloquent violins which open the movement with a startling anticipation of 'Porgi, amor'. A rippling, almost muttered tension builds up, dies away and is replaced by a melody which might be a hymn, calm, pure, out-soaring pain. Its silver language, where very perfection increases the sense of melancholy, is entirely Mozart's own. It will often be heard again, but is heard fully perhaps for the first time in this symphony's slow movement.

Nothing prompts one to think that the newly-elected Prince-Archbishop listened to it, even if he heard it. Yet it is necessary not to read Mozart's relations with him backwards. It was Mozart who was honoured by being given virtually the first commission of his reign: producing the 'dramatic serenade' of '*Il Sogno di Scipione*' (K.126) which welcomed the new ruler into Salzburg. Even this usually dismissed trifle has fortunately been resurrected and performed in recent years (at the Camden Festival in 1968); and even the inevitably ridiculed soprano *licenza* with which it closes – apostrophizing Colloredo – turns out to be effective when staged. Nor is the remaining music for this adaptation of Metastasio's '*azione teatrale*' (written thirty-seven years earlier for Maria Theresia's father's birthday at a time of Austrian military defeat) anything but effective throughout. In passing, it may be noted that the selection of this particular '*azione*', touching on national humiliation and preferring therefore Constancy to Fortune, was possibly not altogether without some wry overtones. Colloredo's election was never, from the first, popular at Salzburg. Whoever selected the

'*Sogno di Scipione*' seems to have shown himself either lacking in tact, or possessed of somewhat mordant humour.

Metastasio intended a solemn, masque-like effect. It is an *azione* with little action and scarcely any 'story'. There was not much Mozart could do to remedy this. In fact he took the opportunity rather to make the work a showcase for his and the singers' virtuosity. Fortune and Constancy became like a rival pair of prima donnas, anticipating the rivals of *Der Schauspieldirektor*. The eventual triumph of Constancy unleashes a highly effective orchestral storm, amid which Fortune calls for '*Orribili disastri, atre sventure . . .*'* with an intensity approaching Electra's vengeance aria at the end of *Idomeneo*. Although Mozart could not stamp the work with the touching grace of *Ascanio*, still less with the sombre power of *Betulia liberata*, he did not fail to use the occasion to exercise his art in fresh ways. Most composers would have given ephemeral music to the frankly ephemeral task, but he creates memorably, gravely, beautiful music for the ghostly chorus of Roman heroes who prelude the serious moment of confrontation between Scipio and his great ancestor. Whether or not Mozart already knew that his new opera for Milan was to be set in ancient Rome, he must have been aware that the elevated style of Metastasio's moralistic *azione* provided a useful foretaste of his return to the world of *opera seria*.

In late October he and his father set out from Salzburg on their way once again to Italy. Within two months Mozart had to have his new opera ready for performance. They stopped at Bozen for one night, chiefly because the weather had broken and there was heavy rain. Mozart rudely summed up the place in the word 'pig-sty', scribbling his usual hasty postscript to Leopold's dutiful letter home; he was occupied with writing of a different sort – but unconnected with the opera. Simply to while away the few hours at Bozen, he was composing a quartet.

That is not a sign of what is so often, and pejoratively, called facility. What was at work was Mozart's incessant, forceful creativity: that vitality which would express itself, as on this rainy night in muddy Bozen, regardless of any commission and even despite the physical weariness of the composer. 'Hungry, thirsty, sleepy, lazy' was how he said he felt; but nevertheless, just as he continued to breathe, so he continued to produce music.

* 'Horrible disasters, dark misfortunes.'

The weather in northern Italy in the weeks before Christmas continued to be stormy and wet. Milan itself was empty of social life; most people would return only with the opening of the theatres, with the first performance of Mozart's new opera. Neither Leopold nor Mozart had any news to offer in their letters home as the autumn merged into a rainy winter. They knew the city well. They had experienced before the inevitable intrigues and delays which surrounded an opera's production. This time there were a few fresh delays and minor mishaps: the prima donna's arrival was held up by muddy roads; the tenor fell ill and had to be replaced by an inexperienced singer; and the libretto was considerably delayed because its poet, Giovanni de Gamerra, had submitted it for approval to Metastasio. It returned altered as well as improved, with at least one new scene. Mozart had no more than six weeks – including rehearsal time – to make the opera ready for performance. The same family, the Galliari, who had designed the scenery for *Ascanio*, would design the sets. The same archducal pair celebrated by *Ascanio* would attend the first night.

Some sense of having been through the whole experience before may well have affected Leopold Mozart, even while Mozart himself worked with increasing concentration on this third and, as it proved, last opera for Italy *Lucio Silla*. When the first night was only three weeks away, he had still fourteen numbers to compose. The prima donna had only just reached Milan. The new tenor – who had the title role – did not arrive until ten days later, and Mozart did not write his arias until then. The first performance was itself delayed on the actual evening of 26 December because the Archduke kept the audience waiting for hours while he wrote, with his own hand, five letters of New Year greetings: '*und NB. er schreibt sehr langsamm*',* Leopold noted with typical sarcasm. The later performances of *Lucio Silla* were probably more successful than the first, but Leopold was throughout concerned not so much about the opera as about Mozart's future.

The weeks in Milan had been dull partly no doubt because Leopold was waiting for a new project to prove successful. And he had to go on waiting, writing home to Salzburg with a circumstantial account of the severe illness which kept him in Italy – while adding a private postscript, to be cut off the rest of the letter, that the account was quite

* 'And *NB*. he writes very slowly.'

untrue: *'Was ich von meiner krankheit geschriben, ist alles nicht wahr . . . '**
The fictitious illness was his excuse for not returning, as due, to Salzburg.
Fortunately for us, Frau Mozart did not detach the postscript from what
would otherwise appear to posterity a most convincing case of Leopoldian grappling with malign fate. And indeed fate was soon to be
revealed as truly malign: sapping the new project not by illness but by
indifference.

In coming to Italy once again, Leopold dreamt once again of an
Italian-imperial post for Mozart. The Archduke Ferdinand had been
guided into rejection of the composer at Milan the previous year; but
his elder brother, Leopold, the Grand Duke of Tuscany (the future
Habsburg Emperor for whose coronation Mozart was to write *La
Clemenza di Tito*) was now approached, with considerable secrecy.
Whether or not it was already clear that the Mozart family had little to
hope for from the new 'sovereign of Saltsburg', Leopold Mozart obviously continued to look elsewhere for Mozart's future, even while
scrupulously writing to Colloredo and doing small commissions for him.
At least on the surface, their relations appear to have still been cordial,
but Leopold's polite mentions of him – seasoned with statistics about the
number of performances of *Lucio Silla* – were probably written in the
likelihood of letters being intercepted and read. Franker references to
fading hopes of the Tuscan court and possibilities of travelling again
were communicated in code, though one so simple that it probably
offered no obstacle to the Prince-Archbishop's agents. Quite possibly
Colloredo's prejudice against the family originated at this period, in the
awareness that they had started to tug at the chain which bound them to
Salzburg and his service.

The success of *Lucio Silla* – for it certainly became, and deserved, to be
a success – was totally ephemeral. Agreeable conversation with the
Archduke Ferdinand was no substitute for employment; but the Archduke Leopold offered neither. The third visit to Italy by Mozart and his
father ended in complete fiasco, and Leopold betrays a sort of desperate-
ness in trying to cheer the family by his assurance of God's plan for
them: *'Gott wird was anders mit uns vorhaben.'†* Almost as if he felt he would
never see the country again, he confessed regretfully in his last letter
home before returning: 'It is difficult for me to leave Italy.'

Although he spoke of God's plans, he continued to make his own.

---

* 'What I wrote about my illness is none of it true.'
† 'God will have other plans for us.'

They continued to follow an almost obsessive line. He could not conceive a career outside the *ancien régime* system. For all his satirical jabs at royal persons who might look homely – or write very slowly – he believed in some essential benefit derived from these people, even after so many disillusioning experiences. He and Mozart were back in Salzburg for the first anniversary of Colloredo's election. As Leopold had talked of doing for many years, he had moved to a new and better apartment in the Hannibalplatz, but this was far from being through acceptance that Mozart would remain with the family in Salzburg.

In July 1773 Colloredo left Salzburg and passed briefly through Vienna. Leopold and Mozart had preceded him; they remained longer, while Leopold hunted for the elusive post which surely there, at the centre of the Austrian imperial world, must exist for his son. It was almost eleven years since he had first travelled there with his two child-performers and been received by the Empress in audience. Still kindly, and still offering nothing, she again received Leopold and Mozart in audience: '*Die Kayserin waren zwar sehr gnädig mit uns, allein dieses ist auch alles . . .*'* Even Leopold's faith in the Habsburg family must have faltered, when he recollected that he had at different times approached in vain three of her sons and now, for the final time, herself. Mozart, who mockingly dated a letter in aristocratic style '*Wien, aus unserer Residenz*' seems to sum up the last remaining possibility in a piece of doggerel verse: '*Dan ich bin gar Capax zu gehen nach Constant-inopel.*'†

Composer to the Sublime Porte: Leopold might have caught himself momentarily musing on the title before he realized Mozart's joke. Not only was the whole concept of Turkey an exotic one that steadily appealed artistically to the rest of Europe, but in 1773 Turkey was still the particular ally of Austria, respected by Maria Theresia though shoddily treated by Joseph II. And Mozart had a personal reason, as he was probably aware, for associating himself with Constantinople: it was on St John Chrysostom's day that he had been born, it was after him that he was partly named, and the saint was patriarch of Constantinople.

In reality it became necessary to travel – not there but back to Salzburg. However, Leopold and Mozart did not hurry to leave Vienna where they were enjoying social and musical life with friends like the Mesmers, enjoying it so patently that Frau Mozart and Nannerl – left behind with a new member of the family, a fox terrier, 'Miss Bimbes'

---

* 'The Empress was certainly very gracious to us, but that's all there is to it . . .'
† 'For I am certainly quite capable of going to Constantinople.'

(Bimperl) – obviously expressed some wish to come to Vienna themselves. Leopold was able to explain why this would not have suited, but Nannerl's request about buying items of dress in the capital he was willing to consider. Local gossip about his staying on in Vienna he disposed of with pungently speedy sarcasm: it was too good of the Salzburg citizens to be so anxious about his return, proposing doubtless to illuminate the town in his honour – which might be useful in searching at night for the lock on the hall door.

At the very end of September he and Mozart were indeed back: to a place lit by no gleaming prospects and made probably the more distasteful by neighbourly, if not civic, awareness of the Mozart family's failure to establish their son elsewhere. Leopold was perhaps paying for his earlier tendency to keep Salzburg informed of the infant prodigy's success. Like Dr Burney's correspondent, other people might opine that the boy was proving 'more extraordinary than excellent'. Sardonic as Leopold might be about Salzburg, he was now to spend the rest of his life there; he never again left German-speaking territory and only once more visited Vienna.

For Mozart the long summer visit to Vienna had probably been much more exciting than disillusioning. The city seemed at once less constricting than Salzburg and less alien than Milan. The prospect of opera there – comic opera or national German opera – remained an attraction. Above all, he is likely to have felt the charm of being received in a rich yet quite unaristocratic, cultured circle – well represented by the Mesmer family – which was as music-loving as it was friendly. Five years later they were still exhorting Leopold to send Mozart to Vienna: '*Hier ist doch immer ein guter Platz für ein grosses Talent.*'* Concerts in the Mesmers' handsome garden in the Landstrasse, hearing Dr Mesmer perform on a novel instrument, the glass harmonica, and then trying it oneself, meals in one or other of the family houses, where could be met people like Heufeld, the influential manager of the Deutsches Theater: an accumulation of such small, half-social things might symbolize the enjoyable freedom offered by life in the capital city. When Mozart in mock-princely fashion despatched that letter from Vienna '*aus unserer Residenz*', perhaps he accidentally revealed that his mind was already thinking of the possibility of the city as the place where he would reside.

Reflections of the advantages of agreeable Viennese social life are apparent in the six quartets Mozart wrote at Vienna in these months.

* 'Yet there is always a good place here for a highly talented person.'

The quartet was still a comparatively new form for him. He had written a first group three years earlier and a second group at the end of 1772, probably in and on the way to Milan. The Vienna group has always been recognized as influenced by Haydn's latest quartets – some of which Dr Burney had heard played 'exquisitely' in Vienna in 1772; and his descriptions of Viennese musical life are themselves sufficient, incidentally, to explain Mozart's attraction to what Burney called 'the imperial seat of music'. Haydn, whom Mozart had probably not yet met in person, represented the most up-to-date music at Vienna – for all that he himself was seldom able to be there – replacing the somewhat stiff baroque world of Maria Theresia's composer, Wagenseil (by then crippled by illness and in retirement). Echoes of Haydn in the group of 'Vienna' quartets make them less personal, but they pay tribute to strong awareness – and speedy assimilation – of the achievements of the greatest composer Mozart was to know. He had not altogether ceased perhaps to look for a musical father. Haydn proved indeed a movingly generous one when the two composers came eventually to meet; and Mozart's printed dedication to him of his own next group of quartets (twelve years later) made a literally filial request: '*ed esser loro Padre . . .*'.*

Probably the 'Vienna' quartets of 1773 were no formal commission but represent music to be played – as Haydn's was – in cultured, domestic circles. Friends and acquaintances of the Mozarts during that summer included young Anton Teiber, a gifted violinist later serving the Viennese court, and Franz Kreibich, who held the post of first violin in the Emperor Joseph ɪɪ's own string quartet. One of the younger members of the Mesmer family (perhaps a violinist), was musically 'really talented', Leopold wrote, and he would willingly have trained him further himself. So dominant is the violin in Mozart's thoughts at this moment that it seems remarkably apt to find him – when the organ of a monastery near Vienna proved unsatisfactory – taking Teiber's violin and performing on that.

The brighter and the more amusing such memories (Leopold had spoken of Mozart's 'cheek' in coolly borrowing and then playing before the monks on Teiber's violin), the duller Salzburg must have seemed. For Mozart a somewhat barren time, even musically, followed the Vienna months. His compulsive urge to write for the theatre would never find fulfilment at Salzburg. In some strange way the boasted commission to write an opera for Venice had come to nothing. Since *Lucio*

* 'And be their Father . . .'

Silla, his nearest approach to the theatre had been to write some choruses for a rather hectically highflown play, *Thamos, King of Egypt*, which its author, a certain Baron von Gebler, was intending to produce in Vienna. Most of Mozart's music for this was written, and can be discussed, somewhat later. Not until the end of 1774 did he receive a new opera commission: for an *opera buffa*, to be performed the following year at the Munich court. As far as Mozart's future was concerned, it was one more success of the type he had too often experienced: glittering but brief, without any solidity or substance when the applause had died away.

Lucio Silla was never repeated; until very recently (when it has been both performed and recorded) it had never been heard again since the first performances in Milan, but Mozart thought sufficiently highly of it to preserve several arias. Eleven years later, one of Anton Teiber's sisters sang an aria from it at a public concert organized by Mozart in Vienna; it was easily the oldest piece of his music included and perhaps stood for him as among the earliest that was totally professional.

It is unfortunate to learn from E.J.Dent (in *Mozart's Operas*) that the opera is 'not even as good as *Mitridate*', because this – if true – only confirms the excellence of that first Milanese success which remains virtually unheard. About *Lucio Silla*, it is more pertinent to recognize that it was musically the most ambitious work Mozart had created. He must have read its antique Roman libretto carefully: consciously or unconsciously choosing what he would stress and what virtually ignore. The simple core of the plot is the firm mutual devotion of the affianced lovers Cecilio and Giunia, '*la fida sposa*', threatened by the tyrant Silla ('Sulla' in English) who has banished Cecilio and wants to marry Giunia, having told her that Cecilio is dead. The lovers triumph by constancy, and through their example Silla reforms himself in proper eighteenth-century moral fashion, as a ruler was expected to do.

The remoteness of the setting is compensated for by the easily understood, sympathetic situation of the lovers. As for the moral hint to rulers, Mozart was perhaps weary, after *Il Sogno di Scipione*, of all such allusions. The classical framework, associations of Roman grandeur, a tyrant turned abruptly magnanimous – none of these is treated other than perfunctorily. It may well have been a quite undisguised blessing that the singer of Lucio Silla was too inexperienced to be allotted much music. To a pair of subsidiary lovers, Silla's sister and Cecilio's friend, are given the light, bright, somewhat hard arias which provide a contrast to the muted, affecting music–often dramatic and nearly always painfully intense – which haunts the main pair of usually grieving lovers.

From Giunia's first aria onwards, a tender death-wish quality mingles with their outbursts of stoic defiance. 'Dalla sponda tenebrosa,'* she bids her father and supposedly dead betrothed come; and though the mood sharpens here to one of brilliantly aggressive coloratura hatred of Silla (with almost joyful pecking at the line '*la pena tua maggior*'),† awareness of mortality is marvellously conveyed throughout the subterranean graveyard scene where she comes to pray before her father's urn and discovers her lover alive. Before this dramatic moment, Cecilio has an extraordinarily solemn, disturbing recitative – one of many *recitativi accompagnati* in the work – 'Morte, morte fatal . . .', where deep strings punctuate his shuddering sensations as he moves among the cold, marble tombs. Giunia's prayer is barely orchestrated; she wails her grief, and only very slowly do plucked strings accompany the spaced-out, sighing syllables of her almost hopeless *sospiri*. The lovers' duet on discovering each other is urgent, more sombre than exultant; Mozart does not forget where they are meeting, what they have experienced and what they have yet to endure.

In what follows, his empathy makes Giunia's music the more interesting, just as her situation is emotionally the more complicated – regardless of any attempt to characterize her. It is Giunia's fast, apparently showy aria, 'Parto, m'affretto'‡, which Mozart revived for Madame Teiber in 1783: an aria which accelerates the opera's pace at a point when it might be dangerously slackening and which illustrates as well Mozart's instinctive gift for translating words (and often stale words, at that) into vividly fresh music which blossoms out of their suggestions. The aria's tempo was obviously prompted by its opening phrase, but Giunia is also bracing herself for the desperate moment of appearing before the Senate, to whom she is hastening; her voice reaches, as do her emotions, to an extremity which makes more than merely decorative her coloratura '*spasimi*', and which justifies the lingering, sweetly-repeated '*morir*', for death is preferable to continued sufferings.

Thus within the ordinary conventions of a *da capo* aria, Mozart builds something at once psychologically and musically satisfying: the more brilliantly the aria is sung the more effectively is Giunia's agony conveyed. But for her final aria, *opera seria* forms give way before such tragic-

* 'From the shadowy shore.'
† 'thine the greater suffering.'
‡ 'In haste I go.'

ally plangent feeling – '*Fra i pensieri più funesti di morte*'* – that it is shaped hardly more than recitative. More than one critic has spoken of Donna Anna in connection with its grieving power – and indeed Giunia, with her several invocations to her dead father, does perhaps slightly anticipate her. Even more, however, does this aria's minor key, and its expression of a state of mind beyond all hope except of death, anticipate Pamina's '*Ach, ich fühl's*', itself shaped emotionally rather than formally.

Lucio Silla is proof that Mozart did not look on the *opera seria* form as antiquated or ludicrous. Under his hand it grew animated, capable of effects intensely moving as well as beautiful. If in *Lucio Silla* all is not yet consistent, the story only sporadically interesting, the character-types insufficiently realized, still there is evident an emotional power which will blaze out fully, unmistakably in the masterpiece of *Idomeneo*. And the ultimate proof of Mozart's ability to animate the form came in the last year of his life, when he was given the commission for one final *opera seria*, *La Clemenza di Tito*, which even in plot has clear echoes of *Lucio Silla*.

A side effect of *Lucio Silla* was a miniature work which poses something of the same problem in appreciation. For the castrato, Rauzzini, who had sung Cecilio, Mozart wrote a motet '*Exsultate, jubilate*' (K.165), sometimes abbreviated for performance merely into an Alleluia and probably so rarely played in a church setting that its lack of religious feeling is automatically assumed ('Besides, there is nothing religious about the tune' was the authoritative pronouncement of Wyzewa and Saint-Foix). Certainly the work is a tribute to Rauzzini's voice, which must have been lyrically sure in its ability to leap and trill – perhaps more like an instrument in timbre than what we think of as vocal. Yet the motet is not just a too-familiar Alleluia: between that final carolling burst of joy and the rightly joyful opening, comes a solemn, unmistakably religious Andante. The idiom should not disguise the seriousness, for otherwise much of Mozart's later religious music will – wrongly – appear profane. Just as virtuosity is used to express Giunia's emotions, so in the '*Exsultate, jubilate*' it serves an entirely devotional purpose; and perhaps in the very joy is a thank-offering for the success of *Lucio Silla*.

* 'Amid most baneful thoughts of death.'

4

Success in Milan might seem less significant than success in what was virtually one's native land. The applause at Munich in 1775 at the first performance of Mozart's first public opera commission north of the Alps—*La Finta Giardiniera* (K.196)—was probably even greater and more enthusiastic than that given to *Lucio Silla*. Cries of 'Viva Maestro' followed each aria; the Electress of Bavaria and the Dowager-Electress both called out 'Bravo' to Mozart across the hall. At the end of the performance applause and more shouts of 'Bravo' continued to resound. The next day the music-loving Bishop of Chiemsee, who had probably played some part in getting the commission for Mozart, sent a message congratulating him on the incomparable success of the opera: '*Bey allen so unvergleichlich ausgeffallen ist.*'*

Among those applauding had been, as well as Leopold Mozart, Nannerl – witnessing her brother's success for the first time since childhood, perhaps as recompense for not having been allowed to come to Vienna two years earlier. Among those absent was notably the Prince-Archbishop of Salzburg, who was due to visit Munich but who contrived to miss any performance of his musician's opera. His visible embarrassment on being congratulated later by the Elector and his family on Mozart's success gave profoundly bitter pleasure to Leopold. By now it had become obvious that the Archbishop actively disliked the Mozart family. As for Mozart's attitude, he reminded his mother (left alone at Salzburg with Bimperl, to whom he sent a customary '1,000 kisses') that there was little reason for hastening home: the breath of fresh air away from Salzburg was doing him good.

Munich was where, at least traditionally, he had performed in public for the first time. There the Elector had delayed the Mozart family on their European tour of 1763 so as to hear Nannerl play the clavier. The same Elector, Max III Joseph, was responsible for commissioning *La Finta Giardiniera*. It was not surprising that rumours of Mozart's Munich success now reached Salzburg, with the additional spice that he was considering entering the Elector's service. Leopold affected total indifference to childish Salzburg gossip on the point. Perhaps it did not seem a suitable moment for Mozart to try and make a permanent move to Munich.

Two years later, dismissed from Salzburg, he would be standing in a

* 'It has succeeded incomparably with everyone.'

87

narrow antechamber at the Bavarian court, desperately hoping to catch Max Joseph on the way to hear mass before going hunting. His own reporting of the incident, with the exchange between himself and the Elector, vividly conveys the benevolent indifference of yet one more ruler when offered Mozart's services. Max Joseph interrupted Mozart's tactful praise of 'Your Serene Highness, who is himself a great . . .' by saying: '*Ja, mein liebes kind, es ist kein vacatur da.*'*

On the evening after the first performance of *La Finta Giardiniera*, Mozart and Leopold had waited in very different mood for the Elector and Electress to pass through a room adjoining the auditorium. The enthusiastic reception of the opera reflected credit on patron, audience and composer. The royal personages were very gracious; Mozart was offered their hands to kiss. Some days later the Elector asked to hear some of Mozart's contrapuntal church music, and that was all. Two more performances of the opera were given at Munich. A few years later it was translated into German and was quite widely performed as a *Singspiel*. When Novello was in Vienna in 1829 he found Italian-German editions of the opera being advertised, having earlier expressed a fear that along with the other early operas, 'these *germs* of Mozart's incomparable Genius are now irreparably lost'. Although Mozart may have revised some parts of *La Finta Giardiniera* for the German version, he does not seem to have taken great interest in it and never utilized any arias from it.

It was commissioned as the *buffa* piece for the Munich carnival and its plot is indeed farcical to the point of imbecility. Nor does its apparent incomprehensibility become much clearer or more satisfactory in stage performance. Yet the text (probably written by Gluck's librettist Calzabigi) had already been successfully set to music in 1774 at Rome. Ironically, some of the unsatisfactoriness may even be increased by Mozart's music, deepening the unhappy situation of the heroine Violante (a marchesa disguised as Sandrina, a female gardener) and making the opera's overall effect no more consistently comic than is, for example, *The Two Gentlemen of Verona*. Perhaps in an attempt to escape from *commedia dell'arte* prototypes, and to achieve a 'romantic' comedy, the librettist not only included two elevated *seria* parts of a faithful, deserted lover (a castrato role) and an extremely petulant Milanese gentlewoman, but seriously sketched Violante's situation as emotionally and physically painful. If the audience began by associating

---

* 'Yes, my dear child, there is no vacancy here.'

female gardeners with something particularly funny, it was – like most audiences – mistaken. Whether or not there existed real female gardeners at the period, they did appear in art: sometimes as companions to male gardeners in highly floral Bow porcelain figures, and once as executed by Falconet, to Boucher's design, for Madame de Pompadour. Faintly rococo and decorative touches – rather than any close contact with the soil – also colour Violante-Sandrina, but like a Shakespearean heroine she suffers through having disguised herself.

Stabbed in a fit of jealousy by her nobly-born but otherwise ignoble lover Belfiore, and supposed dead, Violante decides that she and her major-domo should disguise themselves as gardeners. She still loves Belfiore, but is pursued amorously by her aged employer, the Podestà, disliked by his chambermaid, treated spitefully by the Milanese gentlewoman, and is both hurt by and hurts Belfiore, who grows demented in the uncertainty whether Sandrina can truly be Violante. Some of this is expressed humorously – as the finale inevitably unites three pairs of lovers – but Violante's long *scena* when she is lost in a wood as dark as the plot at this point is more deeply tragic than anything even in Giunia's music. The aristocrat stripped of privilege, with her disguise assumed to be real, she is not only an unhappy woman seeking her lover but an alienated victim of the society represented by the largely unpleasant other characters. It is almost as if Countess Almaviva were doomed to be driven mad in being mistaken for Susanna as part of a conspiracy against her.

Absurdly clumsy in plot but accomplished in music, *La Finta Giardiniera* is, all the same, a hint towards that perfect mingling of the sad and the joyful which is *Le Nozze di Figaro*. Mozart's own private creative world was no more one of unrelieved *buffa* than of total *seria*. The mixture so poorly concocted in *La Finta Giardiniera* was something he had had no opportunity to write for earlier, but his response to it – even in this unpalatable form – was instinctive. The best of *La Finta Semplice* was fused to *Lucio Silla*, it might be said, with the advantage that the composer of *La Finta Giardiniera* – celebrating his nineteenth birthday before the last performance was given – was now mature as man as well as musician. Drama should shape the music, and music should dictate the mood of the drama in ways that were difficult if not impossible in the accepted categories of opera.

Musically, the novelty of *La Finta Giardiniera* lies in no single aria (tenderly beautiful though several of them are), but in a new freedom to advance the action through the music, each character contributing his or her response within one melodic line, again anticipatory of *Figaro*. The ensemble becomes a device for comic and dramatic effects. As well as individual arias, there are also moments of declamation against music, almost in the style of the *melodrama*, and suggestive of affinities with the later *Zaïde*. More unexpected still, but typical of the opera's free idiom, is the culmination of the imbroglio when Sandrina and Belfiore appear bewitched; while the other characters contribute an ensemble of amazed patter, the lovers sing with enchanted, uncanny, proto-Straussian sweetness which indeed gives an effect of disassociation.

It is true that the people in the opera do not possess 'character' in the usual sense of the word. But they have attitudes of mind and – more important – styles of voice. It is this mingling of would-be heroic tenor and truly touching heroine with, on the one hand, *buffa* servants and, on the other, a castrato lover strayed from *opera seria* that makes the work so deeply Mozartean. The mixture is that to be encountered finally in *Die Zauberflöte*, and Mozart already sees that this mixture can be blended to make marvellous, musical unity.

Out of the confused threads of the characters' conflicting viewpoints at the end of Act I, he weaves a finale which may already be compared with that at the end of the second act of *Figaro*. The Podestà's plight, his chambermaid's jealousy of Violante, Violante's misery and her major-domo's concern, Belfiore's recognition of her but his pledge to the Milanese lady, herself eager to revenge his fickleness, while rejecting her *seria* suitor: absurd or touching, conflicting and unreciprocated, these emotions voice themselves individually or in brief ensembles before they are finally welded into one elaborate septet, soaring and dropping in its recognition of powerlessness before the situation in which each person can only appeal to the gods above: 'Numi, che incanto . . .'*

Not for five years, five lean and often deeply distressing years, did Mozart receive a commission to write another proper opera. Then it was again for Munich, under a different Elector. Again Leopold and Nannerl were in the audience, but Frau Mozart was dead and no letters were sent back to Salzburg describing the first night reactions. Those weeks in Munich, composing and witnessing *Idomeneo* in rehearsal and performance, were the ones which Constanze Mozart was to describe nearly half a century later as the happiest time Mozart had ever known.

Even if *Idomeneo* (which remained one of his own favourite works) had

* 'O Gods, what a spell . . .'

not been – as well as a success – a triumph of Mozart's creativity, it would probably still have marked for him emergence from a period better forgotten: an active yet ultimately futile time in which he gained his freedom, travelled as far as possible from Salzburg, only to have to come back and beg for reinstatement at the Archbishop's court. The 'Musikus' returning to Salzburg in March 1775, after a breath of fresh air provided by Munich, could scarcely guess that five years hence he would have advanced not at all, would indeed be the more tightly bound to the ruler whom he formally addressed as 'Your Grace, Most Worthy Prince . . .', but who privately provided him with a target to be peppered by such shots as 'Arch-booby', 'the Mufti' and 'our Salzburg Midas'. At each epithet *ancien-régime* Leopold trembled, but Mozart in fact was playing out his own Figaro and Leporello role in real life – to explode at last in a definitive cry of '*Non voglio più servir*'.*

In 1775 he might feel it strongly, but feeling had to give way before duty. The Archbishop, who had been embarrassed by his musician's success at Munich, selected him a few weeks later to write the music for a *serenata* to entertain the youngest of Maria Theresia's sons, the Archduke Maximilian, returning via Salzburg from a visit to Paris. A suit of the Archduke's clothes had been Maria Theresia's present to Mozart at the age of six; and another childhood memory might be stirred by the choice of libretto for the *serenata*, Metastasio's *Il Re Pastore*, which had been played in London during the Mozarts' stay. Neither the subject nor the object of the entertainment greatly inspired Mozart. His *serenata* is, for once, truly a showcase of unrelated characterless arias, without any binding unity of drama; it deserves the criticisms usually levelled at his other early operatic works, and operatically it is not merely untypical but a retrograde step – in retrograde Salzburg – after *La Finta Giardiniera*. The story of a king's heir, brought up a shepherd, who prefers pastoral love to a throne and is finally rewarded by obtaining both is one of Metastasio's frankest expressions of eighteenth-century establishment beliefs; not accidentally was it originally performed at Schönbrunn, '*alla presenza degli Augustissimi Sovrani*' (the parents of Archduke Maximilian). Its warbling shepherds and shepherdesses with ubiquitous flocks, well-washed and well-behaved, among which moves Alexander the Great, represent the convention Mozart liked least; and he, who had met so many kings and rulers, probably never encountered a shepherd. Although several of the arias are virtuoso vocal displays – sometimes,

---

* 'I wish to serve no longer.'

like the famous one, 'L'amerò, sarò costante,' accompanied by a solo instrument – the orchestration is really the interesting aspect of *Il Re Pastore*; it would not be too paradoxical to claim its sparkling *molto allegro* overture as the most successful, and the most Mozartian, music of the whole affair.

Since a long time would elapse before Mozart again had an opportunity to write opera of any sort, he might well now concentrate on instrumental work. Yet to suggest divisions of interest in this way is almost certainly wrong. Nor had he, of all composers, any need to hoard his creativity. Commissions might briefly stimulate or totally absorb him, but he had always energy for independent work – inspired by an occasion, a talented performer (including himself) or by a private challenge. Some of the most remarkable of Mozart's music in the years which followed his final Italian visit, while he tried to resign himself at least temporarily to Salzburg, had no known external cause – nor any recorded contemporary performance. Some of it, like the symphony in G minor (K.183) written in late 1773, is disturbingly private; there the intensity and almost harshly expressionistic power – a driving agitation declared in the opening bars and still surging through the finale – might well disconcert an audience who expected superficial pastime melodies. It is usually claimed as Mozart's first symphony in a minor key and critics have naturally associated it (though others have denied the association) with his penultimate symphony, of 1788, also in G minor (K.550). Evan apart from its key, one might look backwards as well as forwards. The wild if tentative urge to expression which can be felt unexpectedly in Mozart's very first symphony has deepened into a torrent, controlled but only the more powerful for that control, a dark tide carried by forcefully rhythmic strings which finally closes over the few interludes of relief, so that the symphony ends very much as it began. In the nineteenth century Jahn called it 'almost gloomy', but rather it is stormy and strong-willed in its dynamism. As an 'overture' to anything, it could prelude only *Don Giovanni*; and in its weighting of the symphony with personal feeling it might have inspired Tschaikovsky. Even for its key, however, Mozart's earliest symphonies are not irrelevant, it would seem, for there is record of a non-surviving symphony in A minor (K.16a) written just about the period of his first symphony.

Consciousness of full creative power – and neither vague influences from the '*Sturm und Drang*' movement in Germany nor direct influence from Haydn – seems the motive force behind the G minor symphony.

The same consciousness is certainly unmistakable in a closely contemporary work – Mozart's first piano concerto (K.175) – a majestic entry into a new form, intended for public performance by himself, and something of a continued favourite with both the composer and his audiences. Its thrilling, bold opening movement may well reflect Mozart's thrill in creating for the first time such an elaborate structure to display his own talent as a soloist – instead of, as previously, executing the concertos of other men. By the standards of a much later piano concerto, like K.503, the orchestral beginning is not long, though already far from perfunctory, and the piano breaks in as if the soloist must be heard on this theme. A report on Mozart's clavier playing at the time of *Finta Giardiniera* praised neither its sweetness nor its grace but its 'great weight', which perhaps this concerto is intended to display. And though it turns tender in the slow movement, there is a rising sense of excitement as piano and orchestra not so much exchange dialogue as thrash out in turn through the last movement viewpoints which contrast and in the end complement each other. In 1783 Mozart, who had just played it at a public concert in Vienna, reported that it was still popular, though by then he had supplied it with a new third movement (K.382). Indeed, his steady interests in performing this, the first of all his piano concertos, is the best tribute to its quality.

It was soon followed by concertos for other solo instruments. That for bassoon (K.191) was presumably written for a specific player, possibly Baron von Dürnitz, a Munich amateur who commissioned various works, for which he seems not always to have paid. The obvious limits of the instrument – and perhaps the commissioner's wishes – prevented the result from being a profound work of art, but Mozart demonstrates its range and mood with enchanting, amusing effortlessness. If in the first movement it has a stuttering, bubbling *buffo* role, largely content to share the orchestral texture, in the second it suggests somehow nocturnal melancholy and becomes in the final movement a lively, yet not merely comic, hero. Perhaps Weber's inspiration for his own enchanting bassoon concerto grew out of awareness of Mozart's, to which it is certainly a sympathetic successor. Mozart probably never wrote another concerto for that instrument, but back in Salzburg in 1775 he produced a series of concertos for the instrument associated since childhood with his father, the violin. A violin takes the solo part in 'L'amerò, sarò costante' – probably to show off the skill of the Archbishop's first violinist, Brunetti. The Archbishop himself sometimes played, and the prominence of the violin in an aria of *Il Re Pastore* might particularly interest the Archduke Maximilian, who condescended to play the violin at an evening party in Salzburg on the day after the performance.

In the following months Mozart wrote five violin concertos, probably all for Brunetti to play at court. Not only had he by his side the author of the established *Versuch* on violin-playing but he of course – like Archbishop and Archduke – was also a performer. Nevertheless, the first of this series has none of the stirring personal qualities of the first piano concerto. Brunetti was an acquaintance rather than a friend, and Mozart's attitude to the violin remained somewhat ambiguous: perhaps forever coloured by realization of its being very much his father's instrument. Remarkably for him, he seems to have had little confidence in his own ability to play it, and also to have disliked writing for it that was too patently virtuoso. Even the later violin concertos of 1775 lack 'difficult' virtuoso passages, being more singingly poignant and eloquent. When Mozart was in Mannheim two years later, he reported hearing the famous violinist Fränzl who played difficult music – 'you know that I am no great lover of difficulties' – without his hearers being aware it was difficult. Leopold had not yet received this letter when he wrote urging Mozart to perform a violin concerto, but adding and underlining that he could imagine his son's violin hanging unused, *'allein die Violin hängt am Nagl'*.

Brunetti was only one of the people Mozart was specifically writing for in the uneasy period before his first dismissal from the Archbishop's service in 1777. Apart from other professional soloists, like the oboist Ferlendis, there were Salzburg amateurs who in more ways than one were connected with – are indeed remembered by – Mozart's music. Some might have works written for them to play, as had Countess Lützow (née Czernin), an accomplished pianist, and Countess Lodron, both numbered among the friends Mozart greeted in his letters. For Countess Lützow the piano concerto in C (K.246) was written, and for Countess Lodron, along with her two daughters, an unusual concerto for three pianos (K.242). To be played for, rather than by, Elizabeth Haffner was the 'Haffner Serenade' (K.250), to celebrate her marriage in July 1776. The grandeur of the occasion – the marriage of the burgo-master of Salzburg's daughter – is in itself hardly reason enough for the greatness of this 'serenade', which far surpasses occasional music and is in scale alone like an eight-movement symphony: more perfect in fact than any symphony Mozart had yet written.

The challenge implicit in the 'Haffner Serenade' was to create profoundly serious pleasing music, to build a permanent structure despite
the ephemerality of the celebration and do justice to what may be seen
as a sacramental rite as well as an excuse for high jinks. The mood of
the music – apart from the first and last movements, and in the latter
only its second half – is unexpectedly dark and quite free from conventional or rustic merry-making. The prominent violin in the second
movement plays a slow, tender serenade, perhaps to the bride, and the
last movement opens with a hymn-like Adagio. It may seem absurd to
call the whole serenade a secular non-vocal wedding mass, but at least it
might be called a wedding masque; and preceding the joyful noise of the
actual finale, music seems solemnly to consecrate the man and woman
now united in marriage. Amid the emotions set flowing around them
may even be detected a hint of wistfulness. '*Mann und Weib/ist ein leib,*'*
as Mozart was to write after his own marriage.

Twenty years old, unmarried, increasingly dissatisfied with Salzburg
and his service there, he gave a quite distinct account later in 1776 of his
state of mind, to Padre Martini at Bologna. The letter is a corrective to
seeing him as a carefree child of nature, happy amid creativity and
musical friends. 'I live in a country,' he writes, '*dove la Musica fa pocchis-
sima Fortuna . . .*'† The theatre (i.e. opera) is bad, and his own present
activity he sums up in an almost consciously careless phrase: '*Io mi
diverto intanto à scrivere per la Camera e per la chiesa.*'‡ Even the 'Haffner
Serenade' becomes by implication only a way of filling in time for the
composer who waits – for what? Perhaps for Padre Martini to engineer
some fresh invitation to Italy: '*Ah! che siamo si lontani Cariss.ᵐᵒ Sgr. P:
Maestro . . .*'§ He goes on to explain the peculiar brevity of masses as
they had to be composed at Salzburg, and with guarded hostility thus
comes to the most important, and the most problematic, of his patrons,
the Prince-Archbishop.

The Church continued to offer Mozart his best opportunities for writing for the voice. Of Salzburg court composers, Eberlin was dead.
Adlgasser, praised together with Michael Haydn in the letter to Padre
Martini, was to die in the subsequent year. Litanies, offertories and
motets by Mozart were performed perhaps even more frequently than

---

* 'Man and wife/are one body.'
† 'Where Music rarely prospers.'
‡ 'I amuse myself in the meantime writing Chamber music and for the church.'
§ 'Oh! how far away we are from each other, dearest Signor Father Master!'

his masses. Nannerl still keeping her little diary as dryly at twenty-six as she had at eleven, occasionally notes a litany by her brother amid such events as the Archbishop's consecration of an Abbess, the arrival of an elephant in Salzburg and the deaths of acquaintances. (A terrible, essentially provincial, *ennui* lurks between her meagre lines, sufficient in itself to explain why Mozart found it hard to breathe in Salzburg.)

The brevity required of music for a mass there dates from before Colloredo, though Mozart seems to point to his requirements specifically. While Schrattenbach still reigned he had written more than one *missa brevis*, though perhaps only for Lent. Colloredo made brevity a stringent obligation, even while requiring rich instrumentation of trumpets and drums. In the *missa brevis* in C major (K.259) performed at the end of 1776, Mozart seems to respond to the challenge with witty ingenuity. Not only are there trumpets and drums but space is found for an organ solo between the dramatic 'Sanctus' and decorative 'Benedictus'. All this can be played without holding up the course of the mass, but the celebrant cannot proceed until the Creed is sung. Presumably then as now, he sat throughout it, bowing at the words 'Et incarnatus est . . .', that phrase around which Mozart was to create a complete aria when he wrote the great C Minor Mass (K.427), to be performed in Salzburg at a time when he was no longer employed by the Archbishop. In the Organ Solo Mass of 1776 the whole Creed is despatched in a summary eighty-four bars, contracted to an almost ludicrously bare recital, without one word repeated and only momentarily pausing to usher in the solemn 'Et incarnatus' before hastening on. If Colloredo timed it with a stop-watch, he must have recognized a record. And in the time saved, Mozart could linger over the 'Benedictus' and yet finish the mass within the Archbishop's stipulated three-quarters of an hour.

That was one sort of challenge met, but the satisfaction – like the result – must have been slight. A more fundamental challenge remained in the Archbishop's attitude to the two Mozarts, and theirs to him. On 14 March 1777, the fifth anniversary of Colloredo's election, Leopold fired the first petition in a new campaign: that he and Mozart be allowed to travel for a few months. Receiving no reply to this, he was on the point of petitioning again in June when Colloredo ordered all his musicians to their instruments in preparation for a visit to Salzburg by Joseph II. When the visit was concluded Leopold applied once more; leave for him was refused, but Mozart's was apparently granted, though Colloredo continued to raise objections. In August it was Mozart's turn to take pen in hand, copying no doubt a Leopoldian draft, and beginning with the splendid untranslatable form of address that was so apparently respectful – '*Ihro Hochfürstl. Gnaden/Hochwürdigster des Heil. Röm. Reichs/Fürst/ Gnädigster Landes Fürst/und/Herr Herr!*' – but which he seemed to make dangerously challenging. He asked only for his own discharge from the Archbishop's service: to use his talents to improve his and his parents' circumstances, 'as the Gospel teaches us' – a phrase Leopold must have smiled over in drafting. The Archbishop pencilled a reply, and the formal endorsement of the petition scrupulously preserved his personal sting: father and son were granted permission to seek their fortunes elsewhere, 'according to the Gospel'.

This exchange, which might seem to resolve everything and leave both sides believing they were the victors, was probably never forgotten. For Mozart it was not an end at all, but merely the beginning of a bitter period in which it might well have appeared that the Archbishop's parting taunt was truly a curse: on Leopold as much as on himself, and in both cases striking at the man no less than at the '*Musikus*'.

5

At the news of the double dismissal Leopold became ill. This was not what he had petitioned for at all and he had now to do so yet once again, to be reinstated. Although the Archbishop took him back into service, his nerve was irreparably shaken. 'I beg you not to cringe too much' ('*nicht zu viel zu kriechen*') Mozart was to say after his own final explosive dismissal three years later; but Leopold was too old to change. All his life he had been in someone's service. If Mozart had died in childhood, Leopold would never have really stirred – however much he grumbled – from being the Archbishop's Vice-*Kapellmeister*. Now desperate for re-instatement, he obviously could not leave Salzburg; just as obviously, Mozart must. Leopold was still suffering when he stayed up packing until two in the morning of 23 September. Briefly he went to bed and got up again at six when the carriage set off from Salzburg, carrying not only Mozart but his mother on a long, ill-fated tour which would stop at Paris with her death.

It had been decided that Mozart should not travel alone, and Frau Mozart seemed the obvious alternative to Leopold, despite her lack of experience, her undominating – indeed, undemanding – character and her deep fondness for her own Salzburg circle. 'You were the apple of her eye,' Leopold wrote to Mozart in Paris, by then aware she was dangerously ill and half-suspecting her to be dead even while he wrote; and in the circumstances the simple phrase is poignant. Her role had always been subsidiary to her husband's, and she had probably held only a rather vague place in Mozart's life. Yet in the crisis of 1777, by which time her fifty-seventh birthday was already passed, she set off on travels which proved largely tedious and often lonely – since Mozart spent considerable time meeting people, being entertained or giving music lessons – and she went as much perhaps for Leopold's sake as for Mozart's. At the start of the journey she even enjoyed the experiences. When sending one of the family's typical scatalogical messages that indicated good humour, she added an untypical, operatic '*Addio, ben mio*', which may even have disconcerted Leopold by its gaiety. But then none of them foresaw that failure in Munich would lead to Augsburg, and Augsburg to Mannheim, where after long delays no offer to Mozart was forthcoming, and thence to Paris.

Although she had dreamt of returning home, Frau Mozart obeyed Leopold's fresh orders to accompany Mozart to Paris. She did not speak French but liked gossiping with a few German-born acquaintances and observing the latest fashions for high-piled hair and the carrying of walking-sticks by ladies. She was early in possession of a non-public piece of news, that Marie-Antoinette was pregnant. Her last letter mentions the wonderful summer weather and a visit to the Luxembourg Palace to see both the gardens and the picture-gallery. Yet, rightly perhaps, almost the final words reveal her in as domestic a context as possible: she explains the economy of the supper arrangements by which she and Mozart sat down in the evening to four pasties costing four sous.

From Salzburg Leopold was following and, as far as he could, directing the whole campaign, often with hysteria at not being on the spot to execute immediately what ought to be done. The morning of departure had been terrible for the two members of the family left behind. With tears and headaches Leopold and Nannerl had collapsed on their beds, probably puzzling 'Miss Bimpes' by their misery; a few days later Nannerl reported her as sitting at the door hopefully, all the while still looking for Mozart and his mother to return. Leopold constantly recollected a thousand things he had not told Mozart in the bustle of their leaving. Nor were these items concerned only with the right music to play, the right people to meet or the way to behave; they ranged from stressing the importance of ensuring that a hotel servant always put boot trees in his boots, to questioning whether Mozart had not become lax about going to confession. To such an extent had Leopold grown obsessed about Mozart's incapacity for ordinary life that he even expressed hope that his head was not always full of music: '*nicht immer den Kopf voll der Noten haben*' – a statement he would have dealt pungently with if expressed by anyone else.

Could determination conveyed from a distance have got Mozart an appointment, Leopold would doubtless have succeeded; it was not sufficient, however, and he blamed Mozart for the failure. Scrappy letters from Frau Mozart, telling him not to worry, only drove him frantic with worry. First saying nothing and then pouring over his head a stream of worries – that was how they both behaved, he virtually screamed from Salzburg to Mannheim in exasperation.

This particular scream was prompted by a – to him – quite infuriating event. Mozart had met at Mannheim the Weber family and their young daughter, the singer Aloysia Weber; he had fallen seriously in love with her and wrote to say that he would like to compose an opera for Verona, in which she could make her name. And incidentally, he remarked airily, he and the Webers might all be going to Switzerland and also perhaps to Holland. 'Write to me soon about this,' he asked, a scarcely necessary request to which Leopold responded at once by the longest letter he had probably ever despatched, stiff with self-pity and shrewd advice, cajolery, abuse, and emotional blackmail, culminating in the command: '*Fort mit Dir nach Paris!*'* Like Gibbon, a few years before, Mozart sighed as a lover and obeyed as a son. Unlike Gibbon's, his wound was not healed by time, absence and the habits of a new life; and perhaps it never healed. In old age Aloysia Weber claimed that Mozart had always loved her, an inevitable claim for her to make, but one which may well have contained some grain of truth.

Mozart had rushed away from Salzburg more concerned with escaping than with any planned objective. Leopold was probably still looking up routes in guide books and considering the opportunities offered by various German courts, while discovering at every turn evidence of Mozart's impetuousness. Only two days after his departure Leopold found he had left behind the trousers of his pike-grey suit and they were sent on in a parcel labelled 'one worn pair of trousers and some music'. Frau Mozart was not much more thoughtful, for Leopold soon discovered that she had forgotten her knickers (probably for winter

* 'Off with you to Paris!'

travelling). But something more essential came to light, disclosed in fact by the Prince-Archbishop's action. Mozart was no longer a child-genius to be wound up and made to perform like a clockwork toy; Leopold knew that, of course, but he could not emotionally recognize his son as an entirely independent and now adult being who himself held the key to his own impulses. It must have been hard in fact to realize, as they travelled together over a ten-year period, that Mozart was growing older as well as greater as a musician. Leopold did not really want to realize it. All his emotional capital was, as it were, tied up in Mozart: his life's work, his paternal pride, the proof of that superiority felt but not demonstrated in his own career. He and Mozart were a firm and a team, as well as father and son.

Colloredo, by accident, divided them. He thrust on Mozart a new experience: liberty, which was at once frightening and exciting. Never before had Mozart travelled anywhere without his father, and his immediate anxiety was to prove he could. The first letter he wrote back to Salzburg was on the evening of the first day's journey, to report that all was well. He and his mother were living like princes. All they lacked was Papa, but that was God's will and anyway, *'ich bin der anderte Papa'*.* Certainly Frau Mozart must have felt he was; she was speedily subordinated to him and reduced to writing secretly, while he was having a meal, on the odd occasion that she felt there was something Leopold ought to know. Since she seldom quite grasped what was happening and tended to be optimistic and comfortable by nature (charmed to be called 'Mama' by friendly musicians whom she and Mozart met), she scarcely restricted Mozart's freedom. After the first letter home, Mozart expressed no further sense of lacking Leopold, though part of his delight in experiencing a totally new sort of life was to convey it as it was experienced; hence his haste in communicating his plan to travel through Europe with Aloysia Weber and her family.

The independence of the proposal must have upset Leopold far more than any supposed rashness. In the nerve-centre of operations at Salzburg he probably began to feel like a general whose troops are mutinying. It would be too much to expect him to sympathize with the Prince-Archbishop, and yet Mozart's rebelliousness against the ruler was the same quality which worked against Leopold; the fact that Mozart deeply loved his father, wanted his approval, and welcomed his views on music, only exacerbated the situation. Indeed, it proved much simpler

* 'I am another Papa.'

for Mozart to hate the Archbishop, diverting to him all his blackest thoughts about Salzburg existence, than to establish a consistent attitude to Leopold – from whom his personality had somehow to escape if it was ever to establish autonomy. In some ways the Archbishop Mufti can be seen caricatured as Osmin in *Die Entführung* – a ridiculously oppressive tyrant – and Leopold as idealized in the noble Pasha who generously suppresses his own desire when the woman he has chosen prefers another man.

Actually, Leopold became Osmin-like at Mozart's attempts at independence, especially where love was concerned. And in the flight from Salzburg, Mozart was perhaps unconsciously looking for that sort of experience, as well as for a job. In both he was to be humiliated, yet at least the humiliations were directly inflicted; they became a part of living, and Mozart grew notably – but not unexpectedly – firm under the greatest of all his sufferings, and in the midst of utter isolation, when his mother died. Whatever he endured, he was not enduring the humiliation of being treated as a child. That this was very much in his mind is shown by his reaction to a letter from Heufeld, the Deutsches Theater manager at Vienna, which Leopold had forwarded, in which Heufeld spoke of '*ihr sohn*'.* He would not have disgraced himself, Mozart replied bitterly, had he spoken rather of '*der H. sohn*'.† And with perhaps some glancing application he added: '*Oder er glaubt die Menschen bleiben immer 12 jahr alt.*'‡ Like many parents before and since, Leopold himself did not hesitate to use the emotional blackmail of implying that in refusing to stay in childhood his child had spoilt a previously perfect relationship. At the period of the Aloysia Weber affair, he sentimentally invoked the boy Mozart who had sung to him nightly and stood on a chair to kiss his nose before bedtime – happy times now vanished. To this Mozart sensibly replied that such times were indeed gone (. . . *sind freylich vorbey*') but did he love and respect his father any the less?: '*Mehr sage ich nicht.*' §

In being separated from Leopold, while still feeling accountable to him, Mozart – who was rawly experiencing so much after having been protected so long – also learnt a new art: of writing letters. Previously it had been Leopold who sent home the often detailed reports on their

* 'your son.'
† 'the Herr son.'
‡ 'Or else he believes that people always remain twelve years old.'
§ 'I will say no more.'

travels, to which Mozart had added lively bits of comment or nonsense, the scribble of someone usually preoccupied by writing music. Now it was necessary to report back to his father, to whom he had never before addressed a letter; and seldom before when travelling had he composed so little.

Mozart now emerges unmistakably as a fiercely sentient and sensitive personality, reacting so intensely to what he experiences that writing it down is as much relief as communication. '*Der anderte Papa*,' he of course modelled his letters on Leopold's, but here too he speedily outshone his father in gaiety and in sarcasm, fluent narrative and a gift for conveying dialogue – all achieved by quite effortlessly being himself. Leopold's letters are not inferior in revealing his nature; it is simply that Mozart had a more intensely responsive and attractive nature to reveal. He had also a better theme: the first abrupt confrontation between a genius and the world, in which – almost like Papageno and Monostatos – neither understanding the nature of the other, both retreated. At its sharpest the confrontation took place in Paris; and Mozart's announcement that he was leaving seemed to prompt the musical establishment to offer what he most wanted: the opportunity to write an opera. But no one could be certain his opera would please and he could be certain only that if it did not please in rehearsal it would never be performed: '*Es ist nichts sicheres*'.* That realization – about life in general and not merely about opera production in Paris – was perhaps the profoundest thing Mozart learnt on these travels. Such awareness would colour his music with an increasing insistence. Even the certainty of love is finally sapped by the exception which proves the rule: mortality.

Already on the first step of the journey, at Munich, when everything seemed potential if not truly hopeful, Mozart was confronted by the sad spectacle of a fellow composer, Mysliwecek, with whom he had been friendly in Bologna. Only forty, Mysliwecek had become horribly disfigured by, probably, venereal disease and by the doctors' attempts to cure it. In four years he was to be dead, and meanwhile his moving reception of Mozart, and his friendly attitude to Frau Mozart, '*una signora di garbo*',† made an impression which touched them both, despite a feeling that Leopold would not approve. Mysliwecek recognized not only Mozart's genius but his sensibility: '*Lei è troppo sensibile al mio male*,'‡

* 'It is not certain.'
† 'A gracious lady.'
‡ 'You are too much moved by my illness.'

he wrote on the day after their meeting, which had kept Mozart awake most of the following night.

The same sensibility was at work in a different way when Mozart heard young Mademoiselle Kaiser sing at the Munich opera. 'She often coaxed a tear from me,' he confessed. Mademoiselle Kaiser was pretty and sang well; Mozart never met her off stage, but he was probably more than a little in love with her. She prefigured Aloysia Weber, and he dreamt of writing a German opera in which Mademoiselle Kaiser would sing. Although this impulse was brief, and under Aloysia Weber's spell he was to laugh at having felt anything for Mademoiselle Kaiser, it was a more intense reaction, one may think, than any displayed by his previously boyish flirtations at Salzburg. That the woman he loved should in effect marry his music as well as himself was a natural wish; and that she should respond to his love expressed musically – 'I am no poet' – was equally to be hoped. More than one irony lay behind Mozart's eventual choice of Aloysia Weber's sister, Constanze, to be his wife.

It was soon obvious that, in the Elector's own words, there was no vacancy at Munich, but Mozart – still thinking of some opera he might write, and going often to the theatre – was not particularly depressed. A court as such had no particular appeal to him. All the more therefore did he respond to an idea proposed by the kindly, intelligent hotel-keeper Albert that he should settle in Munich and be supported by a circle of musical philanthropists. Will such people come forward, Leopold shrewdly questioned; and the concept of such enlightened patronage remains perhaps an eternal artistic dream. Nothing came of it in Mozart's case – just as Leopold had supposed – and the next stage was to visit his home town of Augsburg.

If Munich had proved a typically aristocratic rejection, with kind phrases scarcely concealing indifference, bourgeois Augsburg offered an almost brutally philistine reception, largely uninterested in Mozart as a performer and openly rude to him personally. Stinging letters about the people he met were Mozart's revenge, and in them may be detected a shock of disillusion at discovering that human behaviour could be so ludicrous and so horrible. It must indeed have been hard for him to realize that international fame, the applause of Italy, the cultured social welcome he had enjoyed in Vienna and even the friendly private life of Salzburg – none was typical perhaps of ordinary existence. It was not true that everywhere people were glad to meet a musician, or even would naturally be kind to a fellow being. A rough and hasty education was being given to Mozart, as if in preparation for what he would have to endure in Paris.

That Augsburg – 'Augusta Vindelicorum,' Mozart wrote, giving it its ancient name after a particularly biting description of the way a local female infant prodigy played the clavier – should be his father's birthplace may have increased his sense of resentment. There, where the name Mozart was supposed to mean something, he was challenged as a personality more than as a performer – for, in the end, his concert was well spoken of, even if it did not bring in much money. Yet his uncle, Leopold's brother the bookbinder, and his wife, were both kind, and their daughter, Maria Anna Thekla, provided agreeable flirtation; her letters have a saucy soubrette quality, as if Zerlina had written them, and her surviving portrait (perhaps the one she sent Mozart at his request) confirms the impression of sexy liveliness – with one hand shown apparently gathering a rosebud while she may. Mozart laughed with her, but gives not the faintest hint of loving her. She was someone with whom he could exchange schoolboy smut and play the fool. When a certain Father Emilian insisted on the three of them singing a canon together, Mozart delighted her by singing quietly of Father Emilian: '*O du schwanz du, leck du mich im arsch.*'* Those are just the sort of words Mozart later liked to set in canon for singing among his friends. Significantly, none of the Augsburg interlude upset Leopold, except the cost Mozart had put his cousin to in asking for her portrait and a feeling that he had stirred her emotions while himself remaining untouched.

At Mannheim everything promised to be more serious and important. Here the Elector Karl Theodor had created an architecturally magnificent, and also highly intellectual, court at which scientific research, painting and literature were encouraged. The theatre was being personally directed by the Elector towards a new type of national opera and play – away from Italian-style *opera seria* – in which not only the actors and dramatists should be native, but the subject also. Above all, Mannheim was famous for its composers and its orchestra. Its orchestra contained several distinguished players and was by 1777 more remarkable than its composers. The greatest of the Mannheim musicians, Stamitz, had died prematurely twenty years before, though others were still active; of them Ignaz Holzbauer had earlier in 1777 written the

* 'Oh you cock, you; lick my arse.'

music for a German national *Singspiel, Günther von Schwarzburg*. Like most people who saw this, Mozart praised its music as far finer than its libretto. Yet though Mannheim was so famous musically – for this reason attracting also literary figures like Klopstock and Wieland – the style it fostered often seemed mannered and difficult to outsiders. And its public attitude was sometimes prejudiced. Wonderfully performed as the 'Messiah' was there, in fact during Mozart's stay, the audience yawned throughout the first part and the second part was not given at all because it was judged too dry.

Mozart's arrival in this apparent paradise of music was not greeted with much greater enthusiasm. When with Cannabich, leader of the Mannheim orchestra and himself a composer, he went to the 'Messiah' rehearsal, he had the impression of being condescendingly stared at by people who had not heard of him. '*Weil ich klein und jung bin,*'* he flamed afterwards, they thought nothing great and mature could exist in such a person. It must have seemed at first as if Mannheim might be as unpleasant as Augsburg, but the friendliness of Cannabich and the welcome given by the Elector and his family, after Mozart had played the clavier before them, helped to wipe away first impressions. Mozart's vivid ear for dialogue conveys in a few words the typical interruption as well as the condescending style of compliment which probably at any period characterizes royal patronage of artists. As the Elector let Mozart kiss his hand: '*Er sagte, "es ist iezt, glaube ich, 15 jahr dass er nicht hier war." "Ja, Eüer Durchleücht, 15 jahr dass ich nicht die gnade gehabt habe–" "Er spielt unvergleichlich." die Prinzessin als ich ihr die hand küsste sagte zu mir, "Monsieur, je vous assure, on ne peut pas jouer mieux".*'† Instead of money, he received as a present yet one more watch: 'I now have five watches.'

Only gradually did it become apparent that Mozart was going to receive nothing more valuable, and certainly no offer of employment, from the Electoral court. As soon as Leopold suspected it – and as he had never positively advised going to Mannheim, he could always claim the very thought had been an error – he drew up complicated itineraries from his map at home, '*on which all routes are marked*'. He remembered exactly how much a meal in Louvain had cost fourteen years earlier; he thought Mainz might be a good place in which to give a

---

* 'Because I am small and young.'

† 'He said: "It is now fifteen years, I think, since you were last here." "Yes, your highness, it is fifteen years since I had the good fortune –" "You play matchlessly." As I kissed the Princess's hand, she said to me, "Monsieur, I assure you, no one could play better".'

concert; and he worried about how Frau Mozart would manage travelling in the winter, presuming she had left Mannheim.

But none of these things turned out to be relevant. Soon he was writing to ask what Mozart's plans were, having openly lost the initiative which had really not been his since Mozart left Salzburg. It might well be best to stay on at Mannheim during the winter. And when in the new year, on the death of Max III Joseph, the Elector of Mannheim became Duke of Bavaria, this accomplished fact seemed to offer fresh possibilities for Mozart. Leopold had laughingly to deny the rumour at Salzburg that Karl Theodor was going to appoint Mozart his composer at Munich – a rumour much more delightful than true. Meanwhile he had written to Grimm in Paris to prepare him for his son's imminent arrival there.

It was quite casually that the next letter Leopold received mentioned Mozart's plan of staying on at Mannheim in a leisurely way and then travelling through Europe with the Weber family. The Elector's failure to employ him no longer seemed important. The winter was passing very pleasantly; the Cannabich family had become increasingly friendly; he had met Wieland, who was very odd, ugly, but undoubtedly gifted. Mozart and Mademoiselle Weber had been performing in the presence of the Princess of Orange (to whom when a boy he had dedicated the clavier sonatas, Opus 4). Mademoiselle Weber had a most lovely voice and could also play the clavier surprisingly well. She had an excellent reputation; she would make a good companion for Nannerl. The whole Weber family was a joy: the eldest girl could cook, the father in many ways recalled Leopold – and Aloysia Weber was, between the lines of high praise for her character and her singing, a girl Mozart had fallen in love with.

In fact, her father was feckless and cadging, and in no way resembled Leopold Mozart. Her mother, about whom Mozart was perhaps prudently silent, was the driving force of a family with six children. Josefa, the eldest and Mozart's 'good cook', was a brilliant singer, destined to be the Queen of the Night in the first production of *Die Zauberflöte*; Aloysia was certainly talented; Sophie, the youngest of those involved with Mozart, was to be at his deathbed with her sister Constanze, whom he married five years after meeting the Webers at Mannheim. It was to be Frau Weber who went with Mozart on probably his last visit to a performance of *Die Zauberflöte* less than two months before his death, when they took his elder son with them, and all three generations enjoyed their evening.

In 1778 it was probably the whole Weber family whom Mozart loved, loving perhaps too the idea of such an agreeably feminine group, where the father could turn to Mozart for advice and money. The idea of travelling through Europe with them must have appeared a picaresque dream: as if he would share the life of some strolling company that was also an adopted family, amid which he took a dominant position, no longer '*klein und jung*', but the most experienced musician and traveller of them all. When Mozart later wrote from Paris to Weber, twenty-three years his senior, he virtually reversed their ages; he adopted Leopoldian shrewdness and handed out almost touchingly pseudo-paternal advice about Weber's tendency to depression and about Aloysia's future.

With much more briskness had Leopold disposed of her problems, having riddled all Mozart's projects of staying on in Mannheim, and drifting about in the Webers' company, with heavier ammunition than airgun pellets. Cajoling when not commanding, he assaulted Mozart with every form of emotional barrage, dragging in Nannerl's state ('weeping these two days'), his own ragged clothing and – doubtless aware that his image was fading – identifying himself finally with Christ, speaking of being forgotten 'on the Salzburg Cross where I am hanging'. The only way Mozart could atone was by going immediately to Paris. In Paris everyone would be glad to see Mozart; he would gain a great reputation, and would be able to write operas. Thus, posing as both man of sorrows and new-style angel with a flaming sword, Leopold drove Mozart from one musical paradise into what he firmly believed would be a better one.

Such was the tone of the ruthless letters, in which pity was expressed only for Leopold, which reached Mannheim while Mozart was devising arias for Aloysia Weber, as well as for the distinguished tenor Raaff whom he was to meet more than once again. He was distressed but not overwhelmed by their tone; he still wished Leopold could hear the way Aloysia Weber sang his setting of 'Non so d'onde viene' (K.294), an aria he had set as a self-challenge, haunted as he was by Christian Bach's beautiful setting of it. But he and his mother would leave for Paris; Leopold should be obeyed. Once there, however, and all hopefully going well, Mozart would ask him 'a great favour' ('*eine grosse gefallickeit*').

Things went very badly and Mozart never asked it. Obviously it concerned Aloysia Weber. On parting at Mannheim, she gave Mozart two

pairs of mittens knitted by herself, and her father gave him a complete
set of Molière, of which he still owned one volume at his death. Leopold
might be relieved that he never heard more of the great favour, but he
had taken on himself a dangerous responsibility when he pointed the
way to Paris and somewhat savagely separated Mozart from the Webers.
He had interposed again between his son and experience. Could he be
sure that travelling with the Webers and loving, if not reciprocally
loved by, Aloysia, would have been more dreadful than the humiliating
months in Paris and the death of Frau Mozart? Even playing music at a
rural inn could have been no worse than performing – as Mozart had to
– with cold fingers in an icy room before the Duchesse de Chabot and a
circle of her guests entirely indifferent to music.

Leopold had asserted himself in the role of Providence. Already in
May 1778, after scarcely a month in Paris, Mozart piteously appealed to
him to contrive some return to Italy 'where I can revive again'. But
Leopold could advise only staying on, and writing something easy,
suitable for amateurs *'und popular'*. Behind the briefly inspired authori-
tarianism was revealed a timid, powerless little man who could not
extricate his son, and who had now to beg him to mould himself
speedily to French taste. Leopold's concept of Paris was fourteen years
out of date, and Paris in 1778 was musically preoccupied by the war
between Gluckistes and Piccinistes – enjoying the war perhaps all the
more as it filled something of a cultural void. Under the new king Louis
XVI the arts were officially encouraged yet remained generally flavour-
less. The great and favourite sculptor of Louis XV, Lemoyne, died in
1778. Both Voltaire and Rousseau also died that year, and no comparably great figures replaced them. Beaumarchais had written *Le
Barbier de Séville* but not yet the scandalous success of *Le Mariage de
Figaro*.

The 'Paris' symphony (K.297), commissioned for the *Concerts
Spirituels* (concerts organized before and after Easter, when the Opera
was closed) and performed on Corpus Christi, 18 June, was Mozart's
own response to the circumstances: rather hard and contrived in its
brilliance, requiring an almost steely flick of precise, well-drilled strings
and displaying throughout effective if obvious contrasts of *piano* and
fortissimo, as the Parisian public expected. It is a bigger, and perhaps a
more formal, public, symphony than he had written before, and almost
anxiously busy, as though its composer knew that he must provide plenty
of distraction. The last movement opens in exaggerated quietness, and

builds up – quickly – to a crescendo. At the *piano* passage the audience – as Mozart had expected – shushed each other; at the *forte*, they broke into applause. That at least had been a success, and he tried to relive the day of its performance when late on the evening of 3 July he wrote to Leopold at length about it, having begun his letter by warning him that Frau Mozart was very ill.

In fact, he had seen her die an hour or two before. He then sat down and wrote first to Leopold, trying to prepare his mind in this way to lessen the shock, and next to a close family friend, the Abbé Bullinger – marking the letter 'For you alone' – telling him the truth and asking him to prepare Leopold very gently before conveying the terrible news. 'Strength and courage' had been given to Mozart to withstand the ordeal; he prayed for them to be given too to Leopold: '*Gott gebe ihm stärcke und muth!*'* At this moment his care for Leopold was movingly protective and paternal. He controlled his own grief sufficiently to continue writing to his father an outwardly calm letter about how, after the success of his symphony, he had gone off to eat a large ice at the Palais Royal – yet the strain showed in an abrupt outburst about another less recent death, that of '*der gottlose und Erz-spizbub Voltaire*',† 'arch-rogue' perhaps because he was admired by the Archbishop of Salzburg, and 'godless' in tacit contrast to Anna Maria Mozart.

When finally Leopold learnt the truth, Mozart wrote to him again with new maturity and calmly consoling words: speaking out of the depth of experience, for he had had to calm and control himself, as well as actually witness the death (the first he had seen), imaginatively devise the best way to break the news, and arrange the funeral.

The person whose impetuousness and impracticality Leopold had been bewailing a few months previously had managed to do all these things, unaided; and now he was alone. Just how alone he was became clear to Leopold only later, when Mozart revealed how shabbily Grimm had behaved and also when Leopold understood – if he ever did – how praise in Paris was no more substantial or profitable than the ices at the Palais Royal. '*Oh, c'est un Prodige, c'est inconcevable, c'est étonnant,*'‡ Mozart sardonically reported as the typical reaction to his playing, 'and, with that – Adieu'. Grimm meanwhile was telling Leopold that Mozart was 'too trusting' to succeed there. Grimm, now a baron and an established

---

* 'May God give him strength and courage.'
† 'the godless and arch-rogue Voltaire.'
‡ 'Oh, it's a miracle, it's unbelievable, it's amazing.'

littérateur, sniffed an aura of failure around Mozart. Perfunctoriness characterized his few services to the one-time prodigy, whose departure from Paris he openly speeded. Perhaps the final apt comment on Mozart's stay in Paris is the title of the ballet – an interlude in a Piccini opera – for which he composed some music: *'Les petits riens'*.

The mature tone in which Mozart had addressed Leopold and Weber was echoed when from Paris he wrote the only surviving letter to Aloysia; for some reason he wrote in Italian, which perhaps secretly signified for him a language of love. It was, too, the language in which, as he explained, he had written a new aria for her, 'solamente *per lei*';* and the letter is passionately serious, tenderly respectful, yet saying little of his feelings for her and demonstrating rather his usefulness to her by advice on her singing. Flirtatiousness and dirty jokes could not occur, because his emotions were too engaged. The idea of her – to serve and see whom again would be *'l'unica mia consolazione, e la mia quiete'*† – was perhaps the more intensely seized amid a hostile, alien society where his own loneliness was so intense. Leopold's absurd confidence about musical Paris and Mozart had proved cruelly mistaken; and perhaps never again would Mozart quite trust him as a guide, however fond of him as a father.

The defeat at Paris was made the more bitter because there was nowhere else to turn – except back to Salzburg, which meant back to the Archbishop's service. To Leopold it was almost miraculous that the ruler, who was having great difficulty in obtaining a *Kapellmeister* and who had been frankly told by several acquaintances that his dismissal of Mozart was an error, should now be willing to employ him again. Colloredo seems to have been truly eager to do so. Mozart recoiled, grew resigned, and yet as he travelled slowly home – to inescapable-seeming Salzburg – dreamt again of some post at Munich, where Aloysia and the Webers were now successfully settled. His care for their future had not been required; they were doing much better than he. Yet for him that was itself a joy, as was the prospect of seeing them as he passed through Munich. Even Leopold now openly mentioned Mozart's love for Aloysia as something to be accepted; he emphasized the proximity of Salzburg to Munich; he even spoke of Aloysia and her father coming to stay in Salzburg, though he questioned if Herr Weber in prosperity would be as grateful and flattering as he had been in poverty.

* 'For you *alone*.'
† 'My sole consolation, and my repose.'

Although Mozart gladly left Paris at the end of September, he obviously felt a reluctance to hasten to Salzburg, where Leopold and the Archbishop both waited. Uncertainty about his reception from Leopold combined with repugnance to resuming servitude at court; but the way back at least took in Munich, which he reached eventually on Christmas Day. He stayed with the Webers, gratifying that wish to see again '*l'unica mia consolazione*', Aloysia, around whom so many of his hopes and dreams revolved. She must have appeared the sole thing of value surviving from a fifteen-month period of rejection, humiliations and private misery; her presence at Munich might make even Salzburg tolerable while the earlier experiences receded.

Within four days Mozart realized that the whole relationship was an illusion. Like the courts he had visited, Aloysia had no place for him – perhaps had never had – and made this so painfully plain that he could write only a few hasty allusive lines to Leopold (noting he did not write from the Webers' house): 'Today I can do nothing but weep . . . I cannot write . . . my heart really is too reduced to tears . . .' He did not mention her name – just that Leopold's reply would be better sent to a friend's.

The following year Aloysia got an offer from Vienna and left the Munich opera; in 1780 she married the actor Lange, from whom she was later separated. She lived to explain to the Novellos visiting Vienna in 1829, when they asked why she had refused Mozart: 'She could not tell . . . but she could not love him at that time, she was not capable of appreciating his talent and his amiable character.'

Another Fanny Brawne (but with talent), Aloysia Weber was for long supposed a heartless woman who capriciously spurned the love of a genius, yet her words to the Novellos seem simple honesty. She was only sixteen or seventeen when she first met Mozart. Her singing quickly went to his heart ('*um das herz zu rühren wie eine Weber*,'* he was to say a year or two later, indicating where another singer failed to please him) and when she sang an aria like 'Dalla sponda tenebrosa' from *Lucio Silla* he perhaps merged her voice, his Giunia, and the actual girl Aloysia, into one ideal person, the perfect wife. Probably he half-guessed that under stress he was idealizing her; his letter to her from Paris is quite unspontaneous, and certainly not the letter of an accepted, confident lover. In Munich, out of a sort of utter desperation, he seems to have proposed to her; as 'she could not love him,' she rejected him,

---

* 'To touch the heart, as a singer like Weber does.'

which was neither heartless nor capricious. But coming after a series of appalling experiences, the disappearance of this dream must have been the most appalling of them all. The death of parents, the search for a job, are things to be endured. The prospect of life without love is indeed enough to make anyone weep.

Early in the new year of 1779 Mozart reached Salzburg. There was a further emotional ordeal in greeting, and being greeted by, Leopold and Nannerl. Possibly as some sort of protection against too intimate probing, and perhaps as a diversion against too vivid recollections of Aloysia Weber, Mozart brought his lively Augsburg cousin with him. Once back, the most difficult task of all was to address a new petition to the Prince-Archbishop: *'Ihro Hochfürstlich Gnaden:'* It needed seven references to the Archbishop's Grace and graciousness in a very few lines for Mozart to beg to be graciously assigned the post of organist, signing himself 'in the most profound submission'. The last time the Archbishop had responded to a Mozart petition he had delighted Mozart and prostrated Leopold. This time the result must have been almost exactly the opposite. Graciously accepting the suppliant (and considerably raising his salary), the Archbishop took Mozart back into his service as organist. The new year dispelled, apparently irrevocably, a last lingering illusion. It was not in Italy, Germany or France that Mozart would find employment, but in Salzburg, from which it seemed he might just as well never have tried to escape.

Part III
'This *unique* Mozart'

For nearly two years Mozart remained at Salzburg. An uneventful, almost colourless existence it was, glimpsed best in Nannerl's diary, where the weather, walks with the dog, friends coming in to play cards and frequent musical performances at church or court all receive brief notice. A truce with the Archbishop seemed to have been declared, and also a suspension of contact with the world beyond Salzburg. These months were probably the most passive of Mozart's life, more passive certainly than the years ahead. Little more than a decade of activity was left to him, but artistically that decade was to be of constant, sustained achievement: his greatest symphonies, piano concertos and quartets being produced in the years that run from *Idomeneo*, via the greatest operas, to close with *La Clemenza di Tito* and *Die Zauberflöte*.

And for all the outward quietness of the period 1779–80 in Salzburg, Mozart was active – as indeed he always was. He returned with at least one dramatic work to create, but by the autumn of 1779 he had also written two church sonatas, two marches, the Posthorn Serenade (K.320), a divertimento, two symphonies, the famous 'Coronation' Mass (K.317) and the *Sinfonia Concertante* for violin and viola (K.364), as well as sketching a triple *Sinfonia Concertante* (K.App.104) for 'cello, violin and viola.

Yet this period, proving scarcely less fecund during the subsequent year, is marked by something more than productivity. There is felt in most of these works a new confidence in the artist's power to create. The masses and other church music (notably the extraordinarily varied solemn *Vespers de confessore* (K.339)) are more than just mature: they are completely individual and accomplished. The three symphonies written during the same period form virtually a rising graph and all are more sympathetic than the 'Paris' symphony. The last of the three, in C Major (K.338), is not only big in orchestra and concept but imperious in sweeping the listener along, from its almost martial opening to its intensely vivacious final movement. If any Mozart symphony should be nicknamed 'Jupiter', it is this rather than his ultimate one, also in C Major. For all the depressing effect of Salzburg on Mozart, there seem also to have been some instrumental players there capable of stimulating him to produce the subtly rich *Sinfonia Concertante* in E flat – unless this was intended to be sent to friends at Paris or Mannheim.

New confidence was not perhaps to be publicly justified until the success of *Idomeneo* in the early weeks of 1781. Yet part of this confidence is that it could probably no longer be affected by public praise or blame. Mozart never forgot in success that applause usually comes from audiences no more qualified to praise than to blame. Of all the many people he ever met, only one perhaps had sufficient genius – as well as generosity – to make of his praise a significant, valuable thing: Haydn. Not until he settled in Vienna did Mozart come to know Haydn, and he could not realize how overwhelmed Haydn would be at his death. But it was part of the older composer's generosity to pay tribute while Mozart lived – indeed, while Leopold still lived. On Leopold's last visit to Vienna he met Haydn and heard him swear that Mozart was the greatest composer known to him either personally or by repute.

Almost more moving is the testimony in a private letter of Haydn's, written in 1787, virtually declining to allow any *opera buffa* of his to be publicly performed at Prague. That brings him to Mozart. He urges Prague to hold on to – but also to reward properly – such a jewel as Mozart, whose work is so profound, so musically intelligent and so extraordinarily sensitive. The three adjectives perfectly sum up Mozart's art; they make one ponder indeed if there is anything more left to say. Haydn realized only too well how neglected was the composer whom he called, in a burst of chagrin over the whole position, 'this *unique* Mozart' ('*dieser* einzige *Mozart*').

This is the creator who emerges in the outwardly dull period at Salzburg – the last period he would live there, as it happened. Despite the undoubted greatness of much that he had previously written, Mozart had been in effect establishing his own musical individuality, challenging other, usually established, composers and testing – challenging – the range of his own creativity. Of course in some ways he continued to do that, until the end of his life. He had written many operas, but none like *Die Zauberflöte*. He had written much church music, but never a requiem. But he no longer needed to establish individuality or ability as a composer. He assessed his own powers with total accuracy; it is a pity that people in power, whether Colloredo at Salzburg or Joseph II at Vienna, could not take him at his word, even if their ears were defective. The traditionally recorded anecdote of Mozart's exchange with Joseph II after the first performance of *Die Entführung aus dem Serail* typifies Mozart's absolute confidence in his own art. To the Emperor's comment, 'Too beautiful ... and far too many notes',

Mozart supposedly replied, 'Exactly as many, your majesty, as are needed'. More pertinent, and entirely authentic, is the exchange between Mozart and his father during the composition of *Idomeneo*. Leopold urged him to consider the unmusical as well as the musical public, so as to tickle 'long ears'. 'In my opera, there is music for all sorts of people,' Mozart riposted, *'ausgenommen für lange ohren nicht.'** He might have said the same about his church music written for Salzburg just previously. It is unconvincing to suppose that he set out there to challenge Colloredo deliberately, but some of the results seem pointed reminders that in acquiring an organist the Archbishop had not acquired a slave.

Within a fortnight of returning home Mozart reached his twenty-third birthday. In itself it marked no particular step, and indeed by the standards he had set for precocity he might appear almost retarded. Yet on reflection the day may be said to have its significance, for it tacitly celebrated a full year of Mozart's independence and emancipation from Leopold. The previous January he had been at Mannheim – on his actual birthday staying with Aloysia Weber at the Princess of Orange's house – and in the intervening year he had been exposed to many musical experiences as well as personal ones. The theatre, especially at Mannheim and at Paris, had shown him very different concepts of the opera than those old-fashioned categories of *seria* and *buffa*, associated with Italy and earlier journeys with his father. When Mozart referred to a 'duodrama' for which he was intending to write the music, Leopold irritably replied that he had absolutely no idea what a 'so-called duodrama' was. Rightly, he guessed that it was more declamation than singing, but it represented a novelty of which he would perhaps be unlikely to approve, since he had never been consulted. Duodramas and operas in German had not been at all the thing when he was young; and in learning about them he took yet another lesson from his one-time pupil.

Mozart returned to Salzburg with duodramas very much in mind. A few months later the theatre there, conveniently, though only transitorily, was sparked into existence by the arrival of Johann Böhm's troupe of players, and Nannerl was able to add a new activity to her daily record. Most days now closed with a visit to the theatre by one or other member of the family, if not the three of them. Late in the following year came the arrival of another touring company, that of Schik-

* 'But not for long ears.'

aneder, with whom the family quickly became friendly. What these companies usually performed were artistically impure but doubtless entertaining mixtures of play, ballet and pantomime. Such plots as they had might be based on Shakespeare or just on folk and fairy-tale tradition. Not all the productions pleased, even in provincial Salzburg. One of Schikaneder's new productions, flavoured according to him with the best comedy salt, was positively hissed off the stage and the Archbishop walked out before the end. While Mozart had been absent from Salzburg there had also been performances there by a visiting troupe of French actors, among whose repertoire was Voltaire's *Zaïre*, a play for which Michael Haydn had written special *entr'acte* music.

The concept of plays with incidental music represents a typical, experimental merging of categories which was bound to appeal to Mozart for its dramatic possibilities. Long before going to Mannheim he had been involved with such a project through Gebler's play of *König Thamos*, for which he had written some choruses and incidental music during the agreeable summer of 1773 in Vienna. Gebler was consciously aiming at theatrical reform. His play was serious, would-be sublime stuff, set in ancient Egypt and perhaps crypto-Masonic in its steady invocations to the sun. It had been performed at Salzburg in January 1776, but Mozart probably revised and expanded the music for the new performances in 1779 by Böhm's company. At the same time, for the same company, he probably touched up *La Finta Giardiniera*, which was played by Böhm in a German translation.

If *König Thamos* does not appear to have such confident mastery as the remainder of Mozart's work at this period, this is due perhaps partly to its long inception and also to some difficulty for us in appreciating its original effect when sandwiched between portions of Gebler's complicated but uninteresting plot. In Vienna a few years later the play was totally neglected, no longer performed – and that seems no unfair condemnation. Yet Mozart's music is intimately connected with the plot; indeed, it is really an attempt to illustrate it in orchestral terms, with some virtual anticipations of *leitmotiv*. Although the choruses (as well as, of course, the plot) have often been spoken of as anticipatory of *Die Zauberflöte*, the music's mood is perhaps closer to that of *Idomeneo*, while basically the work is altogether closer to a symphonic poem than to an opera. But the trouble is that it does not quite exist in any category. The *entr'actes* were obviously not meant to follow each other closely, as they must in modern performance; the choral moments

1 (*Above*) Leopold Mozart, Wolfgang's father: painting (by Pietro Antonio Lorenzoni ?) *c.* 1765.

2 (*Above*) Leopold Mozart's dedication of a music book 'to my dear son Wolfgang', Salzburg, 31 October 1762, Wolfgang's sixth name-day.

3 (*Above*) Maria Anna Mozart,
Wolfgang's sister 'Nannerl', in
court costume, 1763: painting (by
Pietro Antonio Lorenzoni ?).

4 (*Opposite above*) Anna Maria
Mozart, Wolfgang's mother, *c.* 1775:
painting (by Pietro Antonio
Lorenzoni ?).

5 (*Opposite below*) Hannibal Platz in
Salzburg; the Mozart family lived in
part of the building on the right:
Lithograph after G. Pezold *c.* 1840.

6 (*Above*) Wolfgang Mozart aged seven, dressed in the lilac-coloured court costume given him by Empress Maria Theresa: painting (by Pietro Antonio Lorenzoni ?) early 1763.

7 (*Left*) The Empress Maria Theresa with her husband, Francis I and eldest son the Archduke Joseph. Mozart was received at court in Vienna in 1762.

8 Leopold Mozart with Wolfgang and Nannerl. Water colour by Louis Carrogis de Carmontelle, 1763/4.

9 (*Above*) Tea at Prince Louise-François de Conti's; Mozart is at the harpsichord preparing to accompany the guitarist. Oil painting by Michel Barthelemy Ollivier, Paris, 1766.

10 (*Below*) George III and Queen Charlotte of England in their box at the opera: Contemporary engraving (artist unknown).

12 *London, from the South West*, engraved by Thomas Bowles; one of fifteen views bought by Leopold Mozart during the visit to London in 1764.

13 (*Above*) Johann Christian Bach (1735–1782), painted by Gainsborough in 1776.

14 (*Below*) Part of the motet, 'God is our Refuge' (κ.20), Mozart's setting of psalm 46, verse I, specially composed for the British Museum in 1765.

15 (*Above right*) Aloisia Lange (*née* Weber): from an engraving by Berger, 1785, after Joseph Lange.

16 (*Above left*) Maria Anna Thekla Mozart, the 'little cousin': detail of a pencil drawing, 1777/78.

17 (*Below*) Mozart family portrait, painted by Johann Nepomuk della Croce 1780/81. Mozart's mother had died in 1778.

18 (*Above*) Mozart wearing the Order of the Golden Spur presented to him by Pope Clement XIV in Rome, 1770. The portrait was painted for Padre Martini by an unknown artist in Salzburg, 1777.

19 (*Below*) The Bay of Naples: water colour by Paul Sandby, 1778. Mozart visited Naples in 1770 and recalled the scene in his opera *Così Fan Tutte*, first performed in Vienna, 1790.

20 (*Above*) Constanze Mozart (*née* Weber), painted by Joseph Lange 1782.

21 (*Left*) Mozart's 'Catalogue of all my works from the month of February 1784 until the month of ....' (*Verzeichnuss aller meiner Werke, vom Monath Febrario 1784 bis Monath......................*').

22 (*Above*) The 'Graben', Vienna, engraved by Karl Schutz, 1781. Mozart and Constanze lived first in a building in the centre left, and then in the 'Trattnerhof', right foreground.

23 (*Above*) Ticket for a concert given by Mozart in Vienna, probably a subscription concert 1784/85.

24 (*Left*) Joseph Haydn (1732–1809) drawn by Dance in 1794.

25 Mozart's portrait drawn in silver-point by Doris Stock, Dresden, April 1789.

K. K. priv. Wiedner Theater

Heute Freytag den 30ten September 1791.

Werden die Schauspieler in dem kaiserl. königl. privil. Theater auf der Wieden die Ehre haben aufzuführen

Zum Erstenmale:
Die
Zauberflöte.

Eine grosse Oper in 2 Akten, von Emanuel Schikaneder.

Personen

Sarastro,		Hr. Gerl.
Tamino,		Hr. Schack.
Sprecher,		Hr. Winter.
Erster)		Hr. Schikaneder der ältere.
Zweiter) Priester,		Hr. Kistler.
Dritter)		Hr. Moll.
Königin der Nacht,		Mad. Hofer.
Pramina ihre Tochter,		Mlle. Gottlieb.
Erste)		Mlle. Klöpfer.
Zweite) Dame,		Mlle. Hofmann.
Dritte)		Mad. Schack.
Papageno,		Hr. Schikaneder der jüngere.
Ein altes Weib,		Mad. Gerl.
Monostatos ein Mohr,		Hr. Nouseul.
Erster)		Hr. Gieseke.
Zweiter) Sklav,		Hr. Frasel.
Dritter)		Hr. Starke.
Priester, Sklaven, Gefolge.		

Die Musik ist von Herrn Wolfgang Amade Mozart, Kapellmeister, und wirklicher K. K. Kammerkompositeur. Herr Mozart wird aus Hochachtung für ein gnädiges und verehrungswürdiges Publikum, und aus Freundschaft gegen den Verfasser des Stücks, das Orchester heute selbst dirigiren.

Die Bücher von der Oper, die mit zwei Kupferstichen versehen sind, wo Herr Schikaneder in der Rolle als Papageno nach wahrem Kostüm gestochen ist, werden bei der Theater-Kassa vor 30 kr. verkauft.

Herr Gayl Theatermahler und Herr Neßlthaler als Dekorateur schmeicheln sich nach den vorgeschriebenen Plan des Stücks, mit möglichsten Künstlerfleiß gearbeitet zu haben.

Die Eintrittspreise sind wie gewöhnlich.

 Der Anfang ist um 7 Uhr.

26 (*Opposite*) Play-bill for the première of *The Magic Flute* at the Theater auf der Wieden or Freihaus Theater in 1791. Mozart's name is in small print below the cast list.

27 (*Right*) Mozart's death certificate.

28 (*Below*) The last page of the *Requiem* in the composer's hand.

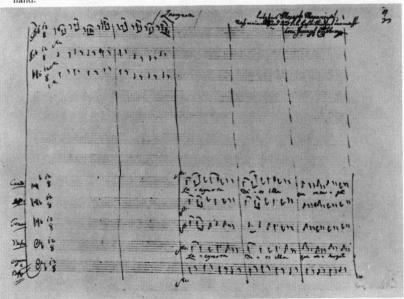

29 Mozart's snuff-box; the nocturnal scene is painted on ivory.

coming after long periods of speech perhaps made a heightened, emotional effect -- comparable to the dialogue of priest and choir in religious services.

At the same time, it seems clear that the music was always additional to *Thamos*, probably no more at best than attractive decoration in Gebler's view. Mozart himself remained fond of the music, and was later to lament that it could not be utilized. To some extent he had served the play too well. It is impossible for the listener not to feel that the music means something exterior to itself: beautiful as is the oboe solo of the second *entr'acte*, its significance as illustrative of Thamos's nobility needs to be realized. At other moments the romantically agitated drama in the orchestra is so obviously depicting something that it is annoying not to know what this is – and something of an anti-climax when one does. It might have been best if Mozart had put Gebler's play aside entirely and conveyed the whole story in musical terms, as he probably longed privately to do. However tedious the plot, its opportunities for grand and dramatic effects were exciting to him. He must have recognized that he was patently experimenting – and in so doing was expressing a sense of confidence. The failure of *Thamos* is not his but Gebler's, and that too he recognized. On future occasions, he had perhaps already decided, the libretto as well as the music should be under his control.

The music for *Thamos* at least survives. None has ever been found for what may well have been a more valuable experiment, a melodrama in the literal sense of the term, the declamatory *Semiramis*, definitely begun at Mannheim on the way home in December 1778. The text had been written by Otto von Gemmingen, a Mason incidentally, who was then living at Mannheim. He clearly intended from the first that his work should combine music and declamation; and both he and Mozart seem to have been excited by the project. That it became more than a project is confirmed by a tantalizingly brief mention of this musical drama in the *Theater-Kalender* for 1785 published at Gotha, a place with marked interest in the form.

The story of Semiramis, something of an ancient Assyrian Catherine the Great in her loves, crimes and ability to rule a great empire, might naturally fascinate the eighteenth century. A play on the subject had been written by Crébillon, but it was Voltaire's tragedy *Semiramis* which gave the story current literary form. More than one German composer had written music to accompany performances of the play. Gemmingen probably knew that, and will certainly have known Voltaire's tragedy.

Perhaps the most obvious opportunities offered to Mozart by the subject were the possibility of Eastern colouring and a central figure who would be a heroine, not a hero. Victim-women and monster-women – Iphigenias and Medeas – were increasingly appearing in opera, as they had previously appeared in plays. As for the melodrama form, Mozart's treatment of this lost *Semiramis* may be partly gauged through its fortunately surviving successor, *Zaïde*, written at Salzburg, conceivably for Böhm's theatrical troupe. If there is nothing tentative about the execution of *Zaïde*, although it is unfinished, this is probably due to the experience of having tackled in Gemmingen's play most of the problems raised by the novel task. At Mannheim Mozart had already enthusiastically responded to a production of the duodrama *Medea* by Georg Benda, *Kapellmeister* to the Duke of Gotha and the leading composer of this comparatively new genre.

The presence in Salzburg of Böhm's company, while he was probably still working on *Semiramis*, might well suggest that an entirely fresh duodrama could be created for performance there. It is impossible to tell whether Mozart turned for a libretto to his boyhood friend, the court-trumpeter Schachtner, or whether Schachtner had already begun a text. Schachtner was certainly the author of what is traditionally called *Zaïde*, though the autograph score has no title, the spoken dialogue is lost, and Mozart never refers to it by name. In fact, Schachtner is nowadays recognized as adapter rather than originator, since Alfred Einstein traced this story of three Christians escaping from the seraglio to an obscure source, *Das Serail*, a *Singspiel* produced in Bozen in 1779. But, to begin with, it seems unsure whether this actually preceded Schachtner's text; and there is no proof that he knew it. More important, the primary source for both works is a common one, another of Voltaire's tragedies, *Zaïre*, the very play performed at Salzburg with Michael Haydn's music in the previous year. That actual performance was probably witnessed by Schachtner. It may be that the players had gone on to Bozen, and that a certain Joseph von Friebert, the author of *Das Serail*, had also been struck by the possibilities of semi-plagiarism, a crime then rarely acknowledged.

Like Zaïde, Zaïre is a Christian living in the seraglio and loved by the Sultan; also apparently like Zaide, she is confronted by an older man who turns out to be her father, and has a potential lover, of whom the Sultan is jealous, who turns out to be her brother. Friebert's sub-title for his piece, 'The Unexpected Encounter in Slavery of Father, Daughter and Son', makes plain how closely he derived it from Voltaire's plot. The end of *Zaïre* brings the heroine's death, stabbed by the Sultan who is still unaware that she is only the sister of his Christian rival. In his remorse he orders the release of all the Christians and then kills himself. Such an end was probably too grim for Schachtner, as it was for Friebert. Perhaps he never quite decided on the details of the dénouement, but it is anyway likely that at the last moment the Sultan showed mercy to his prisoners, and this would possibly have been hailed by a final chorus.

Zaïde is probably the most totally personal work Mozart had so far created. Because its story largely, and its music occasionally, foreshadowed the richer texture of *Die Entführung aus dem Serail* three years later, there is a tendency for it to be treated rather like a preparatory sketch for that opera. Yet some of the most effective parts of *Zaïde* remain quite unparalleled in Mozart's other work: not only the melodrama recitatives but the seriously threatening music of the Sultan, no caricatured tyrant nor mild-mannered liberal *manqué*, but heroically angry and frighteningly dangerous. When Zaïde defies him, her bravery seems unexaggerated in expression, as well as touching. Altogether *Zaïde* is throughout more tense and consistently affecting than the later opera with its alternating moods. Never again (outside *opera seria*) did Mozart so pointedly reduce the place of humour in a dramatic work of his. The sole comic aria – sung by an irrelevant *buffo* slave dealer – no more lightens the general effect than the Porter's soliloquy does in *Macbeth*. One of Mozart's objections to trying to get *Zaïde* put on in Vienna was to be that Viennese audiences preferred comedies, and it is no criticism of *Die Entführung* to say that in it this preference is – without being pandered to – delightfully satisfied.

Zaïde lacks an overture. That may well be deliberate, for *König Thamos*, too, has no overture. Mozart perhaps envisaged *Zaïde* opening with the chorus of slaves which is the first and least remarkable music in it. Throughout he blends aria and declamation, borrowing from the conventions of *opera seria* as well as from the melodrama, and no doubt also from his experiences with the problems of Gebler's play. It is as if *Zaïde* was intended to fuse the advantages of the three types of dramatic form, and be more flexible than any of them. If *Semiramis* was strictly conceived as melodrama, Mozart may have found it offered too little opportunity for the voice; in *Zaïde* the heroine, the hero and the Sultan need to be singers and not just actors who can declaim against a musical background. The captain of the slaves, Allazim (really an ex-Christian, ex-prince, Ruggiero of Palermo) must also be able to sing. Thus Mozart established the material out of which to build a tenderly harmonious trio for father, daughter and son, and a dramatic quartet – when they are confronted by the Sultan – where the vividly expressed, conflicting emotions of the four characters are woven into one magnificent pattern of sound which dies away in *piano* hopelessness. Only the ensembles of *La Finta Giardiniera* (which Mozart was perhaps contemporaneously re-working) hint at such achievement, yet they are slight beside it. Indeed so cumulatively effective is the final quartet of *Zaïde* that there would have needed to be, from a musical viewpoint, some very subtle dénouement to convey the eventual resolution of what seems so irrevocable.

Although there is a long tortured melologue for the Sultan between love and anger, culminating in an aria of explosive force, more remarkable still is the even longer pure melologue for the captive hero Gomatz, following the slaves' chorus at the beginning of the work. Here the expressive possibilities of declamation combined with music – carrying us far beyond the *recitativi accompagnati* of *Lucio Silla* – are explored in exploring the hero's physical and mental weariness. The melologue becomes more psychologically subtle than a conventional aria could be. (Mozart was as keenly aware as any modern objector to opera of the inherent absurdity of people who are exhausted or on the point of death taking long arias to tell us so.) In Gomatz's melologue the music is free from having to follow his sensations and can also depict his longings. When desperately he once again invokes sleep ('*O komm, du Tröster der Müden*'), the music unexpectedly breathes a few bars of beautiful elusive melody, as if conjured up by pity for his despair, throwing over him an enchantment of which he is scarcely aware as consciousness dissolves.

What is finally most remarkable about *Zaïde* is less its experimental mixture than its total achievement. Its typical, stock plot and tepid libretto are transformed by Mozart, but not transformed into the merely charming or exotic. Yet again, the basic situation was one he could seriously respond to and it is there that his imagination finds its inspiration. Love and courage conquer tyranny. Perhaps the father, son and daughter of *Zaïde* who so bravely face a tyrant's wrath might suggest a comparable real-life trio, of whom one at least was by no means reconciled to their own reigning Sultan. *Zaïde* remained apparently incomplete and was therefore never performed at Salzburg. Mozart never had the pleasure of seeing the Prince-Archbishop attend it; otherwise, he might have particularly looked forward to the *licenza*-like aria of

Allazim who addresses the 'mighty ones' of the earth, favoured by fortune but forgetful of those who are 'their brothers'. In these sentiments there is not much aptness to the plot of *Zaïde* but plenty of ironic salt – as Schikaneder might have said – to give topical flavour to its performance at Salzburg.

What was, or was intended to be, performed at Salzburg, is certainly rich enough. It is extraordinary to think of the city steadily exposed, and probably largely indifferent, to the series of musical masterpieces which Mozart created at this period. If his exterior life was boring and un-eventful, at least he was not yet in the desperate, exacerbated and over-worked state to which Vienna would reduce him. His daily existence at Salzburg became the creation of music. The year 1779 takes shape in retrospect – and against the background of major operatic preoccupa-tions – as a succession of virtually monthly masterpieces. By 23 March he had written the 'Coronation' Mass (K.317); in April he finished the Symphony in G Major (K.318) and by 9 July the much finer (in every sense) Symphony in B Flat Minor (K.319).

When the autumn came ('It rained the whole day,' Mozart wrote in Nannerl's diary for 15 September, after an interval of some months), he was working on the never-completed *sinfonia concertante* for violin, viola and 'cello (K. suppl.104) and the fortunately finished, famous and supremely expressive *sinfonia concertante* in E Major (K.364). The year had already included two church sonatas and two marches as well as the Posthorn Serenade (K.320); and in the following year he wrote another, even more boldly magnificent C Major Mass (K.337) and the Vespers *de confessore* (K.339), before producing *Idomeneo*.

At least Salzburg required the performance of church music, and Mozart built in the two C Major masses a pair of similar structures that are memorials to a type of commissioned music which he would seldom be able to write again. Twin monuments in his own style, the two masses are by no means the same and each possibly gains by the existence of the other. With the 'Coronation' Mass (written for the feast day com-memorating the Pope's consecration of the crown on the Virgin's image in a pilgrimage church near Salzburg) we are plunged into a musical edifice as immediately as if entering an actual rococo church: greeted without prelude by the triple cries of '*Kyrie*' which dramatically swell and fall, like walls rapidly curving away. Like such buildings too, Mozart's church music should be recognized as intensely dramatic and intensely spiritual: suggestive often of eternal but unfrightening space which is the Kingdom of God. Neither the music nor the architecture requires faith before it can be appreciated (except for that rarest of all faiths, in art), but they are shaped by faith. The churches are not sense-less riots of colour and gold; they are intended to excite the mind now to praise and now to ponder on the optimistic mystery of God's faith in man. Mozart's masses may joyfully soar *in excelsis* but ultimately they concentrate in utter solemnity on the central moment of belief – central to the Christian religion, musically to the mass itself and, as is the altar, often central to eighteenth-century churches – expressed in the words, '*Et incarnatus est . . .*'

In the 'Coronation' Mass, the jubilant choral surge of the Creed pauses briefly, but for the first time, just before the 'Incarnatus', sung with a steady slowness which merges into the droningly mournful, signi-ficant '*Crucifixus etiam pro nobis . . .*'. In this interpretation, very different from that in the C Major Mass (K.337) of the next year, one mood of solemnity, with no solo voice, infuses the facts of Christ's being born and his dying for us. This mood in turn is changed by the triumphant tone of the Creed itself, as it moves towards affirmation: one God, the resurrec-tion of the dead and life everlasting.

The structure of the mass offered Mozart a clear yet flexible frame-work, a ground-plan on which to build in varying moods, with shifts of emphasis and always experimentally. Commissions for masses can reasonably be compared with the task of designing churches; liturgical requirements at once predominate and also challenge the artist's ingenuity to devise a novel approach to the familiar. Mozart's constant care for the meaning of the words he is setting – sometimes with emphasis on a single one like '*pax*', sometimes lighting up a whole phrase so that the music reflects a shout of jubilation or a plea for mercy – is the best proof of how entirely serious he was, at least as an artist, in his church music. And the range he explored is much more remarkable than any restriction. When he went over the long-familiar words again, new sett-ings must have rapidly suggested themselves.

Nor was it, of course, merely at the prompting of the words as such. The suitably joyful decorated 'Amen' of the Gloria in the 'Coronation' Mass is remarkable enough, and typical of this triumphantly joyful work; but the 'Amen' of the Gloria in the C Major Mass of the following year becomes virtually a hymn of joy itself in its elaboration, with soprano and tenor concentrating in the one word an entirely musical expression of the whole preceding prayer. Nor is the 'Coronation' Mass without its poignancy. After so much concerted singing, the sudden effect of the soprano solo in the Agnus Dei, preceded on the violins by what has sometimes been called a 'strange' anticipation of the Countess's aria *Dove sono*, is to underline an urgent appeal. More vaguely the *Agnus Dei* of the 1780 Mass suggests the Countess's *Porgi amor*. These sacred and profane prayers all express the same desire: either a lone voice, or one later joined by others symbolizing humanity, begs '*dona nobis pacem*'. An extraordinary last sigh of this is left to the soprano in the Agnus Dei of the 1780 Mass, when the piece seems about to close in a now quite confident mood established by the remaining singers; very softly, her voice returns to breathe one final wistful appeal, on which the whole mass ends.

Set across the distance of a year from the 'Coronation' Mass rises the even more splendid, certainly bolder and more idiosyncratic second C Major Mass – rather as Neumann's church of the Vierzehnheiligen is literally set across the river from Dietzenhofer's Abbey at Banz. The particular occasion of the 1780 Mass is not known, but if March is the exact month of execution (as is usually agreed) it may very well have been for the anniversary of the Archbishop's election on 14 March; for once, when it would have been valuable, Nannerl's diary does not cover the date. It would be a pleasing irony if such a marvellous but highly personal work, which proved to be the last mass Mozart ever completed, was for such an occasion. It anyway seems likely that it was (technically as a *missa brevis*) performed in the Cathedral, and the prominent organ passages in it can probably be partly explained if one realizes that they were intended to be played by the Archbishop's organist, Mozart himself. Nothing in this mass is usual or expected. Its softly poignant close is as effective as its opening, with a slow and solemn instrumental prelude to the Kyrie before any voice is heard – an immediate indication of its difference from the mass of the previous year. It is true that that had probably also included an organ sonata (K.329), but the organ sonata (K.336) apparently intended for the second mass is written as if for the piano. That Mozart should later have developed a piano concerto (K.537) out of it is only right. There is no attempt at pious sentiment, any more than at exploitation of the pealing, pseudo-impressive tones of which the organ is only too capable. Like a diversion – and indeed it was intended to occupy the period of the Gradual and Epistle being read – the organ positively glitters tonally, accompanying with enchantingly gay, musical-box melody what might almost be some toy figure turning on the top of it.

This is a frank interlude, an altar raised to talent in one aisle of an otherwise religious building. The Creed is again devised to be in two great blocks of sound, flanking the 'Incarnatus' which is begun only by a soprano. Icy, Christmas-like clarity carves out each syllable of the word: a single angelic voice testifying with lonely intensity at this solemn moment, and then merging with other voices into a grey, unwavering chant as the Passion follows, until the distant, ghostly melancholy which hovers around '*et sepultus est*'. Abruptly, like the unveiling at Easter of statues and shrines covered during Lent, a burst of allegro vivace makes dazzlingly almost visible the miracle of the next words: '*Et resurrexit*'. From then onwards the whole impulse of the piece is ascension, up into an eternity of pale, frescoed dome, accelerated by every twist of capital and pointed at by elegant, swaying gilt figures. Fortissimi shouts of '*Sanctus*' are followed by celestial pianissimi whispering the name of the divinity praised: '*Dominus Deus Sabaoth*'. And yet, amid truly Rococo exuberance, Mozart finds a place for something again quite unexpected: the almost Gothic-Rococo chapel of the 'Benedictus', archaic, even severe music which is thoroughly liturgical as well as religious.

Just such another juxtaposition of traditionally-ancient and modern occurs in the beautifully organized Vespers *de confessore*, which seems altogether close in manner to the 1780 Mass. The Confessor celebrated is not known. St Jerome, though Doctor of the Church as well as Confessor, may be a likely candidate; his feast day on 30 September was the Archbishop's name-day, which may well have been celebrated in church as well as at court. Certainly the Vespers – made up of five psalms and a final 'Magnificat' – form one interlinked, alternating song of praise and faith. They provide no narrative or inherent drama, but Mozart shaped them into a uniquely coherent structure, like a symphony with six movements. Opening and closing in hymns of praise, they explore austerely a realm of faith suitable for a Confessor in the Psalm 'Confitebor tibi' and celebrate in firm laudatory phrases the 'Beatus vir'. The fourth psalm, the 'Laudate pueri', carries one out of the eighteenth century altogether, back to a virtually medieval world of Gregorian plainchant, an evocation of monks singing vespers in some romantically Gothic cathedral. It is also an illustration of Mozart's response to a style of music he might be assumed to have ignored. The more effective for following this thickly-textured sound is the totally 'modern', entirely

Mozartean 'Laudate Dominum', where a soprano voice (equivalent in Mozart's idiom to the purest spirituality) so quietly, confidently and tenderly praises God – in accents that seem, perhaps more than fancifully, to anticipate Susanna's loving, prayerful aria in the last act of *Figaro*. Finally, turning trumpet-tongued, the soprano leads the 'Magnificat', a great choral hymn of almost running rhythm, punctuated by real trumpets, spreading splendour into the minds even of solid Salzburg citizens before they hasten home from church to supper.

Some of them presumably had the opportunity to hear Mozart's instrumental music written during the same period, which shows equal grasp of structure and the same total maturity. Musical experience of Paris and Mannheim is apparent behind all three new symphonies written at this time, though there are no indications of when or where they were to be performed. The first of them, in G Major (K.318) is slight for all its large orchestra, smart, and so Frenchified that it might have been destined positively for Paris. It is easily the least individual and lacks the intimate dreamlike beauty of the Symphony in B Flat (K.319), written four months later. The slow movement of this represents a complete turning away, perhaps consciously, from Parisian elegance, and the whole symphony has a deliberate delicacy and simple singing charm which made it much more private than public. Even its changes of mood and tempo all seem to lie within one single expressive concept. Its mood is woven virtually out of the strings alone, so little prominence do the other instruments have, and even at its most brisk it remains somehow meditative, withdrawn without being sad.

What is delicate, though sure, in its structure becomes massive in the C Major symphony (K.338) of the next year. This was Mozart's thirty-fourth symphony and certainly the greatest he had yet written. Mannheim rather than Paris has given weight to its thunderous, majestic opening; majesty marks, too, the slow movement and the powerful, fast, last movement. But in it Paris and Mannheim are fully assimilated, and it is perhaps the first of Mozart's symphonies that is usually recognized – and played – as typical. Significantly, Mozart himself returned to it in Vienna, when he added a minuet (K.409) which combines delicacy of detail with the grandeur necessary to suit the work. And when sending in 1786 a list of his recent work to Sebastian Winter, the family's one-time valet and 'friend of my youth', he chose this symphony, along with the 'Linz' (K.425) and the 'Haffner' (K.385) to represent him in this category. Even more significant seems the inclusion there of one further symphony, scarcely to be claimed as recent because it was then seven years old: the Symphony in B Flat, perhaps the earliest of his own symphonies in which he detected mature, personal achievement. Winter's employer, Prince von Fürstenberg, seems to have agreed; he selected the two Salzburg symphonies and the 'Linz' for his court orchestra.

Personality and expression are probably felt most vividly of all, though in slightly different ways, in two concertos for solo instruments written at Salzburg, both possibly in 1779. Mozart had insisted that, whatever he did, he would not play the violin at court, and it was perhaps for the Archbishop's violinist, Brunetti, that he wrote the *Sinfonia concertante* (K.364). Almost certainly for himself and Nannerl he wrote the Concerto for Two Pianos (K.365), a less profoundly expressive work, though personal in a special sense, and, as it happens, the last view musically of brother and sister together.

The violin and viola *Sinfonia concertante* has indeed a richly expressive eloquence which – at least in this form – was not exactly attempted or equalled again by Mozart. It joins those other works of this Salzburg period which already justify Haydn's praise of the composer's uniqueness. Freed from any necessity to play the instrument, Mozart is able to write for the violin with an intensity entirely lacking in virtuosity or brilliance, but touching – in the andante middle movement – tragic depths: '*sunt lacrimae rerum et mentem mortalia tangunt.*' The first movement, unhurried, stately in its slowness, has something of the deliberate majesty of the C Major Symphony, yet it is in the subsequent andante that one hears that bleakly tragic tone which remains uneffaced as an impression, despite the cheerful contredanse which concludes the work. Like heroine and confidante of some Racinian drama, violin and viola are engaged in a throbbing dialogue, ultimately the more affecting through its very formality.

The Concerto for Two Pianos does not presume to enter such a seriously elevated world, as is clear from the lilting gaiety of its opening theme; its slow movement is reflective rather than sad and the last movement irrepressibly, almost ridiculously, lively. The two pianos chase each other, echo each other, fall back to allow each other to take precedence – more like gifted kittens than Racinian personages. Even the last movement's orchestration is light enough to have been mouthed by Mozart during rehearsals with Nannerl; round and round during this rondo comes the strong beat of tune, pounced on by the pianos in friendly competitive spirit – as if each pianist dared the other to follow as he or she dashed away with it. Nannerl's real ability as a performer is here briefly glimpsed. It was demonstrated publicly at court, possibly with this actual concerto, when she and Mozart played together before the Archbishop on 3 September 1780. The previous few days, as Mozart kindly noted, with nonsense remarks, in Nannerl's diary, had been fine; but on 3 September, 'it rained the whole day'. As an antidote to boredom and bad weather, the Concerto for Two Pianos is perfectly devised; and it is almost impossible to listen to the last movement without hearing the laughter which must have accompanied its rehearsal.

2

With much greater cause for light-heartedness, Mozart was able to set off, almost exactly two months later, to Munich. He had a short leave of absence from the Archbishop, granted because of receiving the Elector's commission for *Idomeneo, Re di Creta*, due for performance in January 1781. This time his parting with Leopold and Nannerl could not have been very disturbing. The distance was not far, his task was assured, and indeed the most exciting possible he could have been given; and anyway the respite from Salzburg seemed only temporary.

Yet it was this parting which proved decisive. Without knowing it, Mozart was quitting Salzburg for ever; he would return there again only once, and then as a married man, for a brief holiday. Although Leopold and Nannerl followed him to Munich, to witness *Idomeneo*, that was the last taste of family life together; Mozart saw Nannerl again only on his visit to Salzburg, and probably never met the man she married the following year. Leopold and Mozart never saw each other again after Leopold's stay in Vienna, the occasion when he heard Haydn's estimate of his son's ability.

And amid such chances and accidents of the future, there loomed the active hand of the Prince-Archbishop, playing Providence without meaning to, but doing it so much more successfully than Leopold. When Mozart turned from Munich, not back to Salzburg but on to Vienna, it would be at the Archbishop's command. It was merely an accident that it was there that the Archbishop should summon him early in March 1781; he himself had gone there, probably because his own father was ailing. This time, and without Leopold to breathe caution, Mozart entered Vienna confident of conquering it, and privately intending to remain there. Well before he had quarrelled finally and face to face with the Archbishop, he was hinting at his intention of dodging out of service and settling in the city, assuring Leopold, '*dass hier ein Herrlicher ort ist – und für* main Metier *der beste ort von der Welt*'.*

The confidence with which he entered Vienna was partly natural, irrepressible optimism, but it came largely from the success of *Idomeneo*. To play through the opera for Joseph II was one of his first hopes; hopes, too, of a performance in Vienna continued to hover round him, even when rehearsals for *Seraglio* had begun. Indeed, while he described that as '*Meine teutsche opera*' ('My German opera'), indicating its *Singspiel* nature, he referred in the same letter to *Idomeneo*, no less correctly, as '*die grosse opera*' ('the great opera').

Its greatness is fortunately recognized again today, after more than a century of neglect. Yet although it is the earliest of Mozart's operas to have entered the repertoire, it really represents the last – apart from *La Clemenza di Tito* – of a type of opera he had been seeing and writing since he was a boy. Nor are its greatness and maturity so remarkable, when one reflects that it was his tenth operatic work and his third full-scale *opera seria*. Exactly ten years earlier, he and Leopold had been travelling back to Milan with the challenging commission to write *Mitridate*. The composer who could look back over the subsequent decade might well go off alone gaily to Munich in the cold late autumn of 1780. There from November until January of the following year he worked at *Idomeneo*, and the work involved much more than writing music. The problem of the singers – the tenor being old and the castrato at once silly and inexperienced – was only to be expected. But Mozart had also to deal with the administrative and financial arrangements proposed by the Elector's theatre controller, Count Joseph von Seeau – someone long known to the Mozart family. He had to consider the views of the distinguished stage designer, Quaglio. He had to attend rehearsals which went much like most rehearsals, except that the occasional presence at them of the Elector himself must have heightened the usual tension. During this period Mozart was in no way insulated against the demands of daily existence and even the annoyance of a cold. When the news of Maria Theresia's death reached Munich, he had immediately to send home for his black suit: 'I also must *weep*,' he remarked sardonically. When the suit arrived it proved to be too shabby; before he could wear it he needed to have the coat turned and a new

* 'This is a splendid place – and the best place in the world as far as my *Metier* is concerned.'

lining put in. It was necessary, too, to guide Leopold over what clothes he should bring to Munich, and about the Frenchified manner at some households which would require Leopold to kiss the ladies – but only on the chin, to avoid their rouge turning blue.

But, above all, he had to create his opera. It was the total structure of this which concerned him: to make one completely coherent work of art, where a poetic, sensible text married to powerful music should have the greatest possible impact on its auditors. As early as *Mitridate* he had omitted setting passages of the libretto which seemed unnecessary or repetitive. With *Idomeneo*'s libretto, the work of the Salzburg court chaplain, the Abbate Varesco, Mozart was much bolder, indeed artistically ruthless – though no more so than he was at the same time with his own music. The proof, if proof is needed, of his intense sensitivity to the sound and significance of words, is given by his constant letters to Leopold during the months of composition. He proved, inevitably, to have a much better grasp of dramatic essentials than Varesco, who was certainly no Metastasio; and Leopold's own rather timid, somewhat pro-Varesco proposals seem strangely academic beside Mozart's utterly instinctive flair. Mozart apparently never wrote directly to Varesco, probably because most of his requirements meant cutting the poet's text. What he was concerned with was concentration and economy, so that dramatic action would continually, effectively, naturally, unfold. At the same time, his response to the ridiculous was combined with his determination to make each scene psychologically and realistically convincing. As always he was quick to spot absurdity. A real thunderstorm would not be likely to subside during a tenor aria, would it? he asked – and it is exactly this sort of question that no operatic composer before Mozart had seriously bothered to put. In view of his extraordinary sensitivity and sense about every nuance of the story, one may guess that he will not have missed the implications of long discussions with his father about a plot which focused on the relationship between a father and son.

The libretto of *Idomeneo* was derived from an early eighteenth-century French opera of the same title, a tragedy in five acts, which ended in death and madness. Varesco practised some preliminary economy and sense: reducing the structure to three acts, pruning the number of divinities and supernumaries, and ending his text quite calmly with the peaceful abdication of Idomeneo. The core of the story (with obvious echoes of the Biblical one of Jepthah and his daughter, and of the famous classical one of Iphigenia) is the vow of the King of Crete, Idomeneo, who is returning from the Trojan War, to sacrifice to Neptune the first person he encounters if he reaches land safely after a stormy shipwreck. He meets a stranger who turns out to be his son Idamante, grown to manhood during his long absence. Unable to bring himself to carry out his vow, Idomeneo decides to send Idamante away from Crete, but a fresh storm rises, bringing with it a sea-monster and a pestilence which ravage the island. Idomeneo is forced to reveal that his son is Neptune's promised victim and the sacrifice is prepared for, even though Idamante has meanwhile slain the monster. At the moment of imminent death, Idamante is saved by the intervention of Ilia, a captive Trojan princess who loves and is loved by him.

The dramatic knot is untied by the sudden voice of Neptune's oracle, declaring that Idomeneo shall abdicate and Idamante, united to Ilia, reign instead. Standing, as it were, to one side of this main, sympathetic plot is the Greek princess Electra, vainly loving Idamante and furious at losing him; she alone disturbs the muted, almost domestic affection and sadness which unite the three other main characters (for Varesco wisely removed the twist of original plot whereby Idomeneo himself also loved Ilia), but her violently swooping, hissing music is necessary for contrast.

If Idomeneo's rash vow is the core of the plot, it is really Neptune, or the sea, which not only frames it round musically but pulses continually through it. The music never lets us forget that the location is an island, and the sea in a variety of moods governs the very moods of the characters (much as in *Così fan tutte*, another opera set on a sea coast, winds and waves become at once actual and apt symbols of eddying passion). Mozart's music paints the confusion of shipwreck, an almost treacherous calm and the roar of angry waters. It is the sea which demands a victim, and Idomeneo escapes with his life in the first act only to lose his crown in the final act; part-Oedipus at Colonnus, part-Prospero, he relinquishes the magic aura of being king. The sea also expresses symbolically, like waves lapping on the shore, the natural elimination of each generation by a successive one. Although the opera must conventionally close with a cheerful chorus, the more subtle end comes just before, when Idomeneo sings 'Torna la pace al core', and we are returned to the peaceful opening of the opera (before he appeared) when Idamante releases Ilia and her fellow-captives, who celebrate his action with the chorus 'Godiam la pace'.

It is more than an influence from Gluck which makes the role of the chorus important throughout *Idomeneo*, for it forms a steady reminder of the public consequences of the king's actions. The tone of the opera is altogether a good deal more 'democratic' than Metastasio would have cared for. And a further touch of Beethoven-like humanity is given by the fact of Idomeneo's instinctive pity at the first sight of Neptune's victim, before he knows he is his son. By trying to avoid the consequences of his rashness, Idomeneo causes his subjects appalling suffering; nor is it he but Idamante who goes to kill the monster which is devastating Crete – and to this extent he has already abdicated even before commanded to do so by Neptune. Indeed, Idamante is virtually reigning before his father returns; and his private impulse of love for Ilia leads to the public goodness of his releasing the prisoners. Electra has no place on Crete – for all she is a Greek – because her love is selfish and, one might say, unconstructive. When Idamante has the knife at his throat, it is Ilia who hurls herself forward to take his place; she joins that moving series of Mozartian heroines who show us how sincerely they are prepared to die for the man they love. And thus, like Pamina and Tamino at the end of *Die Zauberflöte*, Ilia and Idamante deserve to become an '*edles Paar*' ('noble couple'); and the chorus of Cretans, hailing their accession, rightly calls down Love and Hymen, for in rulers so united lies a guarantee for those ruled: '*Scenda Amor! Scenda Imeneo!*'

But the greatest achievement of *Idomeneo*, for which Mozart worked so hard that by the end he had destroyed the limitations of old *opera seria*, is in presenting an agonizingly real emotional situation – neither exaggerated nor remote – in which conflicting currents of love gradually enclose on their own mental island the four main characters. Some concepts of the ensemble to express a complex situation had been attempted by Mozart in, for example, *La Finta Giardiniera*; but the epic world of *Idomeneo* moved him to the creation of the profoundly desolate quartet 'Andrò, ramingo e solo'. This is the last human stand; now only God's intervention can solve the dilemma. Idomeneo's heart-breaking love for his son, Ilia's love and Electra's desire for revenge, Idamante's own reciprocal love for Ilia and his father, but his determination to go and fight the monster – all these individual emotions are here woven into one plangent cry, as inadequate as human hands to budge the rock of Fate. Idamante must go 'wandering and alone' to seek the monster, and perhaps die. Ilia joins her voice to his, for she too will then die. Idomeneo exlaims against the pitiless god – '*Nettuno spietato*' – as suffering overwhelms him. Electra suffers too, even while she hates. When the four voices have died away in unison, Idamante's returns once more, expressing finally his sad determination and farewell: 'Andrò, ramingo e solo.' This device, the last touch of desolation as the characters disperse and the music mourns, recalls the end of the C Major Mass, written only a few months before, where the soprano softly followed the chorus to repeat the Agnus Dei in one final appeal.

Although it is Idamante who proves the triumphant hero of the opera, it is with Idomeneo himself – no Mitridate, no Lucio Silla, but a loving, unhappy father – that the musical-emotional sympathy most strongly lies. That the part should have been played in Munich by the famous old singer Raaff, a friendly Mannheim acquaintance of Mozart's, is itself movingly apt. Raaff was old-fashioned as well as old; he had naively proposed an aria for himself in place of the revolutionary quartet, and yet at the same time was no longer vocally capable of doing justice to his big, surging, sea-filled aria 'Fuor del mar, ho un mar in seno'* – an aria to which few later singers have, with less excuse, managed to do justice. Raaff was in his middle sixties, some five years older than Leopold Mozart; and Mozart well understood, as he wrote himself, that his grey hairs should be respected: '*So muste man doch seinen grauen Haaren etwas zu gefallen thun.*' Raaff should be respected, though not always agreed with, both because of his one-time fame and because this was to be his last public appearance. Like Idomeneo, he was abdicating ('*Eccovi un altro Re*') and his last aria suitably expressed it in archaic form.

As for an actual new king, there could be no doubt that this was Mozart. He had created the opera he wanted, pleased the singers and won the Elector's approval. All this was established long before Leopold and Nannerl arrived in Munich for the first night. If Paris had represented Mozart's individual achievement amid adversity, *Idomeneo* at Munich represented his artistic achievement, achieved equally by his own efforts. Emancipation from Leopold was now quite complete, and might seem to have been managed as peaceably as Idamante's succession to Idomeneo. Alone ('. . . *e solo*') in the testing climate of what might almost be called Munich-Mannheim – so much had Munich been musically transformed under the new Elector Karl Theodor – Mozart had solved everything, even curing himself of his cold. On 30 December he sat down to send New Year greetings to Leopold, and though the

* 'Escaped from the sea, I feel a sea within me.'

opera was by no means complete, he could report that it had already received the Elector's macaronic compliment: '*das ist eine Magnifique Musik.*'*

The majestic assurance of the overture, heard publicly on the evening of 29 January 1781 in Cuvilliés's enchanting building, the Residenz-theater, was itself sufficient to justify the Elector's praise. And as the evening progressed Mozart could have felt reassured – not about his music but about the audience's ability to recognize its powerful effect. With this triumph behind him, the abrupt summons to Vienna, even though it came from the now hated Archbishop, may have seemed part of new triumphant prospects. Where better than in the imperial capital, to which he had – in some ways – been travelling all his long professional life? Once again he set off alone. Within four days he had reached Vienna and was soon welcomed back into the Mesmer family's familiar garden; in that setting he wrote his first letter to Leopold, announcing his arrival, clearly still in a mood of excited, almost princely confidence.

For the first and last time, he began a letter to his father as if to an equal, '*Mon trés cher amy!*' All Leopold's letters to Mozart from this period are lost, probably having been destroyed by Constanze after Mozart's death. It is impossible to tell if Leopold questioned the form of address, but he is not likely to have missed it, even if he missed its significance. His sensations at seeing *Idomeneo* must have been oddly mixed; they would have been all the more strongly so if he had known that the next time he met his son it would be to meet his son's wife as well. That they should then choose to play over the quartet from *Idomeneo*, and that the tension of it should suddenly reduce Mozart to tears, are extraordinary examples of life catching up with a situation first crystallized in art.

The man sitting in the Mesmers' pleasant garden had once been the boy-king of Rücken, had become a professional composer and was soon to be acknowledged by Haydn as a genius. In *Idomeneo* he had tackled – among other problems – the problem of replacing, without killing, his father. Yet still he was not free; indeed, in Vienna more bitterly than in provincial Salzburg he felt the humiliation and hatefulness of being bound to the Prince-Archbishop. It was this situation which demanded to be resolved, or exploded. Within a very few weeks there came an explosion.

* 'That's a *magnifique* piece of music.'

3

Colloredo had not summoned Mozart to Vienna merely to remind him sharply that he had long overstayed his leave of absence. Mozart was a convenient person to have at hand in the capital, an ornament to display, and also to conceal: he could be ordered to play at the house of old Prince Colloredo, the Archbishop's father, and refused permission to play at the Vienna music-society's regular charity concert for musicians' widows, when every artist traditionally offered his services free.

Thus Colloredo demonstrated that Mozart belonged to him, just as, contemporaneously and equally despotically, Prince Nicolaus Esterházy was demonstrating that Haydn was simply one of his large retinue of servants. Haydn handled his prince tactfully, but then he presumably wished to remain in Esterházy service. Mozart wanted independence, and anyway was too fiery not to blaze openly at his master, himself quick-tempered, and obviously as ready to rage at the mention of Mozart as Mozart was at the thought of him. In Vienna they were lodged in the same house, and since their antipathy had probably reached almost physical loathing, this proximity is likely to have been the final touch needed for an explosion which rapidly echoed all the way to Salzburg, terrifying Leopold.

Yet only an explosion would release Mozart from a servitude he had always detested. If Colloredo had been a reasonable man, Mozart would still have left him, but in a quietly reasonable way. Prince Esterházy was at least a genuine lover of good music; but Colloredo seems to have got little real delight out of Mozart, was virtually jealous of his renown among the Viennese aristocracy and was reduced to the poorest of all pleasures, that of saying no. It cannot have been agreeable to find that the musician placed at table below one's valets, yet above the cooks, was actually the subject of pleas from the nobility that he should be allowed to play at the music society's concert. Eventually the Archbishop gave way, but he refused to permit Mozart to organize a concert on his own behalf. And just as Mozart was privately deciding that his reception in Vienna was too promising to be interrupted by a return to hated Salzburg, the Archbishop – who seems to have been unpopular in court circles – was planning to withdraw there with his household. At table the musicians talked of when they would have to leave, and what arrangements the Archbishop's steward, Count Arco, was making.

Mozart dreamt of asking for permission to stay on in Vienna: giving concerts, taking a few good pupils – and writing an opera. The stage-manager of the new German national opera, the Emperor's particular brain-child, was already promising to find a libretto for him, something with plenty of comedy to please the Viennese public.

Easter came. Mozart's letters perturbed Leopold, as his letters so often had, but it seemed likely that he must, if only temporarily, return to Salzburg. Strong language about the Archbishop, though imprudent, would probably do no great harm. Whatever Leopold wondered and worried over, he cannot have foreseen the next piece of news: '*heute war der glückliche tage für mich*,'* Mozart declared jubilantly, having just announced that he was no longer so unhappy as to be in Salzburgish service.

After two occasions of hearing the Archbishop's complaints of his behaviour, he had been told to move into lodgings. When on Wednesday 9 May he presented himself at the Archbishop's temporary residence, it was for the apparently minor matter of collecting some travelling expenses. Only when he was asked to carry back to Salzburg a parcel for the Archbishop did it emerge that he had delayed his journey until the Saturday. Whatever the Archbishop's parcel in reality contained, it rapidly proved to be dynamite. It was one of those trivial historical accidents which lead to a profound result – the sort of situation of which Saint-Simon's memoirs are so full. One of the valets suggested that Mozart should go in and explain to the Archbishop that he had not been able to get a seat on the coach that day. With that excuse ready, Mozart stepped into the room; and his last interview with the Prince-Archbishop began.

The clash that followed was not fundamentally some inevitable *ancien régime* set-piece. It was the eternal collision between artistic independence and society's wish to control the artist for its own purposes. The abolition of the *ancien régime* did not abolish such collisions. Society always intends to call the tune, however poorly it pays the piper. What it cannot control it hates, with all the hatred that Colloredo directed at Mozart. The reason why he disliked hearing praise of his musician's genius is because he was clever enough to understand that genius represents an uncontrollable element. Dutiful mediocrity (exactly what his other musicians provided, to Mozart's scorn) was, and always is, much safer. Following Plato's advice, Colloredo paid Mozart the compliment

* 'Today was a red-letter day for me.'

of expelling him from his kingdom – a compliment that he recognized Leopold did not deserve; Leopold died still his vice-*Kapellmeister*.

'Now, when is the fellow leaving?' the Archbishop asked, as soon as Mozart entered the room. The third-person address was an *ancien régime* German-speaking form to an inferior, but it was not necessarily contemptuous – as is usually claimed – because it is the very form in which the Elector at Mannheim had congratulated Mozart on his playing. At the moment of presenting his excuses, Mozart was committed to leaving Vienna on the Saturday; he had received his travel money, and perhaps still had charge of the Archbishop's mysterious parcel. Yet Colloredo detected in the delay of those few days the symbol of total, utter rebellion against his authority. If it seemed the last straw, it was also a straw dipped in inflammable spirit: 'He burst out like a fire,' Mozart reported ('*dass gieng fort wie ein feuer*'), giving a marvellously vivid account of the whole scene, with its dialogue, in a letter written to Leopold on the same day. '*Lumpen, lausbub . . . fexen*': the Archbishop's wildly abusive epithets whipped Mozart into insolently sarcastic temper: 'So Your Princely Grace is not satisfied with me?' 'What,' the Archbishop riposted, 'the scoundrel wants to threaten me.' And with no very brilliant phrase, he indicated the door and dismissal: '*dort ist die tühr.*'* Pausing only to say that he would confirm his resignation in writing, Mozart walked through the door and out into freedom. '*Der glückliche tage*' had arrived.

It was not then but nearly a month later that Count Arco actually kicked Mozart when he tried, for about the fifth time, to hand in a memorandum over his resignation. That kick crystallized all Mozart's pent-up loathing and long-endured sense of humiliation. It maddened him, but it released him from behaving reasonably on his side. Meanwhile hysterical, unhelpful, accusatory letters from Leopold rained down, and it was not the Archbishop who was the culprit. Mozart had never shown him any affection, Leopold wrote, going on to compare him – with almost ingenious spite – to Aloysia Weber. These letters, perhaps mercifully lost, possibly destroyed by Mozart himself, combined with the bitter, bickering aftermath of the quarrel of 9 May, must quickly have clouded Mozart's joy in that event. He had done something recklessly brave, for he had little money and very uncertain prospects, but something utterly right. He sacrificed security to his genius: to live a decade of difficulties and poverty, so as to create most of the masterpieces

* 'There is the door.'

by which he is best known. Yet even at the period of doing it, he felt the cost in physical shock, so keyed up by anger and tension that he had to leave the opera-house in the middle of a performance because he was trembling so much. Just when he needed to recover calmness, so as to go on composing, Leopold's dreadful, selfish letters – scarcely more controlled than the Archbishop's epithets – began to arrive; they merely confirmed that in choosing liberty Mozart had chosen a lonely road.

Before kicking Mozart, Count Arco had tried paternally to reason with him. He warned him of the fickleness of Viennese favour with its constant wish for something new. At first there would be plenty of money and praise – '*aber wie lange?*'* There is a sad bravery in Mozart's response that he would not be remaining in Vienna, just as there is a sad truth in Arco's warning. Who knows what opportunities may occur? Mozart asked rhetorically, in the flush of having created the prospect of a future. But from the standpoint of worldly success, Arco put the shrewder question.

Mozart had a few professional acquaintances – acquaintances rather than friends – in Vienna, but it was not easy to get work. With the coming of summer, most aristocratic families withdrew to the country. He had found only one pupil, and she soon followed the usual custom and left the city. Naturally, he had also needed somewhere to live. The lodgings he chose were in themselves one reason for Leopold's hysteria. With percipience heightened by intense fear, he prophesied the worst when he learnt that his son was living in widowed Madame Weber's lodgings. Whether rumours had really reached Salzburg, or whether Leopold argued from the Aloysia Weber incident, as early as July he was telling Mozart that he should move because his name was linked with the now eldest unmarried daughter, Constanze. To this fresh accusation Mozart replied categorically that, though he talked and joked with her, he did not love her. When he wrote that, it was almost certainly true; and in some ways it perhaps remained true. The presence of Aloysia Weber, who had married the actor-painter Josef Lange in the previous year, seems to have haunted the relationship of Mozart and Constanze. If Mozart was not aware of any implications, Constanze later certainly was, and jealousy separated the sisters after his death. He grew seriously, uxoriously, fond of Constanze; she became the wife of his heart, the mother of his children. But he had – in the impetus of his earlier trial flight of freedom – fallen in love with Aloysia first. Perhaps

* 'But for how long?'

none of the three – or four, if Madame Weber be included – could entirely forget that.

And yet it might have seemed a nudge from destiny that only a day or two after denying his love for Constanze, Mozart should receive the promised libretto for a German opera and find that it was called '*Belmonte und Konstanze*'. Indeed, something must have caused his odd little slip when referring to its other title, '*Die Entführung aus dem Serail*', for he mentioned it as '*Die Verführung . . .*': 'seduction' instead of 'abduction'. Perhaps this is not so much an indication of his thoughts about Constanze as about his own position. When eventually, in the following year, Mozart became engaged to her, Leopold accused Madame Weber and Constanze's guardian of being '*verführer der Jugend*' ('seducers of youth'), and this may well not have been the first time that he had made such an accusation. He believed that Madame Weber had all along schemed to marry Constanze off to his son. Possibly Constanze herself – displeasingly flirtatious with other men even after the engagement – flirted provocatively with Mozart in that unusually hot and lonely summer which followed his break with the Archbishop. He was away from his own family and partly estranged from his father. Sympathy from Madame Weber and liveliness from Constanze can hardly have been unwelcome at such a time.

Very reluctantly he left their house, as Leopold wished, though he continued to visit them. He moved to the house of Herr Auernhammer, whose daughter was already his pupil. And here he complained, crudely and cruelly, that not only was the mother stupid and malicious but that the daughter, fat, sweaty and intentionally unclad, was seriously proclaiming her love for him. All this may have been true, yet it strikes such an exaggerated note that it seems more likely that he blackened the Auernhammers to punish and alarm Leopold: there were worse people in Vienna than the Webers, he implied, though perhaps quietly borrowing from his experiences with them to colour the grotesque portrait of the Auernhammer family.

By September he had anyway moved again. Three moves in six months seem typical less of a period of settling in than of Mozart's perpetual wandering from lodging to lodging in Vienna during the rest of his life. To some extent, he never settled there. Prague was to welcome him; thoughts of London, and even Paris, more than once tempted him. Had he lived, he would perhaps have wandered finally away from a city in which he was never truly at home.

With a new lodging in the Graben, not very far from Madame Weber's, and having probably established some sort of understanding with Constanze, he turned to the project of his new opera. He was hastening to write it because it needed to be ready for performance on the arrival in Vienna of the Grand Duke Paul of Russia, and then he learnt that there was no hurry. Not only was the Grand Duke's arrival delayed, but Mozart's opera was not selected for his entertainment. He was greeted with a performance of something more elevated, Gluck's *Alceste*, followed by a masked ball. Afterwards he called on the composer and assured him that though he had heard a great deal of music, none had touched his heart like that of *Alceste*; Gluck himself reported the compliment. His reputation and his already famous operas had effectively delayed Mozart's first public commission at Vienna. The Grand Duke did not remain there long enough to witness the first performance of *Die Entführung* on 16 July 1782, but perhaps more immediately useful, and more flattering, was Gluck's request for a repeat performance of it, as well as his invitation to the young composer to lunch. This kindly recognition from such a shrewd, established figure crowned the opera's success. For, despite some attempts to organize a cabal against it, it had indeed proved a success. By October it had been performed some dozen times and then it was seen, at last, by the Grand Duke and Duchess, passing again through Vienna. Mozart conducted that performance: partly to wake up the orchestra and partly to appear before the royal visitors as the 'father of his child'.

The comparison is his own, and it had particular aptness at that moment. A few weeks after the opera's first performance he had married Constanze Weber, and by October they both knew that she was pregnant. The two forms of paternity must have borne Mozart along very contentedly towards the new year. There were yet further performances of *Die Entführung* before 1782 ended. And of his clavier playing he learnt that the Emperor had remarked '*C'est un talent décidé*'.* He was enjoying being a newly-married man and a prospective father. Settled in new lodgings, in the house of the friendly and rich Baron Wetzlar, he and Constanze gave their own musical parties. They went out socially a good deal, though in a very limited circle compared to that in which Mozart moved as composer and performer. There was one duty visit from which both Mozart and Constanze – though with many polite expressions of regret and a variety of excuses – drew back: to Leopold at

* 'He's definitely got talent.'

Salzburg. An almost bland tone, certainly a quite new air of slightly
distrait courtesy, characterizes Mozart's letters to his father at this
period. He had escaped unscathed from that seraglio. He had carried off
Constanze, despite Leopold's doubts and whatever Madame Weber's
schemes. '*Nimm deine Freiheit und Constanze,*'* as the Pasha tells
Belmonte at the end of *Die Entführung*, and the words unleash the lovers'
rejoicing combined with praise of the Pasha, whose magnanimity is
greater than that which anyone had displayed in real life. Salzburg, the
Archbishop, even Leopold, all had receded far from the core of Mozart's
emotions. He must have felt intense reluctance to return to such vivid
reminders of several sorts of slavery – especially when he looked back on
all he had achieved professionally and privately, in little more than
twelve months.

Freedom is the keyword of *Die Entführung aus dem Serail*. It is of course a
coincidence that the German theatre manager, Stephanie, happened to
choose this libretto (based on somebody else's story, itself merely one
fragment of the century's large concern with liberty in love versus
tyranny, especially in exotic Oriental settings). To Mozart it probably
seemed increasingly significant the more he studied it. He worked
radically on the libretto as well as on the music, even more drastically
than he had with *Idomeneo*, so that if eventually the completed work well
reflects his own experiences, any parallels have ceased to be mere coincidence. Besides, something immediately attracted him to the libretto,
though probably not – at least, not at first – the plight of the heroine,
Constanze. Nor did he estimate its literary merit very highly.

The bare bones of the story Stephanie laid before Mozart concerned
the attempted escape from Pasha Selim's seraglio in Turkey of the
Spanish lovers, Belmonte and Constanze, along with their servants
Pedrillo and Blonde, who are also in love. The Pasha has captured and
loves Constanze. Soon after the opera opens he takes Belmonte into his
service, understanding that he is a distinguished architect. The quartet's
escape is foiled by the Pasha's steward, Osmin, who plays a very minor
part in the original plot. When the prisoners come before the Pasha he
discovers that Belmonte is the son of his bitterest enemy, and death for
them all seems even more certain. However, the Pasha (a modern
Lucio Silla or Tito) shows himself to be a pattern of clemency (his pagan
generosity contrasting with the Christian intolerance of Belmonte's

* 'Take your freedom and Constanze.'

father): he forgives and releases the two pairs of lovers, and all ends happily in a chorus of praise.

Mozart began to work on this libretto when he was still seething at his treatment by the Archbishop and Count Arco. The Archbishop particularly came into his thoughts when the singer of Osmin was chosen, for this was a famous and superbly flexible bass, Fischer, about whom Colloredo had once absurdly complained to Mozart that he sang too low for a bass. Of Count Arco Mozart had written 'I must have my revenge' ('*so muss ich mich rächen*'), and in the Pasha's ragingly rude, contemptuous steward – an 'Arch-fiend' is Mozart's description – revenge is palpably taken: on Arco (= Arch) and on his archiepiscopal master. The part of Osmin was greatly expanded, no doubt partly because of Fischer's talent and popularity. But the almost insanely uncouth figure, ludicrous yet profoundly dangerous, who hates Pedrillo and gratuitously insults Belmonte (even *after* he has been taken into the Pasha's service) is unparalleled in Mozart's later work; he is a brilliantly realized caricature, powered by probably quite conscious revenge.

None of the other personages possesses character in this forceful way. The audience can enjoy disliking Osmin and see him finally crushed by his own master, as he has already been outwitted by Belmonte and Pedrillo, and mocked by Blonde (herself '*Eine Engländerin, zur Freiheit geboren*'*). Only Monostatos in *Die Zauberflöte* comes near this sort of villain, but he is in every way much slighter and more patently ridiculous, and also a coward. Osmin really is no joke; his excited arias savouring the tortures he will inflict on almost anyone have a surly Jonsonian quality which makes him entirely convincing. He is as uncouth as he is evil; and perhaps it is his uncouthness that offends Mozart more.

Though the other people are characterless in varying degrees – Blonde being a soubrette sketch of pert vivacity, but Pedrillo an utter blank – a mood of intensely ardent, often wistful love is woven between hero and heroine, whose arias complement each other before they meet in the opera. This mood is immediately created by Belmonte's opening aria. It is led into directly from the overture and mingles love with longing. His second aria, where throbbing violins evoke his beating heart as Constanze draws near, was described proudly by Mozart himself. Its heroic tenor ring is not heard again until Tamino in *Die Zauberflöte*. More effectively still, Constanze's arias chart her eddying emotions

* 'An Englishwoman, born to freedom.'

around the central fact of her love for Belmonte. First she proclaims her love ('Ach, ich liebte') in a tender aria which Mozart, against his instinctive judgment, was led to make more showily brilliant than he wished, so as to show off the singer's voice. Her second aria is like an echo of melologue from *Zaïde*: the wailingly sad G Minor 'Traurigkeit', subtly orchestrated and affectingly painful in its almost dragging grief – to be caught again only by Pamina in *Die Zauberflöte*.

But it is Constanze's third aria, 'Martern aller arten', which has attracted the greatest attention and criticism, most of the latter misplaced. Still unaware that Belmonte has reached the seraglio, she has declared her love and her grief. Now when the Pasha turns threatening – hinting that he can compel her with tortures of all sorts – she meets his threat with defiance. She grows magnificent, as does the music at this point. To suppose that 'none of the music is quite in character with Constanze' (G. Abraham in *The Mozart Companion* (1956)) is to ignore her 'character' in the last act when she faces death with Belmonte in a comparably exalted state. 'Martern aller arten' returns us almost to the world of Handelian heroines; and it has two moods, clearly caught by the music. After her outburst of defiance, Constanze frankly pleads for mercy ('Verschone mich!'*) and she continues to fluctuate between bravery and a melting plea, underscored by the pleading flute. Ultimately, bravery triumphs; she sees that death can bring freedom: '*zuletzt befreit mich doch der Tod.*' Her sustained coloratura dances twice over the word *befreit*, before the voice descends to the low final note of *Tod*. What she here proclaims, apparently recklessly, she will be able to carry out before the opera ends.

That Constanze represents Constanze Weber is an inevitably tempting supposition, which has been repeated almost as much as the opinion that 'Martern aller arten' is extraneous to the opera. Yet it is the unexpected touch of tyranny in the Pasha which leads to the defiant surge of that aria; and Mozart is more likely to have identified himself at that point with his heroine than thought of his fiancée.

In real life the situation was more complicated than romantic. The opera echoes it most closely when Belmonte and Constanze at last meet – and Belmonte questions whether she has been faithful to him. Constanze weeps at the very thought, while Blonde, to whom Pedrillo has put a similar question, promptly boxes his ears. Mozart positively questioned Constanze Weber's behaviour after they had become engaged; and even

* 'Spare me!'

their engagement seems to have been more engineered by Madame Weber than entered into through mutual rapture. The composer of Belmonte's ardent music might ruefully reflect how very different these matters were in actual fact. The excitement and enchantment which glow through the score of *Die Entführung* do not need to be attributed to young love; the gift of the commission, following so soon on release from Salzburg service, would have been impetus enough, especially as it was combined with a cast of most talented singers. Probably it was the opera – completed well before the marriage – which cast its charm over reality, rather than vice-versa.

What had happened is far from clear, but Mozart's involvement with Constanze rapidly reached a point where Madame Weber and the family's guardian, Johann von Thorwart, stepped in with an ultimatum of the type Figaro faces in *Le Nozze* . . .: '*o pagarla, o sposarla.*'* Mozart had to sign such a document, as he eventually confessed to the furious Leopold. Constanze had her moment of heroism, according to Mozart, when she tore up the document saying she needed no written assurance of his love. In letters stressing the practical advantages of getting married, and perhaps deliberately assessing Constanze's appeal very coolly ('*sie ist nicht hässlich*, aber auch nichts weniger *als schön*')†, Mozart pleaded for Leopold's consent to the wedding. Constanze added a few fearfully humble lines and sent some trinkets to Nannerl, herself at that moment distressed by a love-affair which Leopold seems to have ruthlessly crushed.

It was not only Mozart's uncertain prospects and Constanze's poverty which alarmed Leopold. Her character, as reported to him, seemed bad. Mozart loyally rebutted such rumours; and Leopold was never to know that even while skilfully pleading Constanze's virtue – now she ventured to send Nannerl two caps she had made, now it emerged she never touched wine – Mozart had written to Constanze complaining of an occasion when she had allowed a man to measure her leg. The incident, suggesting some French engraving of the period, easily makes us smile. Yet it has its sadness too.

Mozart had committed himself to Constanze, however her selection had been reached. He knew he needed, physically and emotionally, a wife. Until the months in Vienna he had never properly experienced living alone. After a period of so doing he could say with conviction:

---

* 'Either pay her or marry her.'

† 'She is not ugly, but also less than beautiful.'

'An unmarried man is, in my view, only half alive' ('. . . *lebt in meinen Augen nur halb*'). Leopold could scarcely deny that, if he recollected his own long, happy marriage. Once married to Constanze, Mozart would be firmly faithful to her, for the rest of his life. On 4 August 1782, without waiting longer for Leopold's agreement, he and Constanze were married; on the following day there arrived the notification of his consent.

The uncertain term amid these events remains Constanze herself. In Mozart's perturbed letter to her, he speaks of her having already refused him three times. The apparently trifling affair of her allowing a man to measure her leg may have seemed an indication that she – like the other Weber girls, in Mozart's opinion – was a coquette; and even in the last letters he ever wrote to her, in the year of his death, some uneasiness about her behaviour is detectable. 'Love me half as much as I love you,' is his cry, knowing perhaps that no more could be expected of her.

It is not her appearance, or her musical knowledge, or her intellect, which must trouble us in thinking of her as Mozart's wife – but the quality of her affection, which time certainly did not increase. 'Not quite so enthusiastic as I should have expected,' was Novello's description of her attitude to Mozart in late widowhood. Mozart perhaps never became absolutely sure of her affection, just as he probably never knew whether the wish to escape from her mother was not the most potent reason for her agreeing to marry him.

Madame Weber seems to have been a dubious, slippery sort of person; Weber had not been particularly positive. Their characteristics were not a very desirable inheritance, and Mozart indeed sought to get Constanze away from her mother by lodging her before the marriage with his patroness, Baroness von Waldstätten. She too was a rather dubious figure, a baroness who could have strayed into a Richard Strauss opera: separated from her husband and thus fallen out of society, rich, generous to Mozart, but sadly eager for a music-teacher who might also become her lover. When Mozart playfully addressed her as 'Gilded, Silvered and Sugared . . . Baroness', he virtually defined her Straussian-rococo role. She probably had, and suppressed, a wisp or more of tenderness for Mozart. Gracefully she accepted her place merely as fairy godmother to the pair of lovers. On the evening of the wedding-day she gave a small supper-party for them; and under her somewhat ambiguous protection, the somewhat ambiguous marriage was celebrated.

Freedom, love, generosity: the sentiments pulsing through the final chorus of *Die Entführung* – where the lonely, magnanimous, silent Pasha stands honoured in the centre of the stage – must have echoed that night through the Baroness's house. At least to the composer it might seem for a brief moment that art and life were in perfect accord.

4

Die Entführung aus dem Serail made Mozart famous, without making him rich. But at least, and, at last, it established him with a wide, international public as a great composer. To most of Europe he had been lost sight of, if not forgotten, since his fame as a talented boy-performer. Now, abruptly it must have seemed, he emerged with a new gift. Even the Emperor Joseph II, if a reference by da Ponte is correct, thought *Die Entführung* Mozart's first opera.

He never wrote anything again to equal i.s success at Vienna; it was still being played there in 1788. It was enthusiastically received early on at Prague, a city which retained a much truer understanding of, and response to, Mozart than he was ever shown at Vienna. Soon *Die Entführung* was being performed at Bonn, at Hamburg, at Warsaw, at Weimar, among other places. 'It conquered all,' Goethe was to say a few years later, explaining its widespread popularity. From Bretzner, the original author of the drama *Belmonte und Constanze*, it drew a different tribute: a protest against the audacious misuse of his text by 'a certain individual, *Mozart* by name'. However, Bretzner rapidly came to appreciate that the individual was a composer of genius and praised his later operas. Most remarkable of all was the Prince-Archbishop of Salzburg's verdict when *Die Entführung* was finally performed there: '*Es wäre wirklich nicht übl*' ('really not bad').

That *Die Entführung* was in German naturally aided its popularity in Northern Europe. Yet, from the first, it was appreciated for its music, the more so as Stephanie's libretto lacked all literary merit. At the same time it was not so much the sheer greatness of the music which attracted people as the significant mixture of *genres* which it touched. Comic without being farcical, serious without being stilted or over-heroic, *Die Entführung* provided an almost Shakespearian mingling of what had previously been largely separate categories of opera. There had been exceptions (often in England, with Handel and with Arne's *Artaxerses* (1762)); Mozart's *La Finta Giardiniera*, and even *Zaide* are advances in the direction of breaking down divisions, to achieve a more 'natural' world where the audience will be moved to both tears and laughter in the course of a single opera. One of the very earliest critiques of *Die Entführung* remains one of the most perceptive. It was published by Johann Friedrich Schink in his *Dramaturgische Fragmente* of 1782; he confesses to being no real connoisseur of music but declares that what he finds excellent is music which affects the human heart. He wants not merely pleasing sounds but something to stir all the emotions, joy and sorrow. By that standard, Herr Mozart's music has, he says, his entire approval.

This is probably the earliest serious published tribute to Mozart as a creative artist rather than as merely a talented musician. Unfortunately, it is one of the last to appear in Mozart's lifetime, but Schink should be honoured for seeing the importance of *Die Entführung* without waiting for the supreme demonstrations of *Le Nozze di Figaro*, *Don Giovanni* and *Così fan tutte*. It did not strike him that Mozart's opera was 'a jumble of incompatible styles', but then he was not a musicologist of the type of the late E. J. Dent, whose characteristic judgment this is.

In any good production of *Die Entführung* – or in attentive listening to it on a recording – its structure is revealed as, of course, no jumble. Mozart recognized as a fact of Viennese taste '*dass man in einer opera Seria auch kommische Musik haben will*'.* He then set out to shape the libretto: requiring drastic changes, having the text altered – 'und zwar so wie ich es will'† – down to the last detail. As a first result, the figure of the Pasha assumes a pivotal importance (emphasized rather than diminished by the fact that his is a speaking, not a singing part). The opera shows him learning a lesson: that love cannot be compelled. As a result, he exercises magnanimity, rebukes his steward Osmin, frees the quartet of lovers, and is hailed by a chorus of praise at the end of the opera, much as he was hailed at the opening. All his power comes ultimately to power over himself: Osmin is virtually his *id*, restrained from lashing out as it wants to do. This is very different, as well as much more natural, than Bretzner's dénouement where the Pasha suddenly recognizes in Belmonte his own son, and spares him and resigns Constanze for that reason. Mozart, who had acidly commented at the time of *Idomeneo* on the improbability of a thunderstorm dying down to allow an aria to be heard, must have said some cutting things about a father who

* 'In an *opera seria* people want comic music as well.'
† 'And exactly as I think fit.'

went through a whole opera unaware that his rival in love was his own son. The whole theme of father and son loving the same woman may well in itself have displeased Mozart; it had been a feature also of the original *Idomeneo* text altered for the opera.

The Pasha is reasonable, civilized and ultimately more generous than a Christian, but the lasting impression he gives is of reasonableness. Perhaps he speaks because even Mozart could not write music for the voice of pure reason. The Pasha's love for Constanze remains unurgent and respectful; though he twice says he could compel her, it is significant that he never does. His first appearance is excitingly preluded by Pedrillo's exclamation, '*Der Bassa kommt*' and by the clashing, strongly rhythmic 'Turkish' noise of the janissaries' chorus, yet the figure who thereupon enters is the least Pasha-like of Pashas. '*Grossmüthiger Mann!*' ('Magnanimous man!') is Constanze's immediate reaction, as she sighingly half-wishes she could return his devotion; and merciful, magnanimous – indeed literally great-minded – is exactly what the Pasha proves finally to be.

He is the calm apex of a structure which has on the next level, dependent on him because they are in his power, the lovers Belmonte and Constanze. They are emotionally serious and romantically intense with a love which reaches true tragic force in their duet under threat of death ('*Meinetwegen sollst du sterben*'). Below them and down to earth, in every sense, comes the dependent trio of servants: Osmin, Pedrillo and Blonde, all of whom appear at once comic and also more resourceful than their masters. Belmonte may be all high tenor sentiment, but it takes Pedrillo to pass him off as an architect, get Osmin drunk and then find a ladder by which to climb into the seraglio. It is Osmin who apprehends the lovers and brings them before the Pasha. The Pasha's respectful love for Constanze is caricatured by Osmin's lust for Blonde – and Blonde spends no time sighing but simply laughs at Turkish ideas of how to win a woman. Gaily, she contributes her interpretation to the opera's freedom theme: '*Ein Herz so in Freiheit geboren/Lässt niemals sich sklavisch behandeln.*'* For in fact the structure is fully coherent: whether on a serious or on a comic level, would-be compulsion is defeated by love. Everyone must escape from the seraglio of other people's emotional tyranny; and so as to achieve total harmony, the Pasha has to rise above his own natural impulses, becoming freed from them.

Thus although *Die Entführung* is charming, amusing and light-

---

* 'A heart born in freedom/Never lets itself be treated like a slave.'

heartedly exotic (with an eye especially to pleasing the commonplace taste of '*i signori viennesi*' as Mozart contemptuously called them), it is also perfectly serious and even profound – musically, emotionally and intellectually. Nor is the comic part divergent from the serious. What we are shown fuses into a single world, a rational paradise which excludes only the unforgiving, inhuman Osmin (rather as Electra was excluded from the conciliatory close of *Idomeneo*) who leaves the opera after a last recital of the tortures he would like to inflict. His departure prompts the quartet of lovers to gentle moral reflection ('*Nichts ist so hässlich als die Rache*')* and opens the way to the janissaries' praise of Pasha Selim: those cheerful concluding notes, '*voll vom Jubel, voll vom Ruhm*'† which Mozart might have fancied inaugurating his own career and married life at Vienna.

Everything seemed so favourable, beginning with the Emperor's unmistakable appreciation. Not only did he appear at Mozart's public concerts, but he organized a private competition in virtuosity between Mozart and the famous visiting pianist, Clementi, at which Mozart performed brilliantly, brilliantly dressed too, in a costume which led Clementi to mistake him for some sort of upper servant or official. '*Schön wie die Engeln*,'‡ was how the boy Mozart had described himself and his father in their new Italian clothes, and perhaps he never forgot his first appearance as an opera composer and conductor, seated at the harpsichord in a gold-trimmed scarlet suit, lined with sky-blue satin. Mozart's love of fine clothes – one aspect of his keen visual sense – was at the period after his marriage to be gratified, partly no doubt by his own expenditure, but also through Baroness von Wald-stätten's kindness. In what can only be called a cadging letter, Mozart gave her a strong hint about a 'beautiful red coat' which he coveted and which would be worthy of some mother-of-pearl buttons with yellow stones in the centre that he also had his eye on. '*Ich möchte alles haben was gut, ächt und schön ist*,'§ he wrote, adding a question which has often been asked: 'Yet why is it that those not in a position to do so would like to spend every penny this way, while those who could, do not do so?' The Baroness hastened to promise him a new coat.

Even this slight example points, however, to the basic precariousness

* 'Nothing is as hateful as revenge.'
† 'Full of rejoicing, full of renown.'
‡ 'As handsome as the angels.'
§ 'I should like everything of mine to be good, genuine and beautiful.'

of Mozart's position. Joseph II was a much colder coquette than the Baroness, much less generous and less unconventional. Although he appeared interested in Mozart, he offered him no more than a tantalizing mixture of half-promises and compliments. It was easy for him to enquire affably about Mozart's marriage, but such an act of condescension had no deeper significance. The Emperor himself was both connoisseur of music and performer, as well as being impresario *manqué* and a ruler. The combination was unpropitious. He had been educated to enjoy Italian and Italianate music; the composers for whom he personally felt little enthusiasm included Gluck, Haydn and Mozart – which gives a good idea of his connoisseurship.

He favoured particularly Salieri, Gluck's pupil, someone frankly envious of Mozart; Salieri was established as court composer and as a director of the Opera, and the success of *Die Entführung* must have seemed dangerously challenging. At the Emperor's side there was also his groom, Strack, very much an adroit courtier as well as his master's musical adviser. He too seemed interested in Mozart, but the interest always remained vague. When Mozart grew restive in Vienna, some new hope could often be dangled before him; and several disillusioning experiences never totally quenched his instinctive hopefulness; it seems particularly right that after he became a freemason he should have joined the lodge of 'The New-crowned Hope'. Not until 1785 was a new opera commissioned from him. Not until 1787, after the death of Gluck, was he to gain a court post: he then became '*Kammermusikus*' (though not *Kapellmeister*), at an annual salary of 800 florins. Gluck had received annually 2000 florins for the same post.

Not music but power and money were what Salieri and Strack stood guard over, ensuring that Joseph II did not rashly dissipate either. Their task was much lightened by the Emperor's natural autocracy and miserliness. As for his possibly independent musical judgments, these are rarely as distinctly recorded as the one he sent Count Rosenberg, his director of theatrical entertainments, about *Don Giovanni* (which he had not then heard): 'Certainly too difficult for the singers.' This verdict probably pleased Rosenberg, for he too seems to have spent a good deal of his time in elaborate theatrical intrigues and he certainly disliked da Ponte, the author of the libretto.

The truth is that official Vienna needed to be stormed not by genius but by a pliable, assiduous politician. Mozart's experiences in Paris would have suggested how unsuited he was by nature for such a role; and he had the further disadvantage of overwhelming musical ability. Gluck might be sufficiently established not to fear acknowledging at least something of it; Haydn was instinctively, fearlessly, generous, and anyway wisely kept away from the capital. But to the circle around Joseph II, each with his own word to whisper in the imperial ear, Mozart must have loomed as a nuisance and possibly as a real threat.

There is a tragic basis for the old romantic tale that Salieri eventually poisoned Mozart (the theme of a Rimsky-Korsakov opera of quite painful banality), which is anyway only a crude expression of what was achieved by more subtle means. He poisoned his career instead. And he probably felt real remorse, because at the end of his own life, when he became deranged, he claimed that he had been guilty of Mozart's death – guilty of wishing it, we may guess. As his accomplice, Strack could always raise Mozart's expectations by conveying a crumb of praise dropped by the Emperor in a private moment, while aware that the diet was unlikely to support a man and his family.

It was not long before Mozart was appealing to Baroness Waldstätten about something more vital than a new coat. By early 1783, when Constanze had not yet given birth to their first child, he was being threatened with a law-suit over a loan he was unable to repay. Obviously the Baroness helped him out but, instead of diminishing, the problem of money was gradually to increase. Mozart had no salary for another four years. He could not possibly approach his father for money. He depended on three sources of income, all uncertain: subscriptions for any works printed, pupils' fees and the receipts at his public concerts. When these failed, or should he through ill-health fail, he would be reduced to begging charity from a friend. In that sense, Mozart's friends were good but few.

With the exception of the Baroness, his friends and the majority of his acquaintances were seldom aristocrats. Two important exceptions were themselves rather exceptional. Baron Wetzlar, who was briefly his landlord and became godfather to his first child, was a rich Jew. He early seems to have helped Mozart and remained a friend up to the end of Mozart's life. Baron van Swieten, Dutch by birth, was the son of Maria Theresia's private doctor, a diplomat and composer and a music-collector. Mozart was to make or renew several interesting acquaintances at his house, the most significant musically being the work of Johann Sebastian Bach and Handel. Van Swieten, too, retained his friendly relationship and took some financial care of Mozart's two young sons in the first years of Constanze's widowhood. No high-born patron had come forward positively to support Mozart; and increasingly he was to move in a circle of intelligent, artistic, 'advanced' people who were able to offer sympathy more often than wealth. The career which had opened in the greatest European courts would close in the obscure, suburban theatre where *Die Zauberflöte* was staged. In itself, that shift is far from being a tragedy. Mozart enjoyed his independence, embraced freemasonry, welcomed the sympathy of a few choice spirits – but yet he needed somehow to stay alive.

The best, though most exhausting, solution seemed in the early period at Vienna to lie in his talent as a performer. In that role he probably appeared less challenging to established musicians (at least to operatic composers). In the four years between *Die Entführung*'s success and the production of *Le Nozze di Figaro* Mozart became the most popular performer in the capital on the still comparatively new instrument, the pianoforte.

It was only about twenty years since the first public recitals (in England) on the piano. Johann Christian Bach had taken considerable interest in the instrument; Clementi was famous as a virtuoso performer on it; Haydn was already writing music specifically for it. Like Clementi, Mozart combined virtuosity as performer and as composer. Yet in the latter role he found difficulty in attracting interest. Before planning publication in 1783 of the three new piano concertos (K.413–5) he described them as brilliant, yet representing '*das Mittelding zwischen zu schwer, und zu leicht*'.* Even so, subscriptions for them came in very slowly and they were not eventually published until 1785. But when Mozart announced a concert, a hundred subscribers quickly came forward and on the actual day the hall would be found overflowing. For a time the Viennese public encouraged him to organize such concerts. The applause no doubt took in the compositions, but it concentrated on the performer.

Although ultimately taxing his energy, these appearances – playing his own music to a large appreciative audience – clearly stimulated Mozart. They were preceded by the probably agreeable bustle of his own forte-piano being taken to the theatre or concert-hall. There were often last-minute hitches, and always an acute, yet perhaps still exciting shortage of time: the copyist might not have the music ready in time for Mozart himself to play it through again in rehearsal; pupils' lessons had

* 'The mean between too difficult and too easy.'

to be provided for, as well as some moment in the day when Mozart could try and compose. He would himself take some distinguished visiting fellow-composer, like Paisiello, to a concert so as to hear his opinion '*du kannst nicht glauben wei viel ich zu thun habe!*'* he wrote to Nannerl, sending her hurried greetings for her name-day in 1784. There always needed to be fitted in visitors, letters and meals ('*eine kleine Stunde*',† he gave himself for digestion after lunch) and it is not surprising that gradually his day expanded until he and Constanze were getting up at half-past five in the morning and going to bed well after midnight.

'Not enough time' ... 'in a desperate hurry': increasingly Mozart explained the brevity of his letters to Leopold or his failure to deliver a piece of music by such phrases. He began, but for various reasons left unfinished, more than one new opera. He received a commission for the music to accompany a high-flown ode called *Gibraltar*, and never finished it. Even the self-imposed commission to write a mass in thanksgiving for his marriage to Constanze (as he had vowed beforehand to do) was possibly never completely carried out, though what exists of the superb, majestic edifice of the C Minor Mass (K.427) is wonderful enough.

Being in haste perhaps became synonymous for Mozart with being alive. For a while it was probably exhilarating that there were many more things to do than could ever be done: from the writing of music to the paying of bills. Complaints about having a hard life in his household, made by the maid he and Constanze hired from Salzburg, utterly amazed him when he read them. In art, a last-minute crisis seemed always to be resolved by his virtuosity or creativity. In life, there always seemed hope: some friendly patron would come forward; applause must one day turn into practical recognition. There must be something to be expected from an Emperor who left the theatre as soon as Mozart left the piano.

Mozart and his piano were at this period seldom parted. He is claimed as the first great composer – apart from Haydn – to write great music for the instrument. His own playing of it can only be imagined. Perhaps it would in reality seem delicate and yet disappointing, for he had been formed as a player on the harpsichord and the instrument he knew had not as much power as the modern piano, but was probably more expressive. Mozart himself took special pains to increase the

* 'You can't possibly believe how much I've got to do!'
† 'One short hour.'

volume of his own piano; he had a large pedal-board made to reinforce its tone, and its richness. An early nineteenth-century description of such a pedal-board – which had the keys enlarged to allow easy playing by the feet – mentions among its advantages the possibility for the executant of playing compositions which would otherwise require another instrument. That aspect probably also appealed to Mozart, if only when improvising privately. 'Antiquated' was the adjective used by Beethoven when asked about Mozart's style as a pianist, though he praised his delicacy, and the comment possibly applied more to the instrument than to the performer. It would be interesting to know if Beethoven ever heard Mozart play the smokily romantic D Minor piano concerto (K.466), the very one Beethoven himself apparently played at a benefit for Constanze after Mozart's death. Mozart's own belief was that good playing should be smooth, flowing like oil. Perhaps he felt it should have, too, something of the swell and weight of oil. As early as 1777, when at Augsburg, he had described how he improvised a magnificent last movement for a C Major sonata (K.309): 'es war ein rechtes Getös und lerm.'* Plenty of 'noise' is often required from performer and instrument in his piano music, and not only in the later piano concertos where it is needed to balance the greater prominence of the orchestra.

Indeed concentration on composing for, and playing, the piano led Mozart in the first years of his successful Vienna concerts to an excitingly bold, deeply personal use of the instrument. Several of the resulting works were connected with his pupils. The first piano concerto after the 1783 subscription group was that in E flat (K.449) dedicated to Barbara Ployer. The C Minor Sonata (K.475), with its poignant slow movement flanked by urgent, stormy opening and closing ones, was dedicated to Therese von Trattner. The D Major Sonata (K.448), unusually for two pianos, was written to be played by Fräulein Auernhammer and himself; it treats the pupil as equal to the master, and though it does not attempt to explore as profound an emotional world as the C Minor Sonata, it is powerful in its accomplishment, as well as sparkling. In love though she might be with her teacher, Fräulein Auernhammer was obviously no young lady amusing herself by amateurish picking at the piano. Mozart himself did her justice as a performer, perhaps thinking of her as another Nannerl, and it is only surprising that he completed no more music for two pianos, apart from the fugue in C Minor (K.426).

* 'It was a real din and noise.'

At this period of studying the resources and the potentiality of the piano, it must have seemed particularly valuable to find van Swieten able to introduce him to the art of a new composer, Johann Sebastian Bach. Bach had died in 1750, six years before Mozart was born, and remained an unfamiliar name in Vienna. When serving as ambassador at Berlin, van Swieten had heard of him from Frederick the Great, who actually sang a fugue-subject he had once given the old composer and told how Bach turned it into a fugue of four, five and eventually eight parts. Whether or not van Swieten recalled this anecdote for Mozart's benefit, he certainly showed him Bach's printed *Art of the Fugue* and manuscripts of the *Well-Tempered Clavier*.

Mozart became briefly obsessed with the fugue form, but it was in no way a novelty to him. He wrote to Leopold to send the copies he had of Handel's fugues, for van Swieten was an enthusiast also for Handel and was anxious to have the oratorios and operas especially performed at Vienna. Handel's name must have reminded Mozart of his youthful visit to London. Even writing fugues again might have stirred childhood memories; he had written a fugue in 1766 for his *Galimathias Musicum*, and several more in the following year (now lost). Then, somewhat surprisingly, Constanze conceived a passion for the fugues of Bach and Handel. She pressed Mozart to write down a fugue of his own for her (K.394) and this gave him the idea for a set of six which he intended to write and present to van Swieten. Two more were in fact sketched, but like so much of that period they remained unfinished.

The form which Mozart pursued, and was encouraged to pursue as a performer, was the piano concerto. Altogether, another fourteen concertos followed the 1783 subscription group, the last being written and played in 1791, by which time he was no longer being encouraged to exist, never mind perform publicly. The final piano concerto (K.595) outsoars the pain and penury of his final year of life. Not resignation but serenity is its mood, with a tender, quite private tranquillity, more harrowing than any struggle against fate. The orchestra has retreated to a subordinate position and even the solo part at times does scarcely more than float the quietest of melodies. A celestial calm is created amid frantic, inchoate life. Mozart's music probably only rarely reflects directly immediate circumstances but, by an artistic paradox, often achieves its perfection in contrast to his actual situation. The rondo of the finale has a terrible, lonely gaiety. Serenity almost breaks before the need to smile. It has been compared by Einstein to blessed children playing in Elysian fields, but it sounds comparable to the playing of some solitary child, more like the ghastly game of Maria's son at the end of *Wozzeck*.

The piano concertos do not, even artistically, advance in one undeviating line towards Mozart's, as it proved, last and devastatingly simple statement. Like all his music, they offer extraordinary variety: a variety governed not so much by public taste (though at times this is taken into account) but by his own impetus to approach the form on each occasion in a fresh way, to solve a new problem or express a new mood – above all, to be quite consciously different. The lightness of the orchestral portions of the last concerto contrasts with his treatment a few years before in which the concerto became almost a symphony; all concept of chamber music was forgotten and the effect was virtually that of a symphonic tone poem. Yet a concerto like that in A Major (K.414), one of the 1783 trio, remains enchanting in its tender formality, holding indeed that mean between difficulty and ease which Mozart himself indicated, and not eclipsed by comparison with the later, mysterious, stirring and passionately dramatic concerto in D Minor (K.466). This *'neues vortreffliches Clavier Concert von Wolfgang'** was heard with pleasure by Leopold at Vienna early in 1785, but it seems to prophesy a new style of music, unconcerned with being balanced and agreeable, being instead almost wilfully individual. The sepulchral orchestral opening might suitably prepare the way for a concerto to be played by Don Giovanni on his last night on earth.

Organizing concerts brought Mozart into contact again with Aloysia Weber. Soon she was singing an aria from *Idomeneo* at one of his concerts, and on the same occasion he played one of his three subscription concertos. Even having so much to do did not prevent him from finding more. For the Vienna carnival in 1783 he devised the plot and music for a pantomime, himself taking the part of Harlequin to Aloysia's Colombine. With Mozart as the mischievous rival of Pierrot for Colombine's affections, and Pierrot played by Aloysia's husband, the notoriously jealous Josef Lange, it must have seemed as if the *commedia dell'arte* was almost too pointedly allusive. For Constanze advanced pregnancy made it impossible to be involved anyway, but presumably she was among the audience witnessing this masquerade in which – in every way – her husband played a preponderant role.

* 'New, excellent piano concerto by Wolfgang.'

Strange emotions from the past probably stirred in Mozart while he and Aloysia danced and flirted to his own music; perhaps Aloysia too felt something, if only regret that she had married Lange. *'Wir spielten recht artig,'** Mozart wrote to Leopold describing the pantomime, which remained the entertainment of a single evening, while fresh emotional experiences were gathering for Mozart, Constanze and Leopold, and also for Nannerl. The journey to Salzburg to introduce Constanze was still postponed. The eventual trip cannot have started very auspiciously, for Mozart had barely begged Leopold to be godfather to the expected child (to be called Leopold or Leopoldine) than Constanze gave birth to a son, and Mozart in his excitement informed their friend, Baron von Wetzlar. The Baron immediately offered to be godfather and, when Mozart agreed, greeted the child as *'einen Raymundl'*.† What had been intended to heal the breach of affection provided Leopold with another opportunity to feel slighted. Leaving the unfortunately-named baby behind in Vienna, Mozart and Constanze finally set out for Salzburg at the end of July 1783. They remained there until late October, probably unaware that meanwhile Raymundl had died.

Loathing Salzburg, perhaps fearing the Archbishop, apprehensive about his father's attitude, Mozart must have entered his birthplace again with dread. Nannerl's diary is the only evidence for how the next three months passed: fine August weather, foggy days in October, walks with Miss Bimpes, music at home or at church, and totally colourless references to 'my sister-in-law'. Although Constanze had written ahead rather archly to Nannerl, with a mention of *'unsern lieben bestern Vattern'*,‡ the two women seem from the first to have been wary of each other. It cannot have been easy for Constanze – guessing, if not actually aware, that Leopold disapproved of her family and herself – to face a stay of three months with Mozart's father and sister; but the position was helped by the presence of the talented young Marchand children, a boy violinist and a girl singer, whom Leopold was training. Constanze had known Margarete Marchand in both Mannheim and Munich; her response to Margarete Marchand's friendly message, looking forward to their meeting again, was much more spontaneous than her letters to Nannerl. And once arrived in Salzburg, she perhaps appreciated as

---

* 'We acted very skilfully.'
† 'A little Raymund.'
‡ 'Our dear best Father.'

much as Mozart the intense musical aspects of the family into which she had married. Visiting musicians passed through Salzburg during their stay; there were constant musical parties in Leopold's house. Constanze herself seemed momentarily to borrow something of her sister Aloysia's ability: she appeared in a rather unexpected public role as one of the soprano soloists in the C Minor Mass (K.427), written for her, at its first performance in St Peter's Church (not the cathedral) on the last Sunday of the visit.

Mozart had no doubt spent some of the time at Salzburg writing or revising it. Closely connected in origin with Constanze, it now offered her a chance to triumph before her critical father-in-law; and if she sang the wonderfully pure but demanding 'Et incarnatus est', her voice must indeed have possessed something of the affecting quality of Aloysia's, as well as something of the agility of their elder sister's, Josefa's, (who was to sing the Queen of the Night in Die Zauberflöte). The whole mass – or what survives, rather – is a triumph, but of a subtle not a showy kind. Certainly it is far removed from the brevity required by Colloredo, and Mozart may have enjoyed taking his time to build the vast symphonic bulk of the Gloria, with its solo, terzet and tremendous choral movements, on a sublime scale.

A lyrical quality, tender not exuberant, is immediately apparent in the quiet opening of the 'Kyrie eleison', a hushed hymn of praise into which breaks the first carolling soprano aria of the 'Christe eleison'. The mass in fact requires two sopranos; it would be tempting to think that the gifted Margarete Marchand took the other part, and that hers was the voice which blended with Constanze's in the duet which forms yet another portion of the extended Gloria. In turn it is followed by such a huge, hauntingly serious chorus ('Qui tollis peccata mundi') that one may wonder if the Mass in B Minor or Messiah were not among the Bach and Handel works Van Swieten had lent Mozart. Authority in massing the voices in wave on wave of powerful, strongly organized sound – making a more dense effect than Mozart had attempted before – is combined with the stark pianissimo plea of 'miserere nobis'. Once again, his marvellous faculty for giving fresh musical life to long-familiar words is manifest, as the most powerful of the choral effects positively sculpt a great image of the seated Saviour at God the Father's right hand, 'sedes ad dexteram patris'.

The same faculty is no less wonderfully at work in the surging, strong beat of the Credo, with its excited affirmation and vividly-pointed detail (solidly phrased *'visibilium omnium'* and high, ghostly *'et invisibilium'*). Nothing disturbs its choral unity until the solemn moment of the soprano solo, piercingly sweet and slow: *'Et incarnatus est.'* The world seems hushed to hear this extraordinary mystery, over which Mozart's earlier masses had lingered, though never before for so long. Only when torn from its context, perhaps to display a soprano's ability, does the 'Et incarnatus' seem extraneous. Within its context, it is clearly seen as dramatically effective, essential and moving – though still typical of the sort of church music which non-opera-loving critics believe they have denigrated when they call it 'operatic'. It is, indeed, an aria, a complete ode on the morning of Christ's nativity, in which, as if for eternity, a single voice – usually rising higher and higher with divine afflatus, yet occasionally dropping like an angel into shepherd-inhabited valleys – lovingly adorns while it announces the dazzling truth: *'Et homo factus est.' Factus, factus, factus*: this is the word which the soprano spells out over and over again in a series of jewel-like, soaring sounds, each melting before the radiance of the next until the air is trembling from so much shimmering melody. And there the Credo, as far as we have it, stops.

But the mass continues. The 'Sanctus', interspersed with orchestral fanfares, ringingly salutes the Godhead. The 'Benedictus' weaves four voices (tenor and bass as well as the two sopranos) into a severely beautiful hymn: each voice itself 'coming in the Name of the Lord' as if to join in one stately eventual dance. Beyond the subsequent 'Hosanna' chorus, no more of the score exists. Yet it remains Mozart's supreme mass, as well as being one of the very last of his religious works. Whether its faith is in God or in Constanze, whether written out of love or relief at being partly reconciled with Leopold, it breathes utter conviction. It received a single performance at Salzburg. It was never performed at Vienna (though Mozart utilized parts of it for an oratorio *Davidde penitente*). And on the Sunday evening, Nannerl noted, the family all went to the theatre, and it rained.

The following morning Mozart and Constanze left Salzburg. For Mozart it was a final departure. He would probably not have regretted that, had he known it. Constanze chose to return, though not until 1820, with her second husband, when she settled there until her death. There are so many posthumous ironies involving Mozart and his family; only a minor one, remarkable enough, was Constanze's more careful burial of her second than of her first husband: she buried him in Leopold Mozart's grave.

On 31 October Mozart wrote a short thank-you letter to Leopold from Linz: '*Wir . . . danken nochmal recht sehr für alle empfangene.*'* He turned the page so hurriedly that he left out what exactly they had received; doubtless he meant to write 'kindnesses', but he failed to do so. More genuine kindness was perhaps being experienced at Linz, for Mozart arrived to be offered hospitality and *douceur de vivre* in a style he had not encountered since he was a boy, and then rarely in his own country. The senior member of the aristocratic Thun-Hohenstein family, several of whom had already been kind to Mozart in Vienna, was Count Johann Joseph Anton, who lived alternately in Linz and Prague. His servant was waiting at the city gates when Mozart and Constanze arrived to drive them to the Thun house, for the family would not hear of Mozart staying at an inn. The couple reached Linz on 30 October. By the following day Mozart was committed to giving a public concert on 4 November and, since he had no symphony at all with him, '*so schreibe ich über hals und kopf an einer Neuen . . .*'†

Twenty-one years earlier, in the autumn of 1762, Leopold had taken his two young children on their first long journey, to Vienna. He had stopped first at Passau and there, in the house of the Bishop, Count Thun-Hohenstein, Mozart had given what was virtually his first private concert-demonstration to strangers. And at an inn in Linz, a few days later, he had given the first public concert of his life. Even if in 1783 he could no longer remember when he first met a member of the Thun family, or where he had given his first concert, Leopold is unlikely to have forgotten. But perhaps Mozart remembered very well. Something seems to have impelled his energy to an even more brilliant burst than usual: by 3 November he had created his new symphony (K.425), the 'Linz'. Still with energy to spare, before he and Constanze left the city, Mozart displayed a different talent and drew for her an '*Ecce Homo*'.

Apart from one symphony hurriedly written at Vienna (the 'Haffner', of 1782), he had not written a symphony for over three years. The 'Linz' forms a bridge between the achievement of the last symphonies at Salzburg and the superb final three to be written at Vienna. As if in deliberate contrast to the haste in which it had been written, the 'Linz' opens with solemn, dreamy slowness: the first occasion on which Mozart uses a slow introduction to a symphony. There seems no sense of hurried execution but a wonderful calmness in the whole firm structure, a sense

---

* 'We thank you again very much indeed for all the received . . .'
† 'I'm writing a new one at breakneck speed . . .'

of controlled delight which dances through the minuet and brings the work to a lilting close. Mellow rather than in any way sadly autumnal, the symphony may not at first seem profoundly personal, but in its very beauty there is perhaps personal joy and some relief. The summer visit to Leopold had passed successfully. To linger in Linz, being so hospitably and courteously entertained – while almost certainly unaware of the death of their son – must have seemed for Mozart and Constanze an agreeable interlude before returning to their busy daily existence at Vienna.

What they resumed on their return was very much the previous sort of life, but at an increasingly hectic tempo. They moved house again. Constanze was soon pregnant again – giving birth in September 1784 to another son, Karl Thomas, who survived into the mid-nineteenth century. Mozart's appearances at public concerts became so frequent that for a period he was giving them twice weekly. In March that year he gave altogether – publicly and privately – nineteen concerts. Scarcely was Karl Thomas born than Mozart and Constanze moved yet again. It is not surprising that just before this last move Mozart was suddenly seriously ill. That he recovered at all was probably due to his friend and doctor, Siegmund Barisani, the son of the Prince-Archbishop's physician, who was two years younger than he. Barisani was successfully to save Mozart in another sinister illness a year or two later and then die himself at twenty-nine. That death came, with Leopold's and others' close to Mozart, in a terrible year. In 1784, once recovered, Mozart continued the feverish, basically insecure, increasingly over-worked round of concerts, teaching and composing.

When Nannerl became engaged to a widower of forty-eight, the prefect of St Gilgen and a successor in the post once held by her maternal grandfather, Mozart had barely time to send her a scribbled letter and some doggerel verse before the wedding day. There was no question of his and Constanze attending it, but for Leopold it probably represented a social triumph, even if it left him feeling lonely, particularly – as he mentioned – in the evenings. Yet it was pleasant to address his daughter as Madame de Sonnenburg, deal with the Salzburg people who came to recommend their children to be her servants and send Nannerl and his son-in-law fully-detailed letters ('*Eine kleine Diarium!*'* he exclaimed himself about one of them) which mingled local news with mentions of Mozart, while remaining totally silent about Constanze. Mozart's music, Mozart's career still obsessed him, but at last he seemed to have

* 'A miniature diary!'

discovered a deep affection for Nannerl, perhaps transferring to her and her new family (for she had acquired five step-children) the love which had once all been for Mozart.

Emotionally as well as geographically, Mozart had moved irreparably far away. He was living his own life in Vienna, as Leopold was to see for himself when father and son met for the last time early in 1785. The new apartment (today a museum) into which Mozart and Constanze had moved was expensive but much more spacious than any of their previous homes, and there they remained for nearly three years. Mozart probably had his own study: a small room, with pretty stucco-decorated ceiling of flying putti which looks on to the Schulerstrasse. Already, before the move, he had begun keeping methodical lists of his compositions and his expenses. The former he continued to record up to the end, but the expenses ceased to be noted; however, thanks to these intentions we know he bought a starling, recording not only its price but its whistling ability. (*'Das war schön!'** he wrote, putting down its close echo of the rondo from his new piano concerto (K.453)).

Vienna continued to regard him as performer rather than composer; it was indeed, as he had described it, 'piano-land'. But it was also the capital of a great empire, empty neither of ideas nor of people. Mozart responded intensely to both. A society of intelligent, lively friends, all true equals, had probably always been a dream of his. He admired talent of every kind; and social life, in the sympathetic sense, positively stimulated his own genius. His Schulerstrasse workroom, with its view over an animated city scene, was itself probably more often animated with laughter and talk and bursts of music than heavy with that brooding silence of creativity imagined as essential by nineteenth-century Romanticism.

As a boy, Mozart had devised his kingdom of Rücken. As a man he planned a society or club entitled 'the Grotto', about which almost nothing is known. Possibly it was absorbed by his joining a much more widely disseminated society, when at the end of 1784 he became a Mason. Ideas of brotherhood, with mutual help and mutual contributions of talent, might seem satisfied by Masonry, but Mozart was perhaps more strongly impelled to it by his brush with death a few months earlier in 1784. It offered him a more 'modern' alternative to the religion in which he had been brought up, and which could be personified by someone like Hieronymus Colloredo. Masonry was exemplified by

* 'That was fine!'

several of his friends and acquaintances; he was to benefit from fellow-masons' charity, while contributing his own talent in its service.

Among the people who came to the Schulerstrasse apartment, no two could have been more different in character than Haydn and the rather disreputable, wandering *abbé*-poet Lorenzo da Ponte. Haydn's fatherly encouragement and steady, affectionate conviction of Mozart's genius as a composer were gratefully acknowledged by the publication in 1785 of the six string quartets dedicated '*Al mio caro Amico Haydn*'.* And the dedication also acknowledged Haydn's greatness. In the Schuler-strasse rooms, Leopold Mozart was to hear Haydn swear that Mozart was – not the greatest piano player but the greatest composer known to him either personally or by reputation.

Da Ponte had come to Vienna from Dresden, specifically to work on writing librettos for Salieri, but with an eye to being imperial poet, succeeding the aged, entirely respectable Metastasio. Mozart first met him in 1783 and, knowing of his connection with Salieri, took very much at face value da Ponte's polite interest in producing a libretto for him as well. Since the success of *Die Entführung* Mozart had looked through hundreds of librettos in the hope of finding one which was amusing without being ludicrous and which would – without being tragic – present credible people in varied yet credible situations. Twice he began comic operas, but neither progressed. Da Ponte proved more sincere than Mozart had expected; he was also a lively, able man with a quick pen, genuinely attracted to their collaboration. Two years passed. Mozart still had not found the ideal plot, and it was while discussing the whole thing once again with da Ponte that he threw out a new possibility: could Beaumarchais's notorious comedy *Le Mariage de Figaro* be adapted for an opera? da Ponte thought it could, and delightedly set to work on the libretto. Mozart, too, set to work. On 1 May 1786, despite even more difficulties and intrigues than usual, the first performance of the new opera, *Le Nozze di Figaro*, took place at Vienna. It was not an unqualified success and Count Zinzendorf, the aristocrat who had been among the earliest witnesses in Vienna to the boy Mozart's virtuosity, noted of *Figaro* in his diary after the first night: 'The opera bored me.'

5

Posterity has been unable to agree with Count Zinzendorf, whose ability

* 'To my dear Friend Haydn.'

to be bored still seems remarkable, even by Viennese aristocratic standards. Mozart and da Ponte had quite simply created a masterpiece, though this was probably not recognized unreservedly until the opera was performed a few months later in the more truly musical, more sympathetic and intelligent environment of Prague, a city always grateful for genius. Perhaps the finest tribute offered at Vienna to *Le Nozze di Figaro* came from that most professional and most blasé of audiences, the orchestra, who during the first full rehearsal actually broke into applause at the stirring martial end of Figaro's aria 'Non più andrai'.

An eye witness on that day was the English tenor Michael Kelly, playing the minor role of Basilio in the opera. Like da Ponte, he later wrote his memoirs; unlike da Ponte, he colours with Mozartian vivacity of detail his view of the composer, 'on the stage with his crimson pelisse [surely the gift – one may interpose – of Baroness Waldstätten?] and gold-laced cocked hat'. It was an exciting, moving moment when singers and orchestra were swept into one spontaneous, delighted shout of homage: '*Viva, viva, grande Mozart!*' Here was the applause which really mattered to Mozart, sweeter and more perceptive than anything the Emperor or the public could offer. 'Those in the orchestra I thought would never have ceased applauding, by beating the bows of their violins against the music desks,' Kelly went on, recalling the scene forty years later. 'The little man acknowledged, by repeated obeisances, his thanks for the distinguished mark of enthusiastic applause bestowed upon him.'

For some four years Mozart had been seeking and working towards the perfect comic opera, and it is not surprising that *Figaro* should prove to be exactly that. Collaboration with da Ponte was certainly one aspect of its inspired effect: a collaboration which was to lead to two further operatic masterpieces. But over the same period of time Mozart had been thinking also in terms of the least public, most intimate musical form, the quartet, and here he was inspired by Haydn, personally as well as musically.

Kindly, calm, upright, modest, Haydn is one of those artists (Corot is probably another) whose attractive human qualities may encourage under-estimation of their art and a rather too pat equation between their lack of 'temperament' and the presumed cheerful placidity of what they produced. Mozart made no such mistake about Haydn's music, while warmly grateful for his friendly, admiring attitude to him.

In 1782, after a ten-year interval, Haydn had published a fresh group of quartets (Op.33), the 'Russian Quartets', dedicated to the same Grand Duke Paul who had visited Gluck and attended a performance of *Die Entführung*. When writing to potential subscribers, Haydn stated that these quartets were composed 'in a new and special style'; and this was a pondered statement from a composer whose first string quartet dated from before Mozart's birth.

The 'Russian Quartets' represented a new and special mastery of the form: quartets in which each of the four instruments could speak equally in a movement, creating a conversation more expressive, developed and individual than had been achieved before. It was in this way, rather than by direct, detailed example (though once at least he seems to have borrowed a device, if not a theme, from the 'Russian Quartets') that Mozart found inspiration in Haydn's quartets to create his own fresh series, also 'in a new and special style' that was in part found disconcerting and too artful.

Musically, it was no doubt right that on their publication in 1785 he should dedicate his six quartets to Haydn, with a long, moving dedication in which he hands over '*i sei miei figli*'* and begs Haydn to become their '*Padre, Guida ed Amico*'.† Personally, too, it must have had significance. Haydn and Mozart had probably met for the first time in late 1781, when Mozart had recovered from his quarrel with the Archbishop but was deep in emotional difficulties with Leopold over Constanze Weber. Haydn's paternal attitude to him was more ideal than perhaps any real father's could be (and it continued after Mozart's death, with his offer to train the eldest boy); it must have meant much to the childless older man to have, by adoption as it were, a genius-son. For Mozart – intensely affectionate at all times and at that moment in desperate need of affectionate support – Haydn's kindness must have been as valuable as his musical example. The first of the 'Haydn Quartets' dates from the end of 1782, when Mozart appeared to have triumphed over all his problems and the future seemed excitingly sure. Whether or not he then envisaged writing a series of quartets, he might well reflect on his debt to Haydn; in the eventual published dedication it is he, as much as his work, who seeks in Haydn not only guide and friend, but father.

The personal nature of the 'Haydn Quartets' is much more than a matter of their dedication. The very form is a typical private one, evocative of a world where a household of any rank might easily provide the

* 'My six sons.'
† 'Father, Guide and Friend.'

necessary executants for an evening performance. Joseph II played privately in string quartets. Schubert was typical in being one of a family who could provide a quartet of players within itself. While it is private and domestic, the quartet yet very much represents social music-making: a conversation between four acquaintances or friends, whether or not in other company. Mozart himself performed in this way – preferring the viola, however, not the violin. The reality of his relationship to Haydn, the binding power of music, and the international musical scene at Vienna are all conveyed perhaps most vividly by another page from Kelly's *Reminiscences,* where he describes a musical evening at the house of the English composer, Stephen Storace, when quartets were played by four distinguished non-professional executants: the Viennese composer Dittersdorf, the Bohemian Vanhal, Haydn and Mozart. Though they were not professional performers, all were, however, composers of quartets, and one at least of Dittersdorf's is remarkably novel.

In 1784 Mozart was concentrating particularly on instrumental music: dances, piano concertos, sonatas and a quintet for piano and winds (K.452). It was then that he resumed the writing of the 'Haydn Quartets', three of which he had completed before his visit with Constanze to Salzburg. Amid much other composing, therefore, as well as public appearances, he found time for this fruit of what he was to call in the dedication '*una lunga, e laboriosa fatica*'.* It is interesting that Mozart should declare this about one of the few tasks which he appointed himself. In some ways it was perhaps easier for him to produce the 'Linz' symphony in five days than to achieve the exact self-expression of any of these quartets, the autographs of which are indeed thick with corrections and rubbings-out and cancelled passages. The personal quality of what resulted is the greatest novelty of all, beyond the novel and sometimes daring effects. The string quartet does not cease to retain its social aspect, being music for musicians to play, regardless of a listening audience, but becomes a vessel for the composer's most intimate thoughts.

Mozart's 'long and laborious toil' must have been particularly over the control and direction of energy into the channel of the form. Creative energy has been harnessed so effectively that it carries the quartets into an unearthly region of pure musicality: the essence of Mozart's mind, constantly eddying in mood but ceaselessly energetic, and seeking expression rather than necessarily beauty. There is extraordinary varia-

* 'A long and laborious toil.'

tion of mood between movements and among the quartets themselves, but all are marked by steady contrast of almost growling power and abrupt agitation with streams of intense, radiant melody, like expanses of truly celestial sky sometimes muffled and sometimes revealed amid dark, drifting cloud. The violins have moments of diamond-pointed etching of detail, intricate as cobweb, firm as glass. At times the cello's meditative sombreness colours a passage with almost autumnal effect. The singing slow movements, like the andante cantabile of the G Major quartet (K.387), seem sometimes like pantheistic hymns, anticipating the tone if not the music of *Die Zauberflöte*: sheerly serene glimpses of a 'better land', a '*bess're Land*', far beyond the confines of the Schulerstrasse, or Vienna, or indeed any known world.

These are visionary quartets, quite different in feeling from some agreeable serenade or even a piano concerto for virtuoso public performance. They are full of unexpected effects, from the eerie *pizzicati* (very rarely used elsewhere by Mozart) in the magnificent, darkly moody, D Minor quartet (K.421) to the deliberately dissonant opening of the last of the series, the so-called 'Dissonant' quartet in C Major (K.465). This opening and other portions of the quartets disconcerted many contemporaries – though neither Haydn nor Leopold Mozart. After publication, the quartets were criticized in print as 'too highly seasoned', for all their art and beauty, and Mozart seems to have felt little encouragement to go on writing quartets. Not until 1789 did he settle to a new series of six, the 'Prussian' quartets, which once again he described as 'troublesome' to compose and left only half-completed.

Yet even the famous introductory bars which have given its misleading sobriquet to the C Major quartet – and which are clearly intended to hold rather than disturb the listener – are virtually washed from the ear by the sprightly allegro which follows, led by the first violin. No less intensely solemn than the opening, but ecstatic, is the andante cantabile second movement, where melody seems to create a holy, inviolate climate of harmony: the most sustained sight, in all six quartets, of that blessed '*bess're Land*', to which Mozart already perhaps aspired.

Haydn certainly understood the profundity of achievement which the quartets represented. He heard at least the first three one Saturday in January 1785, only shortly before Leopold Mozart set off on his own journey to Vienna. A few Saturdays later Leopold was present in the Schulerstrasse apartment when Haydn came again, this time to hear the last three quartets. It was then that he paid that spontaneous tribute to

Mozart's ability (his taste and his '*grösste Compositionswissenschaft*')* which must have exhilarated the old man, somewhat bewildered in his daughter-in-law's home, somewhat tired amid the perpetual bustle, and perhaps more conscious than ever before that he belonged in the past.

The winter weather was awful in Vienna. Leopold had caught a chill on the icy journey there. Constanze Mozart's housekeeping was '*im höchsten Grad ökonomisch*',† he wrote to Nannerl; and nobody went to bed before one o'clock in the morning. The regular preparation for concerts and lessons, and more perhaps the sense that he alone had no active part in things, led him to ask himself sadly, '*Wo soll ich hingehen?*'‡ Yet he could not help responding: to Mozart's apparent success and his apparent prosperity, and then to his own grandson Karl (to look at so like Mozart and '*sehr angenehm . . . ungemein freundlich, und lacht so oft mans anredet*')§ and to an excellent dinner given by Madame Weber, of all people. He heard Aloysia Lange sing, and constantly attended Mozart's concerts. These weeks were among the happiest of his life; he had probably forgotten how strongly he had once urged Mozart to return to Salzburg service, and how reluctant he had been to agree to his marriage. When Madame Weber served up a plump roast pheasant in a family party it was difficult to remember that she had been described by him as a 'seducer of youth'. And there was always Haydn's remarkable testimony, which showed that not every human being was envious or an intriguer. Haydn confirmed what Leopold had believed for nearly a quarter of a century.

Perhaps it was chiefly as a gesture of reconciliation, a wish to be close again to his son, that Leopold was led now to become a Mason. He sought admission to the same lodge as Mozart belonged to, and the initiation procedure was apparently speeded up specially for him. The night before he left Vienna, promoted to the third grade, he attended a Masonic festivity with Mozart at the 'Crowned Hope' lodge, when Mozart's cantata *Die Maurerfreude* (K.471) was performed in honour of the Master, who had just been knighted. Haydn too had recently become a Mason, though he never bothered to be fully initiated. Guided by his son for what was the last time, Leopold – who had never been con-

---

* 'Very great knowledge as a composer.'
† 'Extremely economical.'
‡ 'Where am I to go to?'
§ is very delightful . . . uncommonly friendly, and laughs whenever you talk to him.'

spicuous for believing in humanity or brotherhood – took this step into an 'advanced' world. Thus he and his son became brothers, at the moment they were about to separate for ever.

After Leopold's departure in April, Mozart was soon involved in new musical activities, leaving him few opportunities to send his father even brief letters. By late October Leopold had heard a rumour of his planning a new opera; *Le Nozze di Figaro* had in fact been begun. If Vienna had sometimes appeared during his visit too bustlingly noisy, Salzburg soon struck Leopold as depressingly quiet. Mozart had barely time enough to eat and sleep; for Leopold the time had become 'very long' *'sehr lang'*, and seemed yet longer when the local theatre closed. A sharp reminder of his status had come from the Archbishop, angry at his outstaying by many weeks his original leave of absence; his pay was to stop if he had not returned to Salzburg by mid-May (the date was advanced personally by the Archbishop, altering it from the end of the month). He seems to have returned only narrowly within the stipulated time, merely to find existence passing slowly, uneventfully. Once he even wondered hopefully if Mozart might visit him, but that was a fleeting thought.

To fill the days, Leopold wrote to his son-in-law and begged to be allowed to keep at Salzburg the baby, Leopold, to whom Nannerl had recently given birth. The parents agreed. The last and least expected of Leopold Mozart's several careers now began. Assisted by women servants, he occupied himself happily with his namesake-grandson, despatching letters of intimate detail about each stage of the baby's illnesses, the dramatic discovery of his first tooth and the wonderful way he called out *'man, man'* when the moon shone through his bedroom window. Most of all, perhaps, he must have hoped for the day when Leopold would display some sign of having inherited musical talent.

When he learnt that Mozart had chosen Beaumarchais's play for his next opera, Leopold was stirred to little enthusiasm. He was sure the music would be good, he told Nannerl, but was dubious about the play: 'It is a very tiresome play.' This is unfairly severe on a comedy which will anyway have seemed to Mozart the more sparkling after the pages of soggy or ludicrous librettos through which he had for long been wading. From the first he had decided on a comedy, to shift from the romantic *Singspiel* category of *Die Entführung* to some sparkling, Italianate, *buffa* work, with intrigues, comic events and scope for some seven characters.

The vital thing was the comic element: '*Das nothwendigste dabey aber ist recht Comisch im ganzen*,'* he early explained to Leopold.

He began by considering a Goldoni play, *Il Servitore di Due Padroni*, which he had had translated into German, for his first project was to have a German text. As it stands, Goldoni's play is largely a framework of comic incident round one character, Truffaldino, the servant of the title. A first encounter with da Ponte and the arrival in Vienna of some good Italian or Italianate singers probably encouraged Mozart to settle for a totally Italian-style opera. Rejecting servants with two masters, he began to write the music for a libretto provided by da Ponte: *Lo Sposo Deluso* or 'The Rivalry of three Ladies for a single lover'. Apparently even while working on this, and perhaps unsure if da Ponte would adjust it to his requirements, he turned to the Salzburg court poet, Varesco, who had written the libretto, which Mozart had ruthlessly trimmed, for *Idomeneo*. Varesco produced the sketch of a story of quite masterly silliness, *L'Oca del Cairo*, much more absurd than funny. In so far as it is about anything, it concerns a large artificial goose and some complicated intrigues between lovers and a jealous father.

As Mozart worked on it he began to see the inherent futility of the plot; he told Leopold after the stay in Salzburg in 1783, that he had not objected to the '*ganze gans-historie*'† only because he and Varesco had not disapproved of it. Soon even this dubious reason was insufficient for him to persevere. Some fragments of lively music – for example, a trio of two basses and soprano, '*Siano pronte alle gran nozze*' – alone mark the site where the goose-project was decently buried.

Yet in the amusing patter of '*Siano pronte*', where the music so neatly matches the words, there is detectable an advance of technique since *Die Entführung*: something more flexible, and conversational, and potentially more full of character. In itself this trio might almost have dropped from *Figaro*. More certainly anticipatory of the forthcoming opera was the music Mozart contributed in November 1785 to somebody else's comic opera, Bianchi's *La Villanella rapita*. Here the trio, and still more the quartet, which he created are already entirely accomplished and unmistakably Mozartian contributions; one might be listening not only to some sketch for a *Figaro* ensemble but positively to parts of *Così fan tutte*. Vivacious exchanges among the voices build up a music conversation of lyrical vitality – with in the quartet a slightly unusual pattern, for

* 'The most necessary thing is on the whole [to be] really comic.'
† 'Whole goose-story.'

Mozart, of a single woman's voice blended amid three men's – and increasing drama. Each takes a lead, seizing and yielding the conversational shuttle which, as it is thrown back and forward, weaves the fabric ever more closely until at the end one great, glistening sheet of unified sound falls like a triumphant curtain round the listener. Even Count Zinzendorf was stirred to make a complimentary note of Mozart's quartet in his diary when he heard Bianchi's opera for the second time.

Mozart's own electric vitality and intense response to people drew him – drove him – to the theatre. Spectacle, action, interplay of personality, opportunities for artistic speed and economy (and hence wit): all these could be provided by opera and expressed in music. Inevitably he was attracted to the idea of the comic opera – 'recht Comisch' – since this was his own most typical view of life. A sort of natural, animal absurdity never left Mozart, while his energy lasted. Not only was he always the sharp-eyed boy who had remarked at Naples how when the king attended the opera he stood on a stool to look taller than the queen, but he continued to express high spirits with physical exuberance. Having once delighted a Viennese household by playing spontaneous variations on Figaro's 'Non più andrai', he leapt up in different mood and began to jump over the tables and chairs, mewing like a cat. Die Zauberflöte's sublimity is his, but so too are the Natur-Mensch antics in it of Papageno.

Artistically, Mozart becomes each of his characters (it is the secret of their vitality, inherited from him) and is totally involved in the enchanted, yet not artificial world in which they live. But even the slightest opportunity to partake in a musical dramatic atmosphere was seized by him, as the example of his contribution to Bianchi's opera reveals. The writing of dramatic arias, whether as concert pieces or to be inserted in other operas, to be sung often by Aloysia Lange, is part of the same fascination and gift. His own delight in acting was shown by the harlequinade with Aloysia, and also by his dressing-up another year at Carnival as a Hindu philosopher. Perhaps even his delight in fine clothes was part of the fascination with acting and spectacle.

The operatic scene at Vienna seemed suddenly crowded with talents, as well as being enlivened by rivalries and cabals. Da Ponte found a personal rival in a fellow-Italian, abbé and librettist, Casti, who was at least as dissolute and as talented as he was. As well as Salieri, there had appeared in Vienna since Die Entführung's production Paisiello, the composer of a highly successful *Barbiere di Siviglia*, based on Beaumarchais's play which had introduced the character of Figaro. Paisiello and Casti were present on the occasion recorded by Kelly when quartets were played by a group which included Mozart and Haydn. In 1784 another Italian composer, Giuseppe Sarti, had arrived in Vienna, achieving success there first with his comic opera on a Goldoni plot, *I Pretendenti Delusi*. Mozart thought Sarti *'ein rechtschaffner braver Mann'*,* but Sarti was to write a malicious *'Esame acustico'* attacking two of Mozart's 'Haydn' quartets. More immediately, if accidentally, damaging to Mozart was to be the arrival of the composer Vincente Martín, a much younger man than Sarti; Martín and Da Ponte collaborated on a hugely successful opera, *Una Cosa Rara*, which followed closely on *Le Nozze di Figaro* and rapidly obscured its fame with the Viennese public. According to da Ponte, he and Martín became *'cose rare'*, so popular and sought-after were they.

The personality and popularity of certain singers also made their contributions to an almost theatrically animated, though actual, scene. Librettists and composers were nearly as busy turning their mistresses into singers (or vice-versa) as they were in writing operas. Salieri's mistress was the brilliant Madame Cavalieri, the first Constanze in *Die Entführung*. Mozart remained engaged, at least professionally, with Aloysia Lange, but in several ways her position was challenged when Nancy Storace, sister of Mozart's pupil Stephen Storace, came via Italy to Vienna. Although only twenty-two, she was already an accomplished singer, one whose style was tender, yet not unlively, rather than of virtuoso brilliance.

Her success in Vienna was great, but perhaps greater was her effect on Mozart. She was to be Susanna in the first performance of *Figaro*. If something of the character of her voice can be deduced from the deeply-felt tenderness of Susanna's aria 'Deh vieni, non tardar', yet more can be learnt from the scena and aria 'Ch'io mi scordi di te' (K.505), which Mozart wrote specially for her late in the same year, to be accompanied on the piano by himself, recording it in his own list of works as *'Für Mad.-selle Storace und mich'*.† It has often been seen as a love letter in music, but perhaps its strongest impression is of sheer poignancy at imminent part-ing – as if Mozart guessed that he and Nancy Storace would never meet again. She was due to return to England, with her brother and mother.

* 'An upright and honest man.'
† 'For Mademoiselle Storace and me.'

Taking Constanze, but leaving the children with Leopold, Mozart had thought of accompanying the Storace family.

For the final time Leopold intervened, rousing himself out of loneliness and old age to a violent letter of the type he had sent nearly ten years 'Einen sehr *nachdrücklichen Brief'** was Leopold's own description of before when Mozart had proposed travelling with the Weber family. what he now despatched to Mozart in Vienna, declining utterly to take the children, pointing out the disadvantages of going just then to London and generally discouraging the whole project. Mozart had received two such letters well before he recorded completion of the scena *'für Mad.selle Storace und mich'*. Although Nancy Storace was apparently intending to come back after a year's absence in London, she never in fact returned to Vienna.

The operatic possibilities of the opera situation there were amusingly grasped during the very period Mozart was composing *Figaro*. For a fête given by the Emperor at Schönbrunn on 7 February 1786 short works were commissioned from Mozart and from Salieri; they were performed consecutively at either end of the Orangery. Mozart's *Der Schauspieldirektor* was a comedy written for the occasion by Stephanie, the librettist of *Die Entführung*, about a harassed impresario trying to mount a production with two rival *prime donne*; and verisimilitude was strikingly achieved since these two parts were taken by Aloysia Lange and Madame Cavalieri. More topically pointed still was Casti's libretto for Salieri, *Prima la Musica e poi le Parole*. This *buffa* satire on theories about opera libretti was further spiced by the performance of Michael Kelly as an amorous poet, in which he imitated Da Ponte, as Casti intended, in a way which certainly amused the Emperor and even, according to Kelly, da Ponte. However, da Ponte's own *Memoirs* characterize the libretto as quite lacking in wit and style, and claim that the amorous poet's character resembled Casti, rather than himself. Nancy Storace also took part in this opera, parodying a well-known castrato who had sung the previous year at Vienna in an opera by Sarti.

Mozart must have looked on his task as hardly more than a trifle and it was rewarded at exactly half the amount of Salieri's, since he had only provided some musical numbers for a play, not written a complete *opera buffa*. But perhaps there was some private reference for him in the names given to the *prime donne*: Madame Cavalieri, whose 'flexible throat' he had served so well in *Die Entführung*, appeared as Madame Silkberklang,

* 'A very *forceful letter*.'

singing coloratura music suited to her name. Aloysia Lange, whose heart-touching ability Mozart had once praised, appeared as Madame Herz; she is given a G Minor aria of striking depth (*'Da schlächt die Abschiedsstunde'*), which is one further demonstration of Mozart's empathy in music. Slight though the commission might be, and destined for only two or three performances, he could not help characterizing the two types of voice and displaying the range of each, while illustrating the range of his own art: from darkly tragic intensity up to the steepest peaks of silver sound. That he concentrated fiercely, if briefly, on the entertainment is proved by its dynamic overture, alive with powerful contrasts. At once irresistibly witty, fast-paced and yet musically most serious, it is worthy of a more sustained occasion but serves as an apt reminder that when it was written Mozart's mind was really absorbed by the creation of *Le Nozze di Figaro*. It is the twin to that opera's overture.

'A new kind of spectacle,' was da Ponte's description – in the preface to the published libretto – of what he and Mozart meant to offer to the public in their adaptation of Beaumarchais's already notorious play. Not until 1784 had *Le Mariage de Figaro* been performed publicly in Paris, and then only after having passed under the eyes of six censors in addition to those of the king, Louis XVI, who pronounced it *'détestable et injouable'*.* It proved far from unplayable, however detestable, and the king's attitude served merely to emphasize its satirical, egalitarian, revolutionary spirit which was remarked on much more than its comedy. Beaumarchais showed a valet, Figaro, who outwits his aristocratic master; that the master is trying to deflower Figaro's fiancée, his own wife's maid, did not in Louis XVI's eyes remove the offence – of Figaro. Certainly Beaumarchais intended the story to be applicable to late eighteenth-century French society – though he prudently set the play in Spain – and with Figaro's long monologue in the last act he attacked quite openly: *'Parce que vous êtes un grand Seigneur, vous vous croyez un grand génie . . . Noblesse, fortune, un rang, des places: tout cela rend si fier.'*†

The scandalous success so speedily enjoyed by the play was as alarming to the supposedly benevolent, would-be enlightened Joseph II as it had been to his brother-in-law of France. Plans for its being staged in

---

* 'Hateful and unplayable.'
† 'Because you're a great Lord you think you're a genius . . . Nobility, fortune, rank, position: all that makes people so proud.'

Vienna led the Emperor to issue instructions that it ought to be censored or suppressed. By one of those subtle strokes of Austrian bureaucracy to which only Musil could do justice, the final solution was to allow it to be printed (in a German translation), but not acted. The bold person trying to put it on the stage was Emanuel Schikaneder, with whom the Mozarts had become friendly when he had brought his troupe of actors for a season to Salzburg; he perhaps mentioned it to Mozart, who would be likely enough to enjoy reading it, and also to recall Paisiello's success with an opera on Beaumarchais's *Barbier*, to which *Le Mariage* is the sequel. According to da Ponte, when Mozart had selected *Le Mariage* and da Ponte had produced a libretto altering, toning down, or omitting much of the original play, especially the political passages, Joseph II agreed to the opera's performance after an audience at which da Ponte praised Mozart's music.

Da Ponte mentions, too, the annoyance of Casti at this news, as well as that of Casti's powerful protector, Count Rosenberg, the imperial director of the theatre. In letters to Nannerl Leopold Mozart spoke in April 1786 of likely cabals against the opera on its approaching first performance; Salieri was believed to be opposed to it, perhaps through jealousy that the subject had been licensed specially by the Emperor.

To Mozart it must all have been desperately worrying, if he paused for time to worry. Since beginning *Figaro* he had moved his pupils to the afternoons, so as to have the mornings in which to compose. When the commission for *Der Schauspieldirektor* came, that also required to be fitted in. He still gave subscription concerts as well. Late in 1785 he composed a new piano concerto, in E flat (K.482), for performance at one of these. A few weeks after the Schönbrunn production of *Der Schauspieldirektor* he gave some Lenten concerts, for which he wrote two further piano concertos, in A Major (K.488) and in C Minor (K.491); and perhaps that 'new kind of spectacle', *Figaro*, had even then to be completed. An aristocratic amateur performance of *Idomeneo* in April involved him in yet more work; he provided for it an additional duet and a tenor scena and rondo. The two piano concertos of 1786 seem each in its own way bleak and private, receptacles possibly for emotions stirred by the strain of creating *Figaro*. An almost hallucinated, delicate and distant quality marks much of the A Major concerto, a fragile structure of glass where the piano itself is often heard only faintly, while the orchestra breathes a faint haze of hushed strings and clarinets, increasing the ghostly effect, especially in the adagio. In affecting the listener, stirring without conventionally pleasing, the C Minor concerto goes even further. Though the orchestra here is richly prominent, its fire is sometimes banked down and the piano positively thunders on its own wilful path. The opening allegro seems joyless; the finale restless and un-resolved. And no lonelier road can be conceived than that taken by the slow movement, moving in a remote dream which is beautiful but wist-fully so, to the point of pain.

Within a month of the public performance of this concerto, *Le Nozze di Figaro* had its first night, on Monday 1 May 1786. The first novelty offered by da Ponte and Mozart lay in the opera's title, for Beaumar-chais's play was actually called '*La Folle Journée ou Le Mariage de Figaro*', and the German translation of it (Vienna, 1785) carefully preserved this title: '*Der närrische Tag, oder die Hochzeit des Figaro.*' In giving their opera the play's sub-title, they might seem to be merely focusing attention on the fact that it was about Figaro, established throughout Europe as a famous comic character. But it presented a subtle shift of emphasis: away from 'crazy day' intrigues as such and onto the idea of marriage, of indeed love. '*Solo amor può terminar*'* are the words sung by the as-sembled main characters at the opera's close, and they are no translation from the French.

As a result of da Ponte's gifted tampering with the original play – most probably at Mozart's instigation – and as a result, above all, of Mozart's sympathies, Love becomes the presiding god of the whole opera. The almost too mechanically cheerful characters of the play melt and re-emerge as human beings, charged with emotions. Beaumarchais's laughing, fashionably flirtatious Countess (tucking ribbons down her corsage and by no means indifferent to the page, young Chérubin) grows into the wronged, steadfast woman of the opera, seen first praying desperately to the only god she knows ('*Porgi, Amor*'), and eventually triumphant in the dark garden when she comes down, herself now like a goddess, to forgive her husband and provide the final moving touch of reconciliation. Da Ponte and Mozart again soared far beyond the limits of Beaumarchais's Comédie-Française soubrette chambermaid when they created Susanna, still a resourceful, loyal chambermaid, but one who pauses in the garden's darkness to sing a liquid, tender serenade to an absent lover while the light fades and the world falls silent ('*Finchè l'aria è ancor bruna, e il mondo tace*'): 'Vieni, ben mio.' And running Cupid-like through the opera is the fluttering, butterfly-boy Cherubino, a

* 'Only love can bring an end.'

'*farfallone amoroso*'* as Figaro truly calls him, who sings to the Countess and Susanna a song of particular significance: '*Voi che sapete che cosa è amor.*'† Everyone is stirred to some emotion by Cherubino's antics – which include eager grabs at every woman he sees – but it is the Countess and Susanna, mistress and maid united in mutual affection and trust, who really know 'what love is'. Susanna loves and will marry Figaro, outwitting the Count; the Countess loves her husband, despite all his unfaithfulness, and in totally loving him totally forgives him.

What Beaumarchais's play provided was a very firm framework of coherent and outstandingly amusing story, occupying a single day, never shifting from Count Almaviva's house and garden, and offering society a marvellously vivid reflection of its own organization: a small core of aristocracy, supported by personal servants and lawyers, doctors and music teachers, with below these a stratum represented by gardeners, extending into a countrified world, beyond the household yet still part of the Count's feudal domain. The Count's total power over all the other personages is an important aspect; as Figaro dares bitingly to say to him, '*Vous commandez à tout ici, hors à vous même.*'‡ Both play and opera cleverly point up the country setting – so different from the basically urban scene of *Don Giovanni* – where masters and servants are the more dependent upon each other through being isolated. Indeed, half the Count's philandering comes from sheer boredom: '*Libertin par ennui*'§, one of the other characters describes him. The incursions of the local peasantry (given beautifully mock-rustic music by Mozart) add their complications to the story, nearly always arriving to praise the Count at a moment when he is on the point of exploding. In front of them he is forced to keep up the appearances with which he does not bother in front of his household.

Although Beaumarchais laid the scene in Spain, while intending an application to France, the two basic themes of the play were universally applicable. The first, the more obvious, concerned social rank and privilege. It was a shrewd hit when to the Count's complaint that the servants took longer to dress than their masters Figaro riposted that that was because the servants had no valets to help them. Though Mozart and da Ponte were not able to preserve this flash of dialogue, both of them could respond to the egalitarian hint. Mozart especially knew what

* 'Amorous great butterfly.'
† 'You who know what love is.'
‡ 'You are in command of everything here, except yourself.'
§ 'A rake through boredom.'

it was like to be treated as a servant, and society indeed never found a place for him. Da Ponte was a wanderer, equally unplaced in society, and with a sharp ear – as his *Memoirs* reveal – for exchanges between, for example, himself and Count Rosenberg. Like dialogue from one of his librettos is the passage he records of pseudo-politeness in which Rosenberg kept calling him 'Signor poet', while he kept responding with 'Your Excellency'. Da Ponte adds: 'This "Signor Poet" was repeated in a significant tone as though he meant "Signor Ass" or something like it, but my "Excellency" too had its due meaning.' Just in the same way had Mozart bowed with rage before the 'Princely Grace' of his ungracious Archbishop.

Da Ponte claimed to the Emperor that he had omitted things in the original play which might offend decorum, but, despite what is usually supposed, he and Mozart not only kept in much of Beaumarchais's revolutionary cheek (though leaving out the rather laboured hits at the legal profession), but added some of their own. From a brief parting line of Figaro's when he leaves the Countess's boudoir in Act II, '*et puis dansez, Monseigneur*',* they created Figaro's first aria in Act I, threatening as much as mocking his master: 'Se vuol ballare, signor Contino.'

Beaumarchais also advocated another social revolution, one which may not have appealed much to da Ponte but which found instinctive response in Mozart. The position of women, pursued by men and then deserted, treated as playthings rather than as people and always as unintelligent – in a word, women as they have usually been treated by society – stung Beaumarchais into the sort of plea his Marceline makes quite seriously: '*J'étais née, moi, pour etre sage, et je la suis devenue sitôt qu'on m'a permis d'user de ma raison.*'† The ultimate outwitting of the Count comes – not from Figaro but from the Countess and Susanna. It is their plot which brings Susanna to her happy marriage and the Count to kneel before his wronged wife. Reason, wit and ingenuity are enshrined in the women, who are none the less intensely loving; but Beaumarchais found it much easier to convey the wit than the affection. He ended his play feebly, and though he wrote in his *Preface* that '*le plus véritable intérêt se porte-t-il sur la Comtesse*',‡ he could not make this effective dramatically. The result is that his Countess is merely sentimental when she is not being coquettish; yet his intentions remain quite clear. The play represents her triumph.

* '. . . and then dance, my Lord.'
† 'I was born to be sensible, and I became sensible as soon as I was allowed to use my reason.'
‡ 'The real interest is borne by the Countess.'

When Mozart first read *Le Mariage de Figaro* it must indeed have seemed the ideal story for him: topical, modern, neatly plotted and powered by love. On the surface it was amusing; beneath, almost dangerously critical and serious. This quality was not merely preserved but expanded by da Ponte, who ruthlessly trimmed away Beaumarchais's excess characters, often weak concluding scenes, most of his touches of Spanish colour and the confusing motif of the Countess's *tendresse* for Chérubin. Just a few of the gains include the new statuesque importance of the Countess (not seen in the opera until Act ii), the superb close of Act i with Figaro's 'Non più andrai' (quite unparalleled by any speech in the play) and the ragingly haughty aria of the Count, more violently *ancien régime* than anything Beaumarchais had devised: 'Vedrò, mentr' io sospiro Felice un servo mio?'*

Probably da Ponte worked under the closest guidance from Mozart ('*Prima la musica* . . .'),† but he worked with a sort of musical felicity which complemented Mozart's feeling for words. Da Ponte never again encountered a composer with such trenchant ideas of operatic form, and concern with meaning and significance of the text. Da Ponte was *serviable* and speedy, the perfect instrument with which Mozart could virtually write, or at least dictate, what he required. But though Beaumarchais had provided unusually good material, and da Ponte had skilfully tailored it into even better shape, it was of course the music which ultimately put as it were real beings into the resulting costumes, literally animating an opera in a way which had perhaps scarcely been achieved since Monteverdi. '*Un mélange sublime d'esprit et de mélancolie.*'‡ was Stendhal's description, emphasising the uniqueness of mixture in *Le Nozze di Figaro*.

The final convincingness of the characters – characters created by music – comes from their inhabiting a bitter-sweet world, now fast-moving and now sadly slow, now wildly amusing and now hopelessly forlorn. And it is music which shifts and fuses these moods: a ceaseless flow of music which races through the first act with patter, intrigues, and sparkling absurdity but which abruptly pauses, changes character and prepares us for the poignant appeal of the Countess: '*Porgi, amor, qualche ristoro.*'§ Yet she too is part of the same world, borne along sighing into the increasingly rich imbroglio of the end of the second act, closing

* Shall I see, while I sigh, a servant of mine happy?'
† 'First the music.'
‡ 'A sublime mixture of wit and melancholy . . .'
§ 'Grant, O Love, some remedy.'

with that septet which is a triumph of artistic unity while each of the seven characters seeks a different solution out of the complicated maze of plot.

The third act deepens the colour of these characters, now become familiar, and dares also to darken the plot. Has the Count seemed too absurd in his pursuit of Susanna? Will the audience incline to suspect it has heard most of the good tunes and may prepare for a fairly simple dénouement? Mozart chooses this moment for a duel-like duet between the Count and Susanna ('Crudel: perchè finora farmi languir così?'). The more the Count presses Susanna to meet him in the garden, the more her distracted negative answers reveal she does not want to, even while she tries to act her part of pretending she will. More subtle still is her apostrophe – apology for lying, slipped in so quickly that the Count does not hear: 'Scusatemi se mento, voi che intendete amor.'* But he does hear her, as she skips from the room, tell Figaro that they are winning. That is the signal for the explosion of his own aria, packed with real menace and writhing contempt ('tu non nascesti, audace, per dare a me tormento'),† the aristocrat's answer to Figaro's plebeian: 'Se vuol ballare, signor Contino.' This is the blackest moment of the opera; it lightens into the enchanting, touching nonsense of Figaro discovering his real mother and father, but then tilts again to show us – as if imprisoned behind glass – the lonely, humiliated Countess whose aria here begins as an explosion, one of plangent, puzzled grief: 'Dove sono i bei momenti?'‡

Beaumarchais could only write, after his play was written, that the Countess was its real point of interest. Mozart never wasted a word describing his opera, but made the weight of emotional interest unforgettably, tragically actual at this moment. The Countess instigated Susanna's pretence that she would meet the Count at night in the garden, intending to go herself disguised as Susanna and thus trap her husband. She waits uneasily, wondering if Susanna has succeeded, and humiliated further by this very reliance on a servant ('Fammi or cercar da una mia serva aita!') § In this mood, beyond appeal to Cupid, she cries for the pleasure of times past and gone. But then her mood, and the aria, change: there is still hope 'di cangiar l'ingrato cor', ‖ Wind instruments breathe their encouragement, and she sings with new determination

* 'Forgive me if I lle, you who are concerned with love.'
† 'You were not born, bold fellow, to make me suffer.'
‡ 'Where are gone the happy moments?'
§ 'It now makes me seek help from one of my servants.'
‖ 'of changing his ungrateful heart.'

while the orchestra accompany her with fortissimi. At '*cangiar*' again, her voice rises to the highest note of all, confident she can change the Count's heart. An aria which opened in utter despair closes in total triumph. The music has carried the Countess out of the glass prison of frustration. She emerges a woman – not a weak derided object – given purpose by her love. When a fresh incursion of peasant girls bring her flowers as their '*padroncina*', they hail that status as Countess Almaviva which is about to be fully regained. The last act, after tenderness and buffoonery, consecrates her in this role, most movingly. Before the assembled household, the Count kneels to ask her pardon triply, '*Contessa, perdono, perdono, perdono*'. Yes, she forgives him: '*E dico di sì.*'

The marriage of Figaro is the marriage of so much. Ultimately it is a marriage of words and music which makes it probably the most perfect of all operas. If Mozart inspired da Ponte, he himself was no doubt inspired by the vision of an ideal world – reached after considerable struggle – where men may meet as equals, rewarded by love from women who are also at least their equal. A marriage of love is meant to be a marriage of true minds as well. The happy ending of *Figaro* is not something perfunctory but something really achieved after the complications of a long, tormenting day '*giorno di tormenti*'. The opera closes in peace and harmony and happiness, in a night more merciful than the bright bustling day in which it opened.

The social message of *Figaro* was received with near delirium by society in one place. Mozart travelled for the first time to Prague, very early in 1787, by which time Vienna had forgotten *Figaro* in its craze for Martín's *Una Cosa Rara*. At Prague, to his delight and astonishment, everyone was enjoying, whistling, dancing to, and talking about, *Figaro*. The success of *Figaro* there was the sort of success every artist dreams of; and for once the greatness of the work of art was nearly matched by its reception. In a word, it was '*figaro und Ewig figaro*',* as Mozart wrote.

This was the opera which Haydn, even in sleep not forgetting Mozart's music, would find himself happily dreaming of on a wintry night in the depths of the country, a few years later. The north wind, he complained, had roughly awoken him from a dream in which he was attending a performance of *Le Nozze di Figaro*. But for Mozart too by then the exhilarating sense of success – tantalizingly experienced at Prague – had become only a dream.

* 'Figaro, everlastingly Figaro.'

Part IV

'Lacrymosa dies illa'

TRAVELLING back from Prague in February 1787, Mozart might feel excited not only by *Figaro*'s recent tremendous success there but by the even more promising future. He was coming back with the commission for a new opera, to be written specifically for Prague, due for performance in the autumn of that year. Although he had had to abandon the project of going to England, he had discovered so much nearer home an almost ideal, and beautiful, musical haven. In all his previous travels Prague had remained unvisited. Now there was revealed this *'sehr schöner und angenehmer ort'** with sympathetic people, who felt irrepressible enthusiasm for his music and frank longing for him to delight them by returning.

In the autumn Mozart and Constanze indeed returned to Prague. The new opera, *Don Giovanni*, and its composer were received in the theatre with triple cheers, according to the *Prager Oberpostamtszeitung*, which went on to say that everybody involved in the production had strained every nerve to do justice to the composer. *Don Giovanni* was a success, and was probably the more pleasing to Prague since it was truly the city's own opera; not until May 1788 was it heard at Vienna. Before 1787 ended Mozart was able to write to Nannerl, assuming that she had probably learnt of *Don Giovanni's* reception, *'mit allem möglichen beyfall'*,† and giving her a fresh piece of good news: the Emperor had at last taken him into imperial service. Count Rosenberg signed, and Constanze's one-time guardian Thorwart witnessed, the document which appointed Mozart not *Kapellmeister* or composer but simply *Kammermusikus*, for which place he received an annual salary of eight hundred gulden. The office was really a sinecure, made vacant by the recent death of Gluck, whose own annual salary, it may be recalled, had been more than twice that amount.

Gluck's death was merely one among several which touched Mozart in a strangely foreboding year. Between the two visits to Prague, and therefore in the very period of the conception of *Don Giovanni*, Mozart lost two close friends. More fundamentally disturbing still was the sudden news of Leopold Mozart's death. *Don Giovanni* (or *Il Dissoluto Punito*) turned out to be no light-hearted successor to *Figaro*; it opens

---

* 'Very beautiful and pleasant place.'
† 'With tremendous applause.'

with a father's murder and closes only after the protagonist has been dragged down to hell.

Himself no conscious Don Giovanni, Mozart was nevertheless being inexorably pursued even while he remained feverishly active. 1787 is the year of *Eine kleine Nachtmusik*, and the *Musical Joke*, as well as of the intense elaborate concert aria, 'Bella mia fiamma' (K.528), sung by some hero or prince who girds himself to face *'acerba morte'*.* His imperial appointment came too late, or offered him too little for survival. He had only four more years to live: years marked by increasingly brief bursts of hope, frequent moves, desperate encouragement to the ailing Constanze and desperate appeals to his brother-mason Puchberg for the loan of some, any, money. 'I have been living in misery,' Mozart wrote brokenly to him in 1789, underlining the word: 'in *Jammer* gelebt.'

Yet each terrible year, from 1787 onwards, saw him defying circumstances in the sole way he knew how, by creating new masterpieces. The last three symphonies date from 1788. In 1789 he wrote the Clarinet Quintet (K.581) and began *Così fan tutte*, which was performed in 1790. In a single year, the final one of 1791, he offered the last, the most private, of the piano concertos, then *La Clemenza di Tito*, followed by *Die Zauberflöte*; he began the Requiem, but the commission was perhaps too fearfully apt for an exhausted man, however strong his creativity, and he died without completing it.

Even his pet starling died, in the summer of 1787, and he buried it in the garden of his new suburban lodgings. Its death prompted a rhymed epitaph of doggerel lines which yet have disturbing resonance in such a year of deaths:

> *Noch in den besten Jahren*
> *Musst er erfahren*
> *Des Todes bittern Schmerz.*†

Mozart had become a mason partly to exorcize his fear of this ultimate experience – to see it as the doorway to a better, happier world – but he felt death the more keenly as a blow to those who lived on. A solemn sympathy was apparent in the masonic funeral music (K.477) which he had written at the end of 1785 on the deaths of two noble brother-

---

* 'Bitter death.'
† While still in his youth
He had to learn the truth
Of the bitter pain of death.

masons, Duke George of Mecklenburg-Strelitz and Count Franz Esterházy von Galantha. They were members of his own lodge in Vienna, though he can hardly have known them very well. Yet, although they were not bitter personal losses like those which fell so heavily on him in 1787, the deaths were those of two brothers by adoption. The music speaks for a grieving fraternity, indifferent to the high rank and imperial positions of those mourned but conscious that their claim is that of having a shared humanity, masonic humanity. One is reminded of Sarastro's reply in *Die Zauberflöte* to the priest who questions Tamino's suitability for initiation because he is a prince: '*Noch mehr, er ist Mensch.*'*

For those who live on, every effort must be made to achieve what Mozart himself recommended, writing in English in the album of a fellow-mason at Vienna in March 1787: 'Patience and tranquillity of mind . . .' The efforts that he was to make to preserve tranquillity – some sort of central creative calm out of which works of art could proceed – were truly tremendous, but they were efforts; and the marks of a struggle are on much of Mozart's subsequent art.

It is right to think particularly in terms of his greatest operas, where emotions and characters are so patently involved. A certain irrecoverable freshness and rapture lie over the rococo-Turkish *Entführung*, as if to be young and free, and in love, was then enough. Though in every way so much more complex, *Figaro*, too, is ultimately optimistic: sheer human love, confident in Susanna, more timorous in the Countess, tender in both, finally wins through. There is not much love in *Don Giovanni*, and what there is proves largely ineffectual. The opera is as ironic as, and no more funny than, *Measure for Measure*, and indeed Shakespeare was to be specifically associated with it (because of its ghostly effects) by a perceptive reviewer at Frankfurt as early as 1789. An element Mozart had not introduced since *Idomeneo* frighteningly enters *Don Giovanni*: the supernatural, become the more frightening because it is embodied not in some god but in the return to earth of a revengeful dead man. *Die Zauberflöte* gives full play to the supernatural, ultimately beneficent and guiding humanity into a profoundly transfigured world, finer than the known one. But irony is at its most brilliant in the Jane Austen-flavoured *Così*, where emotions are severely quizzed to a point at which everyone looks ridiculous; and humanity is left to guide itself by the only beacon it has, which is reason. In such alien

---

* 'More than that, he is a man.'

worlds, whether ironic or sublime, Susanna's 'Deh vieni'* might sound too simply human and too humanly trusting, for all its beauty.

'*Non temer*'† is the opening phrase in the poignant farewell aria, 'Ch'io mi scordi di te', that duet for Mozart and Nancy Storace which had been written only a few days before Mozart left Vienna on his first visit to Prague. Yet some sort of apprehension, or perhaps tension rather, was already present in the symphony in D Major, finished nearly three weeks before the aria, presumably destined to be played at Prague and now known by that title (K.504). Not since the 'Linz' had Mozart written a symphony, but since then he had written *Figaro* and was soon to receive the opera commission which resulted in *Don Giovanni*. In mood the 'Prague' symphony seems closer to the latter opera; it opens forebodingly, and though there is a brightening of effect as adagio gives way to allegro, an almost feverish grandeur continues to be felt in it. Strong contrasts of *fortissimi* and *pianissimi* are a culmination of the lessons learnt from music at Mannheim, but Mozart now uses them utterly individually, moulding the listener's reaction as if guiding him to feel rather than merely be astonished, as was the tendency of the 'Paris' symphony (also in D Major and also of only three movements). Throughout the Prague symphony there seems an urge for reverie which has constantly to be stirred and become rousing. Even the reverie of the slow movement grows strangely unquiet, like a graceful dance on the edge of something gradually disclosed as unsure, perhaps dangerous. Fever in the third movement is marked by flashes of flute and oboe which are answered each time by the thunder of the full orchestra, until at last a torrential rain of triumphant sound ends the symphony.

While Mozart was still enjoying his rapturous reception in Prague Count August Hatzfeld, his close friend and exact contemporary, died quite suddenly at Düsseldorf. He was a gifted violinist, recorded in one obituary notice as having played Mozart's quartets (doubtless those dedicated to Haydn) in a way which enchanted the composer. Probably not until returning to Vienna did Mozart learn of his death. It was a shock almost like a reminder ('*Er war eben 31 Jahr alt; wie ich*'),‡ and Mozart's first reactions to it were recorded in a letter to Leopold which Nancy Storace's mother mislaid. Indeed, Mozart must still have been under the impact of the news when he parted from the Storace family,

---

* 'Ah come!'
† 'Do not fear.'
‡ 'He was just thirty-one years old, like me.'

after a public concert at Vienna when Nancy Storace sang 'Ch'io mi scordi di te – Non temer, amato bene'.* Perhaps he himself accompanied her, in which case the overwhelming suitability of the aria to the occasion must have been almost too much, especially for someone already emotionally shocked.

Hatzfeld had died. The Storace family had set out for London and Mozart perhaps guessed he would never see them again. Other friends remained, including his doctor Sigmund Barisani, two years younger than himself, and the Jacquin family. The father was Dutch by birth, a distinguished botanist whose three children, Gottfried, Joseph and Franziska, were all musical. Franziska was Mozart's pupil and Gottfried, in his early twenties, stirred an almost paternal affection in Mozart, who lectured him seriously on leading too dissipated a life. Gottfried's hecticness was perhaps physical in origin; he was tubercular and doomed to die not long after Mozart. It was to Gottfried that he had written excitedly from Prague, reporting the success of *Figaro* and giving him a new nonsense name thought up on the journey there. Almost like some echo from the lost kingdom of Rücken are the names Mozart had devised, turning Constanze into 'SchablaPumfa', himself into 'Punkitititi', Gottfried's sister into 'Signora Dinimininimi', while Gottfried became 'HinkitiHonky'. '*Das ist ihr Name, das sie es wissen,*'† Mozart added.

High spirits in Prague had been followed by an inevitably more sober mood back in Vienna. Mozart's inscription about 'patience and tranquillity' in a fellow-mason's album was typical in its seriousness of the entries made by friends in his own album, notably in the same year. Friendship's trials, love as the soul of genius, the power of music, and the value of friendship again: these are the sentiments which people like Gottfried von Jacquin and Barisani expressed with naive but strong feeling, tinged with a romanticism which would probably have struck the generation of Leopold Mozart as very odd and high-flown.

Leopold had gone on a last visit to Munich for the carnival of 1787. Back at Salzburg he irritably explained to Nannerl that her enquiries about his perfect health were impossible: '*Du bedenkst nicht den Unterscheid zwischen eine alten und jungen Mann.*'‡ He was certainly profoundly aware of the difference in his own body, and even his arch-pessimism was modified, as in fact the worst really approached. At least little

---

* 'That I forgot you – Do not fear, dearest love.'
† 'That is your name, as you know.'
‡ 'You don't consider the difference between an old man and a young man.'

Leopold, his grandson, was in excellent health, and Leopold still communicated to Nannerl the minutiae of existence in Salzburg, but now it was with obvious weariness. In March he was taken seriously ill. Mozart had the news by 4 April, when he wrote an alarmed letter to Leopold which yet made every effort – every parental effort, one might say – to much in Mozart's mind: '*Ich bedauere* ihn *nicht – aber wohlherzlich mich und alle die welche ihn so genau kannten wie ich.*'* He reminded Leopold of their common Masonic belief about death, '*den* schlüssel *zu unseren wahren Glückseeligkeit . . .*'† To face the prospect of death without fear; to realize its possible imminence, and yet never to appear gloomy to others. These were the tenets Mozart held, and encouraged Leopold to hold. And yet he hoped for better news of his father. Early in May Leopold did indeed feel, at any rate, no worse; he looked forward to settled weather and fresh air, as the summer approached.

Don Giovanni must have been at least under active discussion at Vienna. It had been agreed that da Ponte, desperately concocting librettos for Martín and Salieri at the same time, should also write the one for Mozart's Prague opera. During May Mozart made several entries in the list of his own works. The first was on 16 May, when he completed the G Minor string quintet (K.516), a work taut, economical and almost violently intense – the product, it might be thought, of someone waiting for news which he suspects will be bad. But Mozart had many reasons for feeling strain, some of which are perhaps exorcized, rather than expressed, in a work which has more affinities with his penultimate symphony than just key. Two days after entering the quintet, Mozart noted a song completed; other songs followed on 20, 23 and 26 May. On 29 May he noted the completion of a piano sonata in C Major (K.521), written for four hands. On the previous day Leopold Mozart had died.

It was to Gottfried von Jacquin that Mozart first hastily communicated the fact, adding it as a bleak postscript to a short semi-business note: he had come home to find the news just arrived: '*Sie können sich meine Lage vorstellen!*'‡ A few days later he wrote to Nannerl, saying how sudden and to him quite unexpected the death had been.

* 'I don't feel sorry for *him* – but I do feel really sorry for myself and for all those who knew him as well as I did.'
† 'The *key* to true happiness for us . . .'
‡ 'You can imagine the state I'm in!'

While still a boy he had announced that he would keep his father in a glass box after he grew old – as Leopold once fondly recalled – but since then Leopold had frequently accused Mozart of virtually bringing on his death. In Mozart's growth was Leopold's decline, but perhaps he had not thought that Leopold would ever really die. He had rebelled violently against Leopold, been reconciled, and then grown inevitably distant again. Mozart's letters became shorter, while the intervals between them were becoming longer; but Leopold never stopped looking for them, as Mozart must have realized. Mozart's move out to the suburbs from the fine Schulerstrasse apartment was probably the last fact Leopold learnt about his son: the household was in financial difficulties and Mozart was turning into exactly what Leopold had always half-feared he would be, a failure.

Although Mozart was spared knowing these final gloomy reflections, he must have felt in sudden retrospect how much he had indeed failed his father. He had not kept him in a glass case in old age, having long ceased to be the ideal son. He had failed in Munich, in Mannheim and in Paris; and though he had not yet failed comparably in Vienna, still he remained without any official appointment or recognition. In his marriage too he had failed Leopold; and even in his children, for no namesake grandson survived. A third boy, Johann Thomas Leopold Mozart, born in October 1786, had died less than a month later.

But in contrast, what sacrifices Leopold had made for Mozart, concentrating all prospects of career, all his musical knowledge, all his love and paternal pride on a marvellously-gifted boy. It would not be enough to say that he had encouraged Mozart; he had created him. Indeed, and undeniably, it was from Leopold that Mozart had inherited his basic gift for music. And now Leopold was dead.

The next entry Mozart made in the list of his own works was on 14 June. He had composed what he called a *Musical Joke* (K.522), for strings and horns, a joke not about clumsy musicians but about a composer who cannot impart meaning or coherence to his music, and the result is at once strange and amusing. Saint-Foix in discussing the piece (in *The Symphonies of Mozart*) suggests that Mozart was possibly satirizing some composer of the period. This may well be correct. The composer would be himself. Those explosions of physical horse-play, which, with him, often followed tension, find some comparable expression here; yet perhaps there is deeper significance in the *Musical Joke*. Mozart had never had the slightest difficulty in composing, but then he had never written a piece of music without some awareness of Leopold and his approval. Virtually everything had been despatched to his father at Salzburg, operas as well as chamber music. In 1784 Mozart was sincerely eager to know Leopold's opinion of his three latest piano concertos. When Leopold heard him playing other new works the following year at Vienna, his enthusiasm was tremendous: '*vortreffliches* . . . *herrliches* . . . *Magnifique*.'* Whatever his beliefs about Mozart's failures as a son, Leopold had never faltered in sustained conviction of his greatness as a composer.

Never again would Mozart be able to turn to Leopold for appreciation, encouragement or advice. Even his supreme creativity was perhaps disturbed by the abrupt loss, emotionally so much more profoundly shattering than it might seem, just because he had taken Leopold's existence increasingly for granted. Hatzfeld represented one type of identification, being exactly Mozart's contemporary; Leopold represented something more intimate, tied so tightly to Mozart's earliest memories of existence that with his death something of Mozart's own individuality might seem to have died. That Leopold's death occurred while there lay before him the Prague opera commission, with its challenging onus to create something as fine as *Figaro*, was perhaps, if only briefly, terrifying. And if one aspect of the loss seemed tragic, another might bring almost a sense of relief, to be followed by guilt. Mozart had loved his father. He was deeply indebted to his father. But he had fought hard to free himself from Leopold; and now he was indeed free.

Hurried arrangements, not altogether satisfactory ones, seem to have surrounded the inheritance of Leopold's property, for Nannerl and her husband were on the spot and were also far better placed financially than Mozart, who now needed money desperately. Nannerl perhaps took some things out of the public auction of all Leopold's effects, and despite Mozart's specific plea did not apparently sort out all his manuscripts to return to him. But Sonnenburg and Mozart agreed that Mozart should receive his estimated half-share of the estate in cash, and a thousand gulden – the agreed sum – were despatched to Michael Puchberg, Mozart's fellow-mason, friend and creditor, after he and Constanze had left for Prague and the first night of *Don Giovanni*.

If the *Musical Joke* represents some disturbance in the balance of Mozart's own creativity, a perfect return to order is declared by *Eine kleine Nachtmusik* (K.525), which was his next piece of completed instru-

* 'Superb . . . splendid . . . *Magnifique*.'

mental music, entered in his list of work some two months later. Mozart is Mozart again, in a famous serenade beautifully, economically, wrought for no known occasion. Possibly it was written with an eye to the forthcoming visit to Prague, by then drawing quite close, and certainly it has the felicity, if not the depth, of everything Mozart wrote for Prague. Perhaps, as has been mentioned earlier, it represents some movement of calm intermission while creating the great night-piece of *Don Giovanni*, itself proceeding amid Mozart's usual hectic existence ('*ich gar zu viel zu thun habe*,'* he scribbled hastily to Nannerl at the beginning of August).

Earlier in the year Siegmund Barisani had written his entry in Mozart's album: verses which declare Mozart equalled only by Bach and Haydn, and then go on to stake a claim to Mozart's remembrance as the friend who has twice 'served to save him for the world'. On 3 September Barisani unexpectedly died, aged twenty-nine, and on that day Mozart wrote the last, the most poignant, of the epitaphs death would wring from him in the year. Under Barisani's entry, he recorded the loss of this 'dearest best friend and saviour of my life . . . He is all right where he is: – but I – we – and all those who knew him well – We will *never* be all right – until we have the happiness of seeing him again in a better world – and *never* to part'. A month later Mozart was approaching Prague. A few days afterwards he was joined there by da Ponte who, however, stayed only a week and was not present on 29 October, when Mozart himself conducted the first performance of what the libretto called *Il Dissoluto Punito / osia il D.Giovanni*.

In old age, though not in his *Memoirs*, da Ponte stated that in *Don Giovanni* Mozart 'determined to cast the opera exclusively as serious', and that he began in that vein before da Ponte persuaded him to change his mind by introducing some comic relief. The year's experiences might have driven Mozart to blackest tragedy, regardless of da Ponte's pleas about the need to be adequately amusing. Instead, with perhaps even more profound reaction to all that had happened, he produced the ironic mixture of *Don Giovanni*, where a lecherous, murdering anti-hero is punished for his sins, but only after having attracted our smiling admiration for his perpetual cheek and bravery. Life in the Spanish city where the opera is set will be better but much duller after Don Giovanni's disappearance. This paradox is increased, accidentally or otherwise, by the comparative failure of any other character in the opera

* 'I've got far too much to do.'

to stir sympathy – or, indeed, to have personality in the way possessed by the characters of *Figaro*. And if Mozart really determined from the first to make his new opera 'serious', he is unlikely to have been deflected by Da Ponte. That it will be serious is proclaimed by the opening bars of its overture, commanding silence before setting an eerie, agitated scene, tossing the auditor between dramatic drops of pianissimi and stormy, rising fortissimi, with snatches of melody passing like gleams of moonlight over a ghostly graveyard.

Nobody listening to this overture could doubt that they were being prepared for something quite novel, very different from the sparkling bustle of the opening of *Figaro*. The overture to *Don Giovanni* ends softly, and a night scene is revealed with a muffled figure pacing amid the darkness: the Don's servant, Leporello, singing rebelliously about how sick he is of servitude while keeping watch outside the house of the Commendatore, whose daughter will shortly rush onto the stage clutching her masked, would-be seducer and declaring – in thrilling, threatening tones – that she will never let him escape. Those words come true in the person of her aged father, entering in turn, demanding that Don Giovanni fight him. Music conveys their duel, pauses as the old man falls, and dies with him. There the corpse lies, awaiting the return of Donna Anna, whose lacerating grief is shudderingly conveyed through soughing strings: '*padre mio, caro padre, padre amato*',* before she swoons. The death of the Commendatore is the beginning of Don Giovanni's bad luck; most of the other characters pursue him vainly throughout the opera, but it is the statue of the Commendatore which supernaturally comes at last to take his hand in a grip from which Giovanni frees himself only by being hurled to hell.

The extraordinary and popular Don Juan story had gone through many transmutations before being tackled by Mozart and da Ponte. It had inspired a Spanish seventeenth-century play, as well as a play by Molière (whose works Mozart possessed, the gift of Constanze's father), a ballet by Gluck and still more recently a Venetian opera, with a libretto by a well-known librettist, Giovanni Bertati. Da Ponte can virtually be proved to have borrowed a good deal directly from Bertati, and something from Molière, but the real impetus for the opera may well have come from Mozart's re-reading Molière, perhaps on analogy with his good fortune when he had read Molière's modern successor, Beaumarchais.

* 'My father, dear father, beloved father . . .'

Molière's *Don Juan* was a tragi-comedy which was originally played with great success – like *Le Mariage de Figaro* – and also, like that, it caused a scandal, being virtually suppressed, and then much toned down when eventually printed. The eponymous hero is blasphemer as well as cynical seducer, and an amusingly brave man. When his valet tells him that he is being warned by heaven, Juan calmly replies, '*Si le Ciel me donne un avis, il faut qu'il parle un peu plus clairement, s'il veut que je l'entende*'.* As well as Molière's play, there were two other contemporary French versions of the story, both laying emphasis in their same subtitle on an unfilial element: *Le Fils criminel*. In Molière's play, Don Juan's father visits him vainly with grave warnings, worthy of the Commendatore; Juan, who has killed the Commendatore before the play begins, openly hopes for his father's death. '*Mourez le plus tôt que vous pourrez*,'† he calls after him, as the old man departs.

Perhaps Mozart knew unconsciously that he was looking for something quite shockingly distinct from the unity and loving harmony which breathe finally from *Figaro*. The story of *Don Giovanni* is – as its main title proclaims – a story of dissoluteness punished; and whatever the earlier transmutations and variations of the tale, a murdering, blaspheming lecher (one of those '*esprits forts qui ne veulent rien croire*,'‡ says his servant in Molière) is always punished at the end. Mozart was not altogether an *esprit fort* in this sense, but he had probably tended more and more to reject the ritual Roman Catholicism of his boyhood in adopting the more modern and ethical religion of Freemasonry. In his imagination he was also probably at least something of a Don Giovanni, easily-aroused and highly-sexed. ('If I had to marry all with whom I have joked,' he had written to Leopold, when denying his love for Constanze, 'I'd have easily had 200 wives.') In so many ways he had rebelled against Leopold who, even on a quite trivial pretext, once solemnly proclaimed that Mozart's behaviour had given him three tastes of '*Todes Angst*', 'fear of death'. Mozart must have wept for Leopold's death, the more bitterly perhaps in feeling that somehow he was indeed the cause of it.

His Don Giovanni is a rebel against society, itself represented by the aristocratic, chilly pair of Donna Anna and her ineffectual fiancé Don

---

* 'If Heaven gives me warning it'll have to speak a bit more clearly, if it wants me to understand.'
† 'Die as soon as you can.'
‡ 'Bold spirits who don't want to believe in anything.'

Ottavio, the more bourgeoise-seeming Donna Elvira, who still loves and pursues the Don who ravished her and now despises her, and the peasant-plebeian Masetto and Zerlina who – unlike Anna and Ottavio – openly show some affection for each other. These disparate elements are all seen ironically, each emotionally perturbed by the maverick presence of a young gentleman who behaves in such non-gentlemanly ways (*'Giovane Cavaliere estremamente licenzioso'** is the libretto's description of him in the list of dramatis personae) but with such attractive energy. Inevitably he disturbs the three women (symbolizing his pursuit, as Leporello sings in the catalogue of his master's conquests, of *'donne d'ogni grado'*)† but he also puzzles Ottavio, who wonders how a *'cavaliere'* could possibly be the Commendatore's murderer, and he misleads Masetto before eventually beating him up. As a result, society – temporarily – coheres, uniting against him, while Leporello only very reluctantly remains in his service. The end of the first half of the opera is a tremendous ensemble, precipitated by Giovanni's third failed seduction (that of Zerlina), in which he defies the vengeance threatened by Anna, Elvira, Zerlina, Ottavio and Masetto, with a heroic refusal to show fear, 'even if the world should fall'.

An ambivalence previously detectable emerges here unmistakably, part of the twisted genesis of the opera. For his bravery Don Giovanni compels admiration – not execration. Mozart is too close to him to condemn his villainy, responding rather – as do the spectators – to the Don's lonely defiance. To increase our sympathy, Don Giovanni is the only person in the opera who is allowed to be amusing. No spark of humour enlivens Ottavio or Anna, the latter still remote from her fiancé in the wonderful but unresponsive aria 'Non mi dir', in which she coldly, if not cruelly, rebuts his accusations of cruelty. Elvira's love is ridiculed, almost too painfully, by both Giovanni and Leporello. Masetto is easily beguiled back out of suspicious sulkiness by Zerlina, though she herself is pert and flirty enough to justify all his suspicions; the peasant pair provides the audience with a laugh, but it is a condescending one, lacking all the *rapport* which binds one instinctively to Susanna and Figaro. Much the same is true of Leporello, a buffoon, not a wit.

Don Giovanni literally outwits society. In the somewhat confused second half of the opera – in which da Ponte's haste and his perhaps

* 'Extremely licentious young Lord.'
† 'Women of all ranks.'

desperate patching at Prague seem marked – the Don goes cheerfully on, while the rest of the characters capture what they believe to be him but proves in fact to be Leporello disguised. The sextet which follows reveals society's impotence to deal even with the servant; borrowing some of his master's impudence, even while doffing his clothes, Leporello makes mock apologies to his captors and eludes them all. Sympathy is with Leporello, all the more so since Ottavio's reaction is an aria – of tenderness rather than purposefulness – in which he beautifully says that he is now going to take action, '*a vendicar io vado*'.*

Mozart the music-dramatist, who had carefully applied realistic and psychological standards to the behaviour of the characters even in an *opera seria* like *Idomeneo*, seems here to falter – or to treat the scene with total irony. Ottavio behaves like an Italian tenor in a provincial opera-house, or like a typically useless aristocrat. It is clear that he has no idea of how to take vengeance, and he makes only the lightest of references to the matter when he next appears. Underlining his ineffectuality is the subsequent scene where the Don – who has in the meantime come near seducing Leporello's sweetheart, so he claims to Leporello – invites the statue of the Commendatore to sup with him, defying heaven as he has successfully defied earth.

This is the moment of real conflict, an artistic conflict because – one may guess – it is basically an emotional one. We are amused by the Don's insolent address to the statue '*O vecchio buffonissimo!*'† (whereas Leporello timidly approaches it as '*O statua gentilissima*',‡) but the statue's sudden animation, its nodding head, and sepulchral one-syllable reply, '*Sì*,' have all the conviction lacking in Ottavio. This time no high-spirited bravery is going to save Don Giovanni, and Leporello's real terror touches even him before the scene is over. The moonlit graveyard, where stands the statue with its plinth inscribed as waiting for vengeance, becomes profoundly foreboding; the Don entered it laughing gaily, but quietly creeps away ('*partiamo via di qua*'),§ as if glad to escape while he can. Perhaps for the first time, the audience really feels that for him the day of wrath is nigh: an almost subterranean, certainly semi-ecclesiastical, solemnity sounds in the trombones which accompany the statue's first words.

---

* 'I am going to take revenge.'
† 'O stupid old fool!'
‡ 'O most noble statue.'
§ 'Let's slip off this way.'

This is supernatural music – Don Giovanni's requiem – which will banish from the stage the mere divertimenti airs which the Don requires as he settles to a good last supper. The introduction by Mozart of a real band into Don Giovanni's house is like Shakespeare's introduction of the actors into *Hamlet*: it heightens conviction in the artistic reality of the main characters and events. '*Che ti par di bel concerto?*'* the Don contentedly asks Leporello as he changes the dishes and the band plays tunes first from *Una Cosa Rara*, then from an opera of Sarti's, *I due Litiganti*, and finally – as joke-compliment to Prague – music which Leporello says he knows too well, Figaro's 'Non più andrai'.

Mozart creates a marvellous image, almost a caricature, of 'good life' for an eighteenth-century aristocrat: relaxed, well-catered-for, waited on, serenaded by the best tunes. And then, remorselessly, he crushes it out. Elvira rushes on, swept into the room by plunging strings, pleads distractedly amid mockery from the Don and then rushes away, to encounter the approaching statue of the Commendatore. Her scream leads Leporello to the door. With a scream he too falls back. In the orchestra the Commendatore is heard knocking for admittance. The musicians on stage flee; the lights go out; Leporello hides. What follows is the agony of an unrepentant death; and at the end even Giovanni's spirit breaks, and he is howling in the ghastly musical holocaust – '*Che smania! Che inferno!*'† – in which Mozart purges his own guilt. The subsequent vaudeville effect of the arrival of the other characters, with their rapidly cheerful agreement that such is an evil-doer's fate, scarcely dispels the fatal smell of reactionary brimstone. Anyway, for Vienna Mozart himself removed the final sextet, more confident perhaps after the opera's success at Prague that its often acrid irony need not be softened by this somewhat conventional close.

When he wrote to Gottfried von Jacquin about his new Prague success, Mozart took the opportunity to speak quite seriously about Jacquin's way of life, especially concerning love-affairs – like a friendly Commendatore to a repentant Don Giovanni. He hoped Jacquin had indeed given up what he emphasized as a previous '*etwas unruhigen lebensart*'.‡ He hoped Jacquin was now convinced of the truth of his daily, severe little sermons ('*meiner kleinen Straf-Predigten*'): that the pleasure to be had from fleeting affairs was far removed from the blessedness of 'a

---

* 'What do you think of the fine concert?'
† 'What frenzy! What an inferno!'
‡ 'Somewhat restless way of life.'

true and rational love'. And if that was so, he claimed to have played quite a significant role in Jacquin's conversion.

This letter alone is evidence for the similarity of Mozart's personal beliefs to the belief which powers his operas: the blessedness of mutual love. Perhaps he admonished Jacquin the more effectively for having been through the same sort of experiences himself; and the eventual punishment of Don Giovanni – in the one opera where love is significantly replaced by fleeting affairs – is confirmed as something deadly serious. The letter also reveals a continuing seriousness in Mozart's mood, even in the delightfully distracting atmosphere of Prague.

It was for the famous Prague-born singer, Josepha Duschek, that he wrote the aria 'Bella mia fiamma', after the première of *Don Giovanni* and before returning to Vienna. Frans Duschek, her husband, was a composer. The Mozarts and Duscheks had met long before in Salzburg, when Mozart had composed his first aria for her, 'Ah, lo previdi' (K.272), but it was at Prague that there developed a warm friendship. Constanze was writing to Madame Duschek two or three months before Mozart's death, though the letters are lost. The Duscheks seem to have provided Mozart with not only hospitality but that ideal climate for him of intense musicality combined with jokes and high spirits. It was amusing to be announced as a total stranger to Madame Duschek, who would then discover that the stranger was Mozart, arrived unexpectedly somewhere where she too happened to be staying.

Writing for Madame Duschek's voice was a pleasure of a different kind. Her voice was possibly the widest-ranging and the most dramatic of all the sopranos Mozart wrote for. It is displayed in the really vast and varied 'Ah, lo previdi', where wild bursts of strings intersperse the first portion of recitative, and the aria itself provides a whole series of moods to mirror those of the heroine, Andromeda, desperate, loving, sad, as she longs to die because her lover is dying. Mozart sounded a warning, intended for Aloysia Weber, when he was helping her over the aria, but worth passing on, especially to modern critics: 'Put yourself seriously into the state and situation of Andromeda.' He did not mean his work to be treated as a piece of empty virtuosity unrelated to the scene depicted; he told Aloysia to pay attention too *'al senso ed alla forza delle parolle* [sic]'.* Madame Duschek was some six years older than Aloysia and probably did not need such guidance. The range of 'Ah, lo previdi' must have delighted her; it even includes, as a final display, a bit of

* 'To the meaning and the force of the words.'

rapidly-sung coloratura of the kind which is, or should be, heard more fully in the desperately taxing, extended coloratura which closes 'Bella mia fiamma'. This is altogether more concentrated than the earlier aria, bolder and much more deeply affecting. The voice has to negotiate speedy, terribly difficult runs up the very word *'terribile'* and must also be able to seize the anguishedly low notes of *'acerba morte'*, bitter death the fate to which the protagonist goes – the voice dropping with heart-rending effect before the realization of parting and imminent death. It must have been easy for Mozart towards the end of 1787 to put himself into the proper state to feel 'the force of the words'.

Yet the year was to close, much as it had opened, with him returning from Prague having achieved a great operatic success. Recognition of a sort was coming to him at Vienna, seven years after he had settled there. Gluck's death opened the way for an imperial economy which partly benefited Mozart, but unfortunately perhaps tied him to Vienna at a moment when he might seriously have considered moving to Prague. He spoke hopefully of his salary of only 800 gulden as being given to him 'at present'; but it never rose. Still, there was the prospect of Vienna's reception of *Don Giovanni*. A change of circumstances came too with another change of lodgings; Mozart moved back from the Landstrasse nearer to the city centre. And, after the steady toll of deaths, it must have seemed a welcome affirmation of life when Constanze gave birth on 27 December to their first daughter, who was christened Theresia.

2

By the summer of 1788 Mozart, probably for the first time, openly acknowledged moods of overwhelming despair. They were caused not by the death of others, nor by any failure of his creativity, but by sheer poverty. He tried to fight against the black thoughts (*'schwarze Gedanken'*) which so often assailed him, he explained to Michael Puchberg, frankly begging for a further loan of money; having begged, all he could do was to be silent 'and *hope*'.

In 1788 the three major operas Mozart had written since moving to Vienna were performed all over Germany. A modern composer might think himself very lucky if twelve European cities mounted his work in one year; and he would certainly benefit from the performances. Financially it meant nothing to Mozart that *Die Entführung* was played at

Brunswick, Breslau, Hildesheim, Graz, Regensburg, Frankfurt and Berlin; that *Figaro* was heard at Lübeck, and also in part at Florence, as well as at Graz and Carlsbad; that *Don Giovanni* was played in Leipzig. None of these productions failed to record that the composer was Mozart, sometimes called 'celebrated' in the often quite perceptive critiques which appeared in local papers. Mozart was indeed a celebrity, and when he later gave concerts in cities like Leipzig he received splendid applause – but little profit. From a single concert Nancy Storace once made 4,000 gulden in receipts.

In Vienna even the applause had dwindled. Mozart made several efforts in 1788 to earn money by his musical abilities, as performer and as composer, and none was successful. He was paid for the Viennese première of *Don Giovanni*, but the opera itself failed to please. The very phrase is da Ponte's, but there is direct contemporary evidence too. According to da Ponte, Joseph II found the opera 'divine', though not meat for his Viennese; and when this was reported by da Ponte to Mozart, he said they should give the Viennese time to chew on it. However, though da Ponte went on to claim that in time the opera's success increased, the fact is that after 1788 (when it was played fifteen times) it was never performed at Vienna during Mozart's lifetime. Joseph II's documented reaction to it has already been mentioned: away at the front with the Army, he had declared the music too difficult for the singers. He did not see the opera until its final performance in December. The egregious Count Zinzendorf had by then heard it several times, which perhaps accounts for his eventual – if typical – reaction: he found it very boring. That seemed to sum up Vienna's attitude to Mozart.

Yet *Don Giovanni* had been retailored, if not for Vienna at least for the singers there. The tenor could not sing Ottavio's 'Il mio tesoro' and was equipped with the briefer, easier and more melting 'Dalla sua pace', still expressive of Ottavio's ineffectual, dependent nature (*'quel che a lei piace Vita mi rende'*).* A comic duet, now rarely included in stage performances, was provided by Leporello and Zerlina, presumably to amuse *'i signori Viennesi'*. It is not likely to amuse anyone else, being oddly barren and banal; all that emerges is Zerlina's basically shrewish little nature. But in adding a new aria, 'Mitradi' for Madame Cavalieri, Salieri's mistress (and the Madame Silberklang of *Der Schauspieldirektor*), who was now taking the part of Elvira, Mozart did something which

---

* 'What pleases her gives life to me.'

deepened and warmed the whole opera. It is a soliloquy-aria – for Elvira is a lonely character, herself something of a drop-out from society since being seduced – in which she confesses, despite everything, her continued affection for the man who betrayed her. The slow recitative depicts her tortured state: she sees heaven's vengeance approaching, and yet sighs at its approach. A cry of anguish breaks from her so rapidly that there is hardly a pause between the recitative's questioning close and the flight of the aria into painful, shameful, thrilling realization: 'Provo ancor per lui pietà.'* As well as being a marvellous piece of music, the aria explains in advance Elvira's irruption into the supper-scene on the Don's last night on earth. She joins Mozart's other heroines in truly meaning what she says. Love drives her to do more than feel 'pity': she acts on her emotions, though not even her love-turned-charity can save Don Giovanni.

For Austria the year 1788 had opened with a long-awaited declaration of war, in alliance with Russia, against Turkey. In an oblique way, Mozart was to be involved. Austria had earlier lost Belgrade to the Turks and a wish to recover this fortress-city was one cause, though scarcely a justification, of Joseph II's conduct. Despite, or indeed because of, his well-meant personal concern to be with his soldiers, he proved unable to inspire great victories. His health and popularity suffered. Not until the autumn of the following year was Belgrade taken by the Austrians, under Marshal Lodon. Both the Emperor and the Marshal died in 1790; and in 1791 Austria made peace with Turkey.

Mozart took advantage of patriotic interest in the war to offer the public a bass battle-song, to words written several years before, 'Ich möchte wohl der Kaiser sein' ('I should love to be the Emperor') (K.539), and a contredanse (K.535) with the topical title of 'The Siege of Belgrade', introducing battle-music and a Turkish march. Such things were probably undertaken in an increasingly desperate bid to earn some money. Both pieces were advertised in the *Wiener Zeitung* in March. Much more serious work was advertised there for subscription in April: three string quintets (K.406, 515 and 516), all written during the grim previous year. The tickets for these were on sale from Puchberg, to whom Mozart was already in debt privately.

Subscriptions must have come in very slowly. In June Mozart bravely believed he would find more subscribers abroad than in Vienna, but the scheme petered out. It was Puchberg who was to prove the most gene-

* 'I still feel pity for him.'

rous of all subscribers – to Mozart's existence – never failing to send some money in response to the rising tide of agonized appeals which continued virtually until the end. At death Mozart owed Puchberg more than a year's salary, and that sum probably omits amounts which may always have been called gifts. It is true that Puchberg, who did not press for payment of the debt immediately after Mozart's death, is said to have demanded the money from Constanze later; but he himself died very poor.

In 1788 Johann Michael Puchberg was prosperous. His family had done well as dealers in wine. As a young man he entered a textile manufacturer's firm, and went on to marry the manufacturer's widow. When she died, she left him a further fortune. He does not seem to have been very merciful over repayment of the loans he made to other people, but from at least 1788 onwards his support of Mozart was clearly as generous in its manner as in deed. It cannot have been hard for him to see that Mozart was sinking into a morass of debt and that the 'loans' were really gifts. As well as being a mason, Puchberg was also a keen amateur musician. Mozart always wrote to him as 'Dearest friend and Brother of the Order'; and, almost alone among Mozart's acquaintances in Vienna, Puchberg showed himself to be a true brother and friend. There was not much but gratitude that Mozart could offer him in return, apart from musical opportunities. It seems very right to find him invited by Mozart to the first rehearsal of his next opera *Così fan tutte*, which was to be attended also by Haydn: '*So wollen wir den alle zusammen gehen.*'*

Public indifference over his advertisements of the string quintets might perhaps have warned Mozart that concerts organized by him were not likely to do much better. During the early part of 1788 he took part in one or two semi-private concerts and conducted Carl Philipp Emanuel Bach's *Resurrection* cantata at some performances mounted by Baron van Swieten. But it is improbable that such appearances were very well paid.

By June he was planning a series of concerts, probably for the second time that year. A few months earlier he had written a penultimate piano concerto, in D Major (K.537), the so-called 'Coronation Concerto'. It does not seem to have been played by him publicly until 1789, at Dresden, and was played again in 1790 at the Frankfurt festivities for the coronation of the new emperor, Leopold II. Its irrelevant sobriquet has perhaps too much encouraged the idea that it is just a festive *pièce*

* 'So let's all go together.'

d'occasion. Certainly it has none of the profound passion of the D Minor concerto (K.466) but its simple, limpid, slow movement seems to point the way to the extreme crystalline simplicity of the last piano concerto (K.595). Nor is its opening particularly brilliant or festive; the strings quietly sketch a gentle melody. Some of the glitter of the solo part must anyway be suspect, because the autograph is defective, and Mozart wrote the concerto long before there was any question of celebrating a coronation. Because it is easy to appreciate, it need not be supposed superficial. For Mozart it probably represented a conscious mean between the easy and the difficult; to that extent, it may have been created with performance in mind at Vienna, where ironically it was never played in his lifetime.

More extraordinary to posterity is the fact that the three great symphonies Mozart wrote during the summer, presumably with a view to concerts, seem never to have been performed at all until after his death. In June Mozart and Constanze retreated, with their children, back to the suburbs of Vienna. Their new lodgings were cheaper, and included a garden where the boy Karl was heard by some visitors singing recitatives, while Constanze cut quill-pens for a music-copyist and Mozart extemporized marvellously on the piano. (Theresia Mozart had died some ten days after the move.) The visitors to Mozart were a Danish party of actors, one of whom left a journal describing this August afternoon which seemed to him so wonderful. He found Mozart a small man but a great master; and everything surrounding the master was musical.

The idyllic scene – one of the very last external glimpses of Mozart – was at once true and misleading. Art could not keep reality at bay for more than an afternoon. The delighted Danes returned to the city; and Mozart returned to his problems. Although he had prepared tickets for a new series of concerts, it does not seem that he gave any. He had no particular commissions. He never gave public concerts again in Vienna. Indeed, as he told Puchberg, he had very little reason for going into Vienna at all. His financial affairs were hopelessly involved. He still owed money to the landlord of his Landstrasse rooms and, shortly after Puchberg had helped him over this, Mozart had to appeal to him again, to advance some money against two pawnbroker's tickets.

Yet it was in this very period of experiences blacker than any he had known before, and without any likelihood of things improving, that Mozart created his three famous last symphonies, finished within six weeks of each other. No doubt they were not intended as a consciously planned triad; as previously when he had composed several symphonies within one brief period, the results seem nevertheless consciously varied and contrasted. Because the last of them, the Symphony in C Major (K.551) proved the last of forty-one works in a form which Mozart had been writing for nearly a quarter of a century, and perhaps a little because of that enduring, probably early nineteenth-century christening of it as the 'Jupiter', it has often been treated as Mozart's divine, supreme and final symphonic treatment. The excited phrases of Saint-Foix consecrate this view of it: 'Nothing so great and important had arisen before that which dawned on 10 August 1788 . . . which saw the older music, suddenly revived, united with the new to salute the future:' However, it is possible to appreciate something of the greatness, and the interest, of the symphony without feeling either that it must be treated as the culmination of all Mozart's symphonies, or that it must necessarily be finer for whatever salute it gave to the future.

Mozart, with Haydn, had long before banished the old idea of the pastime-overture symphony which was hardly more than a divertimento. The Viennese creation of the four-movement symphony did more than expand the form, because it gave the slow second movement the opportunity to become more than a reflective passage between first and last, which are lively, often *buffa*, movements. First and last movements now flanked two internal ones; and the slow movement was followed not by an abrupt contrast but by a minuet, so that there was also internal balance. Mozart's earliest four-movement symphonies date from 1767 and the concept was quickly assimilated by him. Of his finest mature symphonies, it is the 'Prague' which is exceptional in having only three movements. Where the minuet movement provided a smiling, courtly contrast (an extrovert slow movement, as it were) the slow movement itself could assume – as it does so often in Mozart – an introverted, holy, even ecstatic quality of great poignancy. The slow movements of the last three symphonies each have much of this effect, in varied ways; and the *andante cantabile* of the C Major symphony is probably the most haunting and unearthly of them all.

No sudden musical leap brought Mozart to the creative plateau where he so speedily set up these three powerful, power-filled structures. To them should mentally be added the Prague symphony. The storming power of its romantic last movement – with the orchestra thundering as if over a threatened ballroom where flute and oboe still bravely pipe on –

is caught again and rolls with tremendous force through the slow but boldly commanding first bars of the E flat symphony (K.543), the first of the three to be completed.

In sheer orchestral power, always controlled and therefore the more effective when allowed to swell, this symphony is the biggest of the three. Its range of instrument is also the widest: there are no trumpets or timpani in the G Minor symphony and no clarinets in the 'Jupiter'. The surge of its strings, its drums and trumpets immediately establish a vast, temple-like building (possibly deliberately masonic in allusion, the symphony's key being also that of *Die Zaüberflöte*); nor is it fanciful to hear a solemn knocking in the orchestra before the adagio beginning gives way to a hymn-like allegro. The listener is borne on, really as though entering an edifice.

Perhaps some equation between the mass and the symphony was felt by Mozart, or perhaps his instinctive sense of drama sometimes achieved comparable effects with the liturgy and the symphonic form. After the sustained choral-orchestral close of the first movement, the light breath of the strings which open the slow movement seems to spread a more intimate solemnity, heightened by the first high notes of the woodwind; this mood itself might appear disturbed, even attacked, by the return of the strings once and then again with more passionate rhythms, and yet the ultimate effect of the movement is a sort of musical, harmonious, exaltation. Mysterious exaltation rather than any conventional gaiety fills the minuet too, coloured by clarinets (the instrument for which Mozart was soon to write a full-scale work) with an autumnal beauty the more piercing for its formality – keeping up appearances like Donna Anna (*'Io moro!'*)* dancing the minuet at Don Giovanni's ball.

The last movement spins the listener round, speeding him out of the building amid constant echoes of a single theme, speeding him not only powerfully but as it were cathartically: tension is released after an emotional experience, if not an ordeal. It should seem a long time since the impressive sounds which created the threshhold of the whole symphony, and yet positive reminiscences of the first movement can be heard; there are pauses and reflective passages in the progress towards the burst of final, full orchestral brightness with which Mozart illumines, even as he closes, the doorway between art and life.

He noted the new symphony in the list of his work, the '*Verzeichnüss*

* 'I am dying!'

aller meiner Werke' on 26 June. On 25 July he listed another new symphony completed, that in G Minor (K.550). For Mozart a month was a long time in which to compose a symphony, and he had meanwhile produced some other works. What is remarkable is not the space of time between the two symphonies, but the almost savage shift in key, scoring and mood. The G Minor seems like a symphony of strings, so prominent are they throughout, while the wood-wind is plaintive against their often violent passion. Beside the grandeur of the previous symphony, its structure is vulnerably frail. After the weight of that assured architecture, it seems scarcely architectural: a skeletal cage for some gaunt, pining bird, rocked – before the symphony is over – by shuddering gusts which bring a deadly chill.

Once before, at Salzburg in 1773, Mozart had written a symphony in G Minor, a harshly expressive work (K.183) which has sometimes been explained as due simply to encountering Haydn's symphonies in minor keys. The explanation may possibly serve for that instance, but will not help much over the quintet in G Minor of 1787, widely recognized as intense and disturbing. The second symphony in G Minor would in itself seem further to confirm Mozart's association of the key with particularly troubled, passionate sensations. That it is the key chosen for Pamina's bleakly tragic aria 'Ach, ich fühl's' in *Die Zauberflöte* makes this quite explicit, and what is unrelieved in the aria is more overwhelming in the symphony because of fragments of lyrical relief when a blessed peace seems about to descend – only to be lost again in the sombre agitation of the strings.

It was on the day after completing the E flat symphony that Mozart had written the despairing letter to Puchberg, speaking of those 'black thoughts' which assailed him amid the pleasant, quiet atmosphere of his new lodgings. Because that symphony appears to explore a less harsh and hopeless world than does the G Minor, it does not exactly follow that Mozart excluded all personal sensations from his music. The E flat symphony's structure of artistic, optimistic coherence may well paradoxically be shaped by the composer's awareness of incoherent, worrying, daily existence. Mozart's position did not improve. If the first symphony shows him capable of outsoaring circumstances, the G Minor seems in part to reflect quite clearly 'black thoughts'.

Such an equation has perturbed some critics who fear too pat a correlation between an artist's life and his art, but the artist's personality can hardly remain unaffected by experience. Of course, Mozart may have privately overcome – perhaps had necessarily to overcome – his actual sensations of misery and despair, before they could find any expression in the music of the G Minor symphony. But it cannot be denied that he had undergone those sensations. It would be a strange obtuseness to refuse them any part whatsoever in the most starkly despairing of his symphonies; and to argue that they are not present there because they apparently play no part in either the E flat or the 'Jupiter' symphonies is to show a poor acquaintance with the human mind. (Some judicious disagreement round this point is recorded by the editors of *The Mozart Companion* with their contributor E. Larsen, who is particularly anxious to believe that Mozart remained 'classic' and that both G Minor symphonies are just examples of Mozart 'seeking to master all the varieties of expression'.) It may be worth adding that even if the 'Jupiter' expresses such a very different mood, this itself could be explicable by the fact that so much pain had been poured into the vessel of the previous symphony.

The argument does not affect the art of the G Minor symphony, a work which remains largely unprecedented, even in Mozart's own explorations. Its piano beginning, followed by a rising agitation, prepares the listener for a new experience, confirmed by the equally soft, singingly soft, slow movement where occasionally the woodwind call like curlews over desolate land but where again the strings gather to rise tensely, almost disruptive in their effect. The opening of the minuet is macabre, so driving, dynamic and dark is it, looming over the unexpectedly tranquil trio which takes on a symbolic quality of bravery: a brief patch of candlelight, snuffed out in the draught, as with eerie rhythmic haste the last movement begins. There seems a profound irony in Mozart's marking this movement 'allegro assai', for there is little enough joy in the protesting strings and the interventions of the woodwind are frankly wistful. Only once does the pace slacken, and then with renewed urgency the whole orchestra is whipped on to desperate speed, itself turned aggressive in its frantically impelled, mercilessly controlled course towards what indeed seems, in the most bitter sense, conclusion.

After the experience of the E flat and G Minor symphonies – different in so many ways and yet so intensely personal – there is something disappointing in the monument of the C Major symphony, the 'Jupiter', noted as finished on 10 August. Even while being much praised, it has been called 'traditional' and, in comparison with the G Minor, 'somewhat reactionary'. The undoubted majesty of its opening and closing movements, with suggestions of almost pompous festivity, seem strangely impersonal, for all their attraction and invention. A wonderfully well-built palace, it might appear too patently well-built, as if for once in Mozart inspiration was not fused with execution, were it not for the andante cantabile slow movement. Within such palace walls that has all the touching unexpectedness of encountering a cradle; and there is throughout it a celestial lullaby quality, from the very specifically hushed opening bars (the strings played with mutes), which float a melody of total tenderness, to the faintly throbbing, no less hushed dying close in which the movement fades on the air. The melody seems all-powerful, despite its mildness, and its singing simplicity brings it un-scathed through disturbed, cloudy moments when something of the G Minor symphony's agitation is heard. The movement seems to speak, or rather to dream, of a peace so perfect that it becomes as poignant as anything in the previous symphony, and suggests its creator has now passed beyond struggling, 'all passion spent'.

But Mozart still meant to live. In November – after the extraordinary summer of intense poverty and creativity – he appeared again at a concert, as conductor and arranger of another man's music, again organized by Van Swieten. This time it was Handel, one of Van Swieten's 'chief comforters', in his own words, who was honoured. Van Swieten appears to have been a cold and even mean man, intelligent in his response to music but not always over-generous in financial help to musicians. What he wrote after Mozart's death suggests that he thought Mozart promising: had he lived he would have attained the goal represented by the Bachs and Handel.

Van Swieten must be admired for his devotion to Handel, whose true greatness as a composer, especially of opera and oratorios (other than *Messiah*), is even now only slowly being recognized. In November 1788 he selected the faultless, lyrical and touching pastoral *Acis and Galatea* for performance in connection with the society he directed, a society of noblemen supporting classical music. Yet in many ways, a performance of at least one of the symphonies Mozart had so recently written might have more truly supported the cause of music; not for the first or last time, 'classical' seems to have got equated with 'dead'. Van Swieten un-doubtedly felt something of this himself, since he got Mozart in effect to modernize Handel's orchestration. It was presumably in this arrange-ment that Count Zinzendorf listened to the work some ten years later and found it charming. Yet perhaps the ravishing work, with its neatly poetic text, still sounded faintly old-fashioned, the more so possibly to Mozart's ear when he heard the actual singers of Galatea and Acis: Madame Cavalieri and Valentin Adamberger, the first Constanze and Belmonte of his own *Entführung*. In fact he conducted only one public performance of *Acis and Galatea* which, was positively for his own benefit. Perhaps it brought some financial aid, encouraging him yet once more to move back – as he soon did – into Vienna.

Nevertheless, by the time another summer came round, he was in an even more desperate situation than in the summer of the year before. And one should not judge Van Swieten too harshly. A fortnight after Mozart sent out a list inviting subscribers to a newly projected series of concerts, only one person had bothered to put his name down: Van Swieten.

3

A new worry developed for Mozart in 1789 and remained with him for the rest of his life. It was not his own health but Constanze's which seemed abruptly to give way. She was the one certain thing in his life, in so far as her health and her affection (closely connected) were certain. The last months before his final illness were spent in doing everything to cure her; and since she outlived him for more than fifty years, she must be accounted to have recovered remarkably well.

In 1789 Constanze was twenty-seven. During the seven years of her marriage she had borne four children and was for most of that year pregnant with a fifth. Pregnancies and desperate poverty may well have begun to affect her health, but she had not in fact had to endure such regular pregnancies as many women of the time. Mozart's mother, for example, had given birth to five children in the first five years of marriage. The nature of Constanze's illnesses remains vague, but some of her troubles – such as a complaint involving her foot – do not seem to have been so very grave. It is sometimes hard to read with patience of her minor stomach upsets, over which Mozart advised her as carefully as if she were a child, when one recollects that her husband was so soon going to die.

Most of the last summer of Mozart's life was spent by Constanze at the small sulphur-springs resort of Baden, some miles from Vienna, and there her incautiously flirtatious behaviour seems often to have worried him almost as much as her health. Her convalescence and treatment also naturally cost money, but Mozart hoped that the result would be to keep her well throughout the following winter. By then not many of his hopes were realized, except for this one.

Mozart's own awareness of Constanze was possibly sharpened from 1789 onwards by fears for her as well as by absence from her. Besides, all else except love was failing. For the first time since their marriage, he was to travel without her, travelling because there seemed more prospect of earning money out of Vienna. Because they were separated so much in these last three years, they needed to write to each other. Constanze's letters are lost, very probably destroyed by her in some fit of shame or indifference. Mozart's mostly survive. By then he had stopped writing to Nannerl and, apart from needing frequently to beg from Puchberg, had scarcely any other correspondent. And so Constanze was the recipient of the last, still amusing, and most deeply affectionate letters of all. They may not help one decide whether Constanze loved Mozart, but they prove how fiercely he felt love for her.

Something of this love perhaps overflowed to include her family, beyond whom and Puchberg, and one or two pupils, there existed only acquaintances. The Weber family had virtually replaced his own family. He had joined it, as he had twelve years before told Leopold he would like to. Aloysia Lange and her husband may have receded somewhat from the original intimacy, though references by Mozart in 1789 to a portrait for which Constanze was then sitting could well be to a painting of her by Lange. Aloysia herself travelled considerably during 1789, singing in various German cities. Her husband was a talented painter, as well as a gifted actor; he had earlier painted both Constanze and Mozart, and his unfinished portrait of Mozart at the clavier is probably the most convincing image of what Mozart looked like.

It was Constanze's other sister, Josefa, and her husband Franz Hofer, a court violinist, who now seem to have become particularly close friends. Mozart refers to them a great deal in his late letters, and not only because Josefa sang in *Die Zauberflöte*. Constanze's younger sister, Sophie, the only unmarried daughter, was also a frequent visitor; Leopold had mentioned her more than once when staying in Vienna, and Sophie was assiduous in visiting Mozart during his last illness. She it was who managed to persuade a priest to come to his bedside when he was dying; and she was there herself when he died. Mozart seems to have become almost fond too of old Madame Weber, as she of him; some sort of reconciliation may have taken place, possibly made easier after

Leopold's death. Sophie later recalled how Mozart used to bring her mother little presents of coffee and sugar. The two women soon reciprocated with the rather tragic gift of a bedjacket, specially designed to be put on frontways, when Mozart's body had swollen and he was too ill to turn in bed; they also made him a quilted dressing-gown for use after his recovery, but it was never needed.

Constanze's health became Mozart's theme: '*gardes votre santè si chere et precieuse a votre epaux*,'* he wrote in his individual French orthography, when he was at Prague on Good Friday 1789. The year had begun with his writing an aria and some German dances, and also the short but perfect piano B flat sonata (K.570), yet one more piece of artistic order created amid the confusion of existence. He was again involved in orchestrating Handel – this time, *Messiah* – for a concert performance at which Aloysia Lange sang and he conducted.

Among the audience was quite possibly the music-loving Prince Karl Lichnowsky, a freemason and a pupil of Mozart's. He held officer's rank in the Prussian Army and was due to travel on one of his periodic visits to the court at Potsdam, where Frederick William II encouraged music no less keenly than had his uncle Frederick the Great. Prince Lichnowsky offered Mozart the chance to travel with him, via Prague and Dresden. At any time it might have been a tempting suggestion, but especially so in the continuing barren climate of Vienna. Mozart had hastily to borrow money to accompany Lichnowsky, and probably to provide for the household of Constanze and their son Karl in his absence. For Lichnowsky's proposal meant a parting of some weeks. Mozart was always affected by such partings, and before leaving he wrote a quite serious poem, expressing how little he would estimate the praise and honour he hoped to gain at Berlin without Constanze joining in. He longed for the moment of happy reunion:

> *aber Thränen – Trauerthränen – fliessen*
> *noch ehvor – und spalten Herz und Brust.*†

When the sad actual day of departure came, he carried with him a small portrait of Constanze, and his own letters to her describe how he greeted this every morning and regularly said goodnight to it ('*Gute Nacht, Mauserl, schlaf gesund*').‡ Well aware of how stupid such things

---

* 'Look after your health, which is so dear and precious to your husband.'
† But tears – tears of sorrow – still flow
  – and split my heart and breast in two.
‡ 'Good Night, little mouse, sleep well.'

might seem at least to the world – '*dummes (für die Welt wenigstens)*' – he asserted how far from stupid they were 'to us who love each other so intensely'. When he wrote this, it was only six days since he had left Constanze, but already it seemed a year. As he travelled on, the more frankly did he express his physical longings for her – with such frankness indeed that her second husband tried to scratch out some of the passages in the letters which graphically describe his excitement at the prospect of being again in bed with her.

Yet even amid these assurances, there sound some hints of anxiety. The concern with Constanze's health hid one other, no less important, obsession: Constanze's attitude to Mozart. When he again and again emphasized his love, his heartfelt love as her husband, he was asking – sometimes openly – for some reciprocal declaration. 'Do you think of me as often as I of you?' he questioned her. Something of the tone of Constanze's replies can be deduced from Mozart's begging her to give more details when she wrote; and he reminded her that the length of her letters should not be regulated by the length of his, often written hurriedly during a short pause on the journey. Whatever Constanze managed to write, she appears to have thought Mozart's absence an opportunity for enquiring – with a sort of coy obtusity – if he had forgotten her.

Mozart neatly tabulated a series of requests to her which reveal, along with assurances of his love, his fears. He asked her to take care of her health and not to be sad, not to go out walking alone and to be careful in her conduct, '*auf* Deine *und* Meine Ehre',* and to pay attention also to *appearances* (his italics). Something in Constanze the married woman and mother kept alive that girl who had shocked her fiancé by her behaviour during their engagement. And it was not just jealousy which prompted Mozart's fears.

As his travels continued, it became clear that they were not contributing to a dramatic improvement in his fortunes. '*But I shall not make much,*' he emphatically explained, having mentioned that the Queen of Prussia had asked him to play for her. A previous concert at Leipzig had been a financial disaster. So, he told Constanze, she must be more delighted to have *him* back than with the *money*. It was a strange stipulation to make between two people who were supposed to love each other intensely. Mozart was, in effect, providing the love on both sides. He had to stimulate, if not create, Constanze's affection for him, even while he clung to her with all the tremendous affection of which he was capable.

* 'for *your* and *my honour*.'

Perhaps it is not surprising that he, as well as she, was taken seriously ill when he got back to Vienna in the summer.

As usual, he had started on his travels hopefully. At Prague there had been old friends to meet, the near-promise of being commissioned to write a new opera and flattering messages from Berlin conveying the King's anxiety that he would really go there. Although Mozart missed seeing Madame Duschek, he learnt that she was in Dresden, his own next stop on the journey. A delightful reunion took place: 'a large party . . . ugly ladies whose kindness made up for their lack of beauty,' Mozart wrote with Jane Austen-style crispness. At a hastily-improvised concert he accompanied Madame Duschek while she sang arias from *Figaro* and *Don Giovanni*; the next day he played the 'Coronation' piano concerto at court. The following day he lunched with the music-loving Russian anbassador and in the afternoon challengingly displayed his ability as organist to a group who included the organist Hässler, the pupil of a pupil of Bach's. The day closed with a visit to the 'truly wretched' opera, to hear Cimarosa's *Le trame deluse*.

A few days later he reached Leipzig, Bach's own city. There he improvised on the organ of St Thomas's Church, where Bach had been Cantor (in charge of choirs and choir-schools) for twenty-seven years. Bach had died in 1750, but a pupil of his was now *Cantor*, and the son of the organist in his time was now organist. These two men manipulated the stops while Mozart played, suitably improvising – among his themes – on a Bach chorale. It was a moving occasion: a spiritual meeting of two supreme musicians from very different worlds, and Bach's pupil is recorded as having felt in Mozart's playing that his old master had come back to life.

Agreeable as all this was, however, it solved none of Mozart's problems. He hastened on to the Prussian court at Potsdam, where he rapidly, tactfully, produced some pianoforte variations (K.573) on one of the king's favourite pieces of music, a minuet by the court composer, Duport. Although probably received politely, Mozart seems to have gained little positive from the days spent there. His letters thence to Constanze are lost. Hers to him at the same period went astray or were delayed, so that his whole stay at Potsdam passed agonizingly without hearing anything from her. He returned to Leipzig, where Madame Duschek had arrived, and together they gave a concert which was splendidly applauded but poorly recompensed. Two of Mozart's finest arias – 'Bella mia fiamma', probably, and 'Ch'io mi scordi di te' – two mature piano concertos and portions of two unidentified symphonies were included in a programme which may make posterity weep for envy of those who heard it, and for shame that humanity would not pay for such a privilege.

Mozart had now been away from Vienna some five weeks and only Berlin remained unvisited. In mid-May, after the Leipzig fiasco, he arrived there. Although in favour with the king, he had not much else to boast of. Lichnowsky had borrowed money from him, and had then travelled on elsewhere. The king did not wish him to organize a public concert at Berlin, though he heard Mozart play at court and may just conceivably have suggested that he might like to leave Vienna and settle there instead. Certainly he gave Mozart two commissions, for some easy piano sonatas for his daughter and for a set of six string quartets, in which he himself would take the 'cello part. And while Mozart was in Berlin *Die Entführung* was performed there once again.

On the evening of perhaps that actual performance the sixteen-year-old Ludwig Tieck, an admirer of Mozart's work despite the then fashionable preference in Berlin for Dittersdorf, spoke to a small, ordinary-looking man in a grey topcoat who was glancing over the music-desks in the orchestra while the auditorium was still empty. As they got into conversation, Tieck said how much he admired Mozart's operas. The stranger appeared interested, remarking that it was good of the young man to be fond of them. The theatre filled; the older man was called away, but Tieck felt some urge to discover his identity. He learnt he had spoken to the great composer himself. More than sixty years later he described this convincingly straightforward and moving incident. Mozart must have been touched, encouraged too, by such a youthful enthusiast; Tieck's artless homage perhaps meant more than King Frederick William's commissions, for he worked only very slowly on them and never completed either.

Travelling much faster than he had come, he was back in Vienna on 4 June, the exact day he had twice mentioned to Constanze. He looked for, and perhaps got, a family welcoming party to drive out and meet him: Constanze ('*Vergesse auch den Carl nicht,*'* he reminded her), and Hofer, as well as Herr and Frau von Puchberg. This is virtually the extent of the circle on which he could rely; within a very few weeks he was relying again on one member of it, Puchberg, '*meinen einzigen Freund*',† in total, humiliating misery.

* 'Don't forget Carl.'   † 'My only friend.'

Straightaway in June he completed the first of the 'Prussian' quartets (K.575), but its completion was probably an effort. Tired and dispirited as Mozart had previously been, he had never before had to face the additional double blow of his own illness and Constanze's. Unprecedentedly he turned back to some of his much earlier sketches for quartets, utilizing these as some spur to inspiration for the quartet in D Major. Not until May 1790 did he finish the next quartet.

The listener to the D Major quartet may wonder as it begins if even Mozart can throw off weariness, worry, and for once perhaps some self-doubt. Its opening is so light, so slight in its pleasingness and faintly insipid. He had called the creation of the 'Haydn' quartets a '*laboriosa fatica*', and then he had been in health and spirits. In the new series of quartets there was also a further technical-creative problem of giving prominence to the royal commissioner's 'cello playing; but eventually this very problem may have provided an impetus, because in the last movement the 'cello leads the way into confident, sustained melody, achieving quite novel texture. Something of Mozart's increasing tendency towards simple, most masterly simple, effects – apparent in the andante cantabile of the 'Jupiter' Symphony and governing the last piano concerto of 1791 – is felt in the quartet's slow movement, but grows with a sense of power steadily accumulating, like ripples of melodic wave, lapping and creaming into liquid beauty.

This gradual growth is perhaps a deliberate artistic contrivance, and the first movement is as markedly light as it is soft (its opening being with the unusual direction 'sotto voce') in order that the finale shall emerge the more boldly; and there the 'cello not only leads but demonstrates its virtuosity, reminding one that the king must have been a highly accomplished amateur performer. With this first quartet finished, Mozart paused.

It was impossible to continue. His own illness prevented him from earning any money. The attempt at organizing subscription concerts died after Van Swieten proved their sole supporter. In July Constanze was acutely ill. For a brief period Mozart seems to have feared for her life, but as she grew better there arose the problem of her convalescence and the Mozarts' new doctor, Dr Closset, recommended the expensive cure of her going to Baden. This time, despite the desperate circumstances, Mozart scarcely dared approach Puchberg to lend him yet more money. Face to face with Puchberg, he had not been able to ask outright, but was reduced to writing him a long letter; and even then he hesitated to send it: '*Ach Gott! – ich kann mich fast nicht entschliessen, diesen Brief abzuschicken! – und doch muss ich es!*'* Finally, on 14 July – the day the Bastille was stormed in Paris – he despatched it. He asked for Puchberg's forgiveness as well as his help. Still he asserted his belief, from the depths of his present despair, that his appalling situation was only temporary; in the long run it would improve.

Puchberg too must have hesitated. For three days Mozart heard nothing from him, and meanwhile Constanze's condition fluctuated alarmingly before improving. On the third day Mozart could wait no longer. He wrote again, imploring Puchberg to send, lend, give him some money; later that same day Puchberg responded with the sum of 150 gulden, almost a fifth of Mozart's annual imperial salary.

And this loan or gift seemed to signal that brighter future in which Mozart went on believing. Constanze was able to go off to Baden, where Mozart spent a few days with her in August before returning to Vienna for a revival of *Figaro*. For this he wrote two new arias for a new Susanna, Madame Adriana Ferrarese del Bene, whose concocted name sufficiently indicated her provenance from Ferrara. The new words were probably provided by da Ponte, who had a fresh personal interest in the opera because Madame Ferrarese was his current mistress.

This revival seems to have been a distinct success. It served as a reminder that Mozart was alive, but not employed. During the autumn he received a large and life-enhancing commission: a new opera was ordered by Joseph II, with da Ponte as the librettist. Madame Ferrarese and her beautiful and possibly more talented sister, Louise Villeneuve, would appear as the two leading singers in it. Probably relying for once on his own invention, da Ponte for the last time proved that working with Mozart truly inspired him. He delivered the libretto of *Così fan tutte*, a modern story about two sisters who do indeed come from Ferrara.

The arrival of Puchberg's 150 gulden probably released the acute block in Mozart's creativity. He wrote not only the new arias for *Figaro* but very soon afterwards provided some for Louise Villeneuve to sing in other composers' operas. The virtuoso clarinettist and freemason, Anton Stadler, was also provided with something at least as much his property: the beautifully mellow Clarinet Quintet (K.581), which Mozart himself called 'Stadler's Quintet', a work touched with autumnal premonition and suitably entered in his '*Verzeichnüss*' on Michaelmas Day.

* 'Oh God! – I can scarcely bring myself to send this letter! – and yet I must!'

No instrument is more Mozartean than the clarinet. He had been fond of it since his Mannheim days and only the year before had used it with haunting effect in the E flat symphony. Its bitter-sweet flavour and its ability to move from almost overcharged cloying tone to bubbling *buffo* noises – stirring the listener to a gamut of sensations, in which pleasurable melancholy predominates – represent much of Mozart's own ability and flavour. 'Stadler's Quintet' moves at times into a deeply romantic world, emphasizing how late in the century it was written; and at the same time, its romantic qualities are a matter of character rather than chronology, linking Mozart to Brahms and Mahler. Such qualities, like the instrument, are carefully controlled. The clarinet is never allowed to upset the balance of what remains an ensemble; and among the subtle effects achieved none is perhaps more subtle than the use of the strings, which sometimes gently but insistently drive like fine rain across the receding note of the clarinet, or elsewhere (as in the last movement) briefly evoke their own private quartet party.

The quintet opens lyrically and the clarinet is quickly heard, mellow, shimmering, ranging: moving among the strings with a sweetness which clothes any obtrusion of its virtuoso abilities. In the subsequent larghetto, it sails reflectively like a silver swan, borne on a tide of hushed strings with such slow grace that it creates an overwhelming tension. So much long-drawn, piled richness, where silver seems gradually turning to gold and the swan becomes a drifting leaf on a lake overhung by the misty, murmuring strings, is almost too piercingly intense in its beauty. It is replaced by a very consciously courtly minuet, the clarinet restricted at first to taking equal part with other instruments – rapid return to a typical indoor eighteenth-century mood, which broadens from courtly into country dance, allowing the clarinet some cheerful flourishes. The last movement is a series of miniature movements, variations on a theme perkily proposed by the strings but turned abruptly sober and then sadly, disturbingly slow, before closing in typical liveliness. The alternating moods of this last movement, where the clarinet too alternates in predominance with the strings, form perhaps one of the most brilliant single demonstrations of Mozart's ability to bathe the listener's mind with every nuance of emotional light and shade; and it seems no accident that the clarinet should be so fully involved in the demonstration.

Even while sketching the Clarinet Quintet Mozart was becoming preoccupied by his new opera. In December he could invite Puchberg

(*'Erschrecken Sie nicht über den inhalt dieses Briefes'*)* to join him and Haydn
at the rehearsals of it. The first performance took place on 26 January
1790. The opera is not a simple cynical joke about faithless women, as
has too often been supposed. Da Ponte to some extent sounded a warning note in his sub-title: 'The School for Lovers'. The nature of love –
that subject which interested both the librettist and the composer in
their different ways – is really the subject of the opera; lovers are seen
learning lessons about the emotions during its course, so that they will
live and love more sincerely as a result. The amusing tone in which most
of this is expressed, by the words and by the music, is simply part of
eighteenth-century enlightenment polish on works of art, which need to
entertain all the more when they mean also to instruct. To that extent
Così fan tutte is descended directly from *Le Mariage de Figaro*; in another
way it anticipates *Sense and Sensibility*.

Mozart had been profoundly humiliated, as well as distressed, by the
fiascos of 1789. His travels had helped him very little. The early summer
had been harrowing to the point where he could no longer work. It
might be said that, through no fault of his own, he was failing his own
wife and child. Yet, he certainly did not fail in affection. There he
remained rich. He saw Constanze installed at Baden and wrote to her
tenderly from Vienna just before the *Figaro* rehearsals began, assuring
her: *'Du hast einen Mann der Dich liebt . . .'*† All he could possibly do for
her, as he said, he did. But Constanze still worried him, and not on
account of her health. She had to be urged to trust in love: *'Habe
Vertrauen in meine Liebe . . . und Du wirst sehen wie vergnügt wir seyn werden.'*‡

Such phrases might almost be exchanges between the faithful lovers
Tamino and Pamina in *Die Zauberflöte*, agonizingly parted only to be
united happily to share and triumph over their ordeals. Constanze's
behaviour, however, was more likely to come wryly to mind during the
setting of *Così*, for she was not only displaying groundless jealousy about
Mozart (presumably about his life in Vienna without her) but was
passing her own time at Baden in a perturbingly flirtatious way. He
reminded her of what she had once admitted to him: that she might be
too 'yielding' (*'dass Du zu nachgebend seyst'*). And, even while trying to
cheer her and expressing his deep love for her, he asked her to stop being
too free with certain men. What had been general exhortation from the

---

* 'Don't get alarmed about the contents of this letter.'
† 'You have a husband who loves you.'
‡ 'Trust in my love . . . and you will see how happy we shall be.'

distance of Prague or Berlin had become humiliatingly specific. To the woman who had represented the one permanent point left, amid his uncertain circumstances and shaken health, he was now writing, longing to see her very soon – but regretting that she should sometimes make herself so cheap.

4

Così fan tutte apparently pleased. Da Ponte, who refers to it as *La Scuola degli Amanti* mentions it annoyingly briefly, but that aristocratic Viennese barometer Count Zinzendorf registered favourably, pronouncing the music charming and the subject quite amusing. Four performances followed quickly on the first night before a sheer piece of bad luck altered everything at Vienna, including the theatrical organization.

On 20 February 1790, the Emperor died. The theatres closed. Da Ponte hastily prepared an adroit ode, lamenting Joseph II's death and praising the virtues of the new emperor, Joseph's brother Leopold II; but neither this nor his writing the libretto for an imperial wedding festivity seemed to help. The changes at Vienna were quite soon to include his dismissal. Mozart, as usual, began by being intensely hopeful, believing that the new emperor – the Grand Duke of Tuscany into whose service eighteen years earlier his father had tried to manoeuvre him – would surely appoint him court *Kapellmeister*. Before the year was over, this hope had crumbled into bitter dust.

Così fan tutte was the last, perhaps the most perfectly plotted, of his 'comic' operas, the culmination of that long quest which had set off on a wild-goose chase with *L'Oca del Cairo*: for a new libretto, with two equally good female parts, one *seria*, the other *mezzo carattere*, 'both equal in *importance* and *excellence*', while the third female character might be entirely *buffa* (letter of 7 May 1783 to his father). Then Mozart had spoken of requiring seven characters. It is one aspect of the balanced quality of *Così* that the three female characters are matched by three male; except for a chorus (not necessarily seen) – and some silent servants – there are no other characters. As a result, the opera's domestic, even suburban (set on the outskirts of Naples) and intimate tone is increased. Its pattern is a dance one, centering on a quartet of lovers who start united, divide, meet again and exchange partners, before ending as they began, while the other two characters act as master and mistress of ceremonies, virtually calling the next figure to be performed.

Two romantically named and soulful sisters from Ferrara, Fiordiligi and Dorabella, have taken a villa on the Bay of Naples, where they are attended by the nastiest and pertest of all Mozart's maids, Despina. Two presumably local officers, also soulful though prosaically named Ferrando and Guglielmo, are the ladies' accepted lovers. A shrewd Neapolitan bachelor, Don Alfonso, much older ('*Ho i crini grigi*')* is a friend of the officers and an acquaintance of the ladies; he is also the pedagogic deviser of the plot, organizing a twenty-four-hour-long school for lovers in which they learn a great deal about the strengths, as well as the weaknesses, of the human heart.

Don Alfonso – usually carelessly described as a cynic – teaches them not merely so as to get a laugh at their expense or to win a wager. First he disillusions the men about their goddesses who, under pressure, turn out to be only too human, swaying in constancy and eventually succumbing to each other's lover when disguised. Then, when the officers rage against two such cheap creatures, he calms them with the cool, quite serious advice: marry the sisters. If women are changeable it is through their heart's need, '*necessità del core*'. The heart has its reasons, and human beings must be reasonable ('*Da ragion guidar si fà*').

Eventually, after the last amusing wrinkle of the plot has been shaken out, the opera ends with the four lovers taking his advice; joined by Alfonso and Despina, they sing a cheerful ensemble recommending everyone to be indeed guided by reason, and thus find calm in the midst of whirlwinds ('*bella calma troverà*'). The faintly marine metaphor is suitable to the opera's setting; and both music and words are magically full of the emotional elements – kind winds, amorous breezes, tempests breaking over rocks and even a pertinent reference to Vesuvius ('*un Vesuvio in petto*'). Don Alfonso turns out to be a bachelor matchmaker; more, the matches he has made, being based on good sense rather than exaggerated sensibility, are likely to endure.

Like *Figaro*, *Così fan tutte* ends happily. Yet it lacks any of the high summer happiness and 'rightness' of *Figaro*. Its flavour is more acrid, its solution more rational than instinctive, and Mozart's identification with his people (themselves less full of character) much more restricted. There is humour enough in *Così*, but the humour tends to be wry and even at times non-sympathetic; the composer seems occasionally to look at the quartet of lovers, increasingly entangled in a wood of the emotions, with something of Puck's untouched amazement: 'Lord, what fools these

* 'I have grey hair.'

mortals be.' Only one person, Fiordiligi, is motivated, and therefore wracked by real love; Mozart's heart goes out to her, and he gives her such sadly touching music when she is driven into a corner by Don Alfonso's plot, plus the cruel pressure exerted by her sister's lover, that he nearly disturbs the opera's cool balance. The experiment ceases to be either amusing or just. Could the man who had fallen deeply in love with one woman, yet later married her sister, too harshly judge Fiordiligi who truly loves Guglielmo but feels the dangerous attraction of Ferrando?

Da Ponte, too, had been in the position of loving two sisters, during his earlier stay in Dresden. He never could decide, he says in his *Memoirs*, which of them he preferred; and he is hardly likely to have forgotten this dilemma when his mistress, Madame Ferrarese, was joined at Vienna by her beautiful sister, Louise Villeneuve. Da Ponte may well have wondered if he had not made the wrong choice. Certainly it would be surprising if he, with his notorious susceptibility, felt nothing for Madame Villeneuve – especially since her sister was not only ugly but, at least in theatrical circles, increasingly unpopular.

However unclear the personal associations which contributed to *Così*, the opera is not merely domestic and middle-class but entirely contemporary. Its sole exoticism is its setting in Naples, a city known, however, to Mozart (*'Heunt racht der Vesuvius starck,'** begins a boyhood letter in dialect thence, to Nannerl) though not known to da Ponte. Apart from the more attractive geographical setting, Naples might be Vienna, for all it affects the actual plot. Five of the six characters are entirely equal socially; and this equality is partly expressed in the exceptional number of ensembles, especially in the first half, which – as usual with da Ponte – is also the better constructed.

There are other touches of the contemporary (i.e. 1790), such as the sister's sensibility, which make nonsense of the average production where Fiordiligi and Dorabella are tricked out in vaguely Louis xv wigs and made generally to appear ready for presentation at court instead of enjoying seaside life. Their world is better represented by Madame Vigée-Lebrun's fashionable portraits, with light, graceful draperies and shady hats in modishly simple style; and where an almost swimmingly sensuous sensibility is equally modish. *'Une âme'* was what versifiers praised in Vigée-Lebrun's portraits. That is partly the target of da Ponte's satire, translated into a sort of gushing emotionalism which, with

* 'Today Vesuvius is smoking strongly.'

typical topicality, is stirred by nature. *'Che vezzosi arboscelli!'** Dorabella exclaims in their own garden after Fiordiligi has commented on the lovely weather, as they hesitate about pairing off with the strange men who are in fact their lovers disguised. A garden, so movingly made the setting for the triumph of true love in *Figaro*, is in *Così* part of the conspiratorial atmosphere which weakens the two women: breezes and trees and warm weather seduce them scarcely less than the men. *'Ah, correte al giardino,'†* Don Alfonso urges the sisters who – up till then – have resisted temptation. Only a few minutes later, Dorabella, the weaker sister, is handing over her lover's miniature during a love duet with her new wooer. And it is hard not to think of one final, ironic, contemporaneous aspect: Constanze Mozart flirting away on walks at Baden, with her tendency to be 'too *yielding*'.

Even more closely than before, probably, did Mozart and Da Ponte collaborate on an opera which was entirely theirs – in several senses. As usual, da Ponte doubtless emphasized the need to be funny; he provided Despina with some disguises – now, glancing at Dr Mesmer, as a doctor armed with a magnet, and now as a lawyer – which are funny to the point of farce, but perfectly planted and mercifully quite brief. Also, this use of Despina draws attention again to the economical restriction of the characters, as well as to her mean little nature (tricking her mistresses is for her a pleasure and a matter of hard cash). Like Leporello, she is a rebellious servant; like him, her first appearance declares it: *'Che vita maledetta è il far la cameriera!'‡* She is exactly the reverse of Susanna – or Susanna seen by a misanthrope (and her bossy behaviour is consciously indicated by her name, which in Greek means 'mistress', as pointed out by Brigid Brophy).

Despina serves not merely as comic relief and, when bribed, as Don Alfonso's accomplice. She anticipates Alfonso's *'Così fan tutte'§* with the female answer of *'Così fan tutti'.‖* When her mistresses tell her despairingly that their lovers have gone off to the wars (this being Alfonso's ruse to test the ladies' faithfulness; the lovers have in fact gone off only to return grotesquely disguised), she breaks into a cynically amused little aria: 'In uomini, in soldati, sperare fedeltà?' Her cynicism comes from personal

---

* 'What charming shrubs!'
† 'Ah, run to the garden.'
‡ 'What an accursed life is a chambermaid's!'
§ 'That's how all women behave.'
‖ 'That's how all *men* behave.'

experience: '*In noi non amano che il lor diletto.*'* That is the type of accusation Marceline in *Le Mariage de Figaro* – and real women increasingly during the century – had made: their pleasure achieved, men desert or despise women. 'Pay them out in their own coin,' is Despina's advice ('*Paghiam, o femmine, d'equal moneta . . .*'). Nasty, short (surely) and brutish, Despina sees the relationship between man and woman, typically in a financial metaphor, as a matter of each trying to win at the other's expense. It is to be a perpetual battle.

And perhaps that was da Ponte's outlook. Alfonso – closer probably to Mozart – recognizes that both sides have their weaknesses. There is no rock-like constancy, no great unshakeable marriage of true minds (Fiordiligi seems, but is eventually unable to sustain her role as '*La Penelope, l'Artemisia del secolo*').† Modern men and women must settle for less. And it is this sobering realization that gradually tints the opera with a chilly hue as the sunny morning opening ('*Mi par, che stammatina . . .*,' Fiordiligi sighs ecstatically, '*. . . quando Guglielmo viene . . .*') ‡ fades before the fact of self-knowledge; the opera ends in the evening of the same day with rueful but useful recognition of human limitations.

This mood is not wintry but autumnal, rather. An autumnal bloom lies over much of the sensuous music, so delicately ironic because the characters sincerely believe in their own sensations (an effect often ruined on the stage by clumsy over-playing and misplaced archness) while they are experiencing them. When the officers sail away at the beginning of the plot, the trio for Don Alfonso and the two sisters wishes them calm seas and a prosperous voyage ('*Soave sia il vento*') with absolute, and enchantingly tender, seriousness; even Alfonso seems to have forgotten that the men are not in fact on their way to the battlefield, so softened is he – briefly – by the emotional, soulful climate.

There is no discrepancy between da Ponte's libretto and Mozart's music; they are complementary. The stingingly dry core of the story makes its effect just because it floats in such a richly beautiful liquid. (Perhaps it may be wrong, incidentally, to say that the Neapolitan setting is not significant; *dolce far niente* weather on a ravishing southern coast is possibly an ironic part of the beautiful atmosphere surrounding unbeautiful behaviour.) Had Rossini set da Ponte's libretto, the result would probably have alienated sympathy, and emphasized the funny

---

* 'In us they love nothing but their own pleasure.'

† 'The Penelope, the Artemisia of the century.'

‡ 'It seems to me, that this morning . . . when Guglielmo comes . . .'

and the mechanical, literally intriguing elements. Rossini was too much of a musical da Ponte. *Così* would have become the sort of heartless opera which it is still sometimes supposed to be, though that supposition is itself contradicted by any comprehension of Mozart – even before any scrutiny of the particular opera.

What is entirely typical of Mozart, and is prepared for in the libretto because it must have been tailored exactly to his requirements, is that one female character should truly express love. Even in *Don Giovanni* there was place for the faithful affection of Elvira, unrequited and in the end unable to save the man she loved. In *Così* it is Fiordiligi who gradually ceases to be, as it were, Dorabella's twin in silly sentimentality and becomes a loving but tortured woman. She cuts herself off from her sister and Despina, who find her scruples ridiculous; and in an opera of so many ensembles, her sad soliloquy-aria ('Per pietà, ben mio') comes as a striking illustration of loneliness. She apostrophizes the only person she thinks can help her: her supposedly absent lover, to whom she apologizes for having been shaken in her constancy. Hers was the slip of a loving heart (*'perdona all'error d'un' alma amante'*), and she is determined to keep faith. Entirely seriously, she decides to dress up in a spare uniform (that it is not Guglielmo's but Ferrando's, the man she is fleeing, is perhaps a psychological subtlety of da Ponte's). She intends Dorabella to take one of Guglielmo's. Together they will follow their men as far as the battlefield – and to death if need be (*'a loro fianco pugnar potremo e morir se fa d'uopo'*).

This is the spirit of Beethoven's Leonore or a Shakespearean heroine, as well as being fully Mozartean. And a tragic duet begins as she takes this resolution. For Ferrando has just discovered Dorabella's fickleness; in his anger he renews his assault on Fiordiligi with miserable fury, determined that she shall yield so that he can be revenged. She has hardly begun to sketch the joyful moment of being united with Guglielmo than the disguised Ferrando bursts in on her.

His violently beguiling appeal is punctuated by her triply-repeated invocation *'Giusto ciel'*; and then, with the bewildered weakness of a battered animal, she yields indeed. A piercing cry of *'crudel'* is followed by utter lassitude: '. . . *hai vinto. Fa di me quel che ti par.*'* Melting music accompanies this pathetic collapse of the heroic figure whose first aria is the wonderfully defiant bravura 'Come scoglio', an impossible boast of human constancy. Fiordiligi's second aria shows her poignantly ad-

---

* '. . . you have won. Do with me as you think fit.'

vanced in self-awareness. Her humiliation is completed by Ferrando's renewed attack, itself made horribly convincing by his own humiliation. The would-be brightening of the duet, as Fiordiligi and Ferrando embrace, expresses the wavering, uneasy feeling of two people who know they are both guilty and unhappy. Even superficially it sounds cheerless and it cannot wipe away the accents of suffering which preceded it.

And perhaps Mozart felt, as everyone must, how worthless, or at least colourless, were the two men who between them wrack Fiordiligi. The whole of this last incident, in which Ferrando presses her far beyond any joking stage, for good reasons of his own, is witnessed by Guglielmo without any impetus to intervene. Such cruel vanity deserves the experience it undergoes. But at this point, the opera's sky is so deeply overcast that it has ceased to be a comedy in any light-hearted sense. A sour stalemate seems all that Don Alfonso has achieved. It is now that he lives up to the responsibility he undertook in engineering the plot, by virtually ordering the two men to marry the women. And after what we have seen of Fiordiligi's ordeal, he may well sing, '*Tutti accusan le donne, ed io le scuso*'.*

Fiordiligi has, however, a sister: that is, her character has a reverse side. Dorabella, who cannot even plead the excuse of being a servant, is Mozart's most unattractive woman: flighty from the first, deeply stupid and gradually slipping in her *mezza seria* role from the showy mock madness which she displays on the officers' departure ('*Smanie implacabili*') into a Despina-ish amorality: '*È amore un ladroncello*.'† Mozart, who had written to Constanze that it was through prudent behaviour that a wife held her husband, pinned up an example by contrast in this possibly ironically named person (in pidgin Greek a 'beautiful gift'):

> For I have sworn thee fair – more perjur'd I,
> To swear, against the truth, so foul a lie.

Shakespeare's attitude to trust betrayed, and his mind altogether, are strangely relevant to Mozart. In the progression of the operas, from *Die Entführung* onwards, there is much of the same pattern of evolution as in Shakespeare's plays: the exciting lovelorn mood of that opera might be compared with *Romeo and Juliet*. The confident optimism of *Figaro* is captured by *Much Ado* or, perhaps more closely, by *As You Like It*. Parallels between *Hamlet* and *Don Giovanni* have already been drawn by

---

* 'Everyone accuses women, and I forgive them.'
† 'Love is a pilfering rogue.'

Brigid Brophy (in *Mozart the Dramatist*). The royal-festive *Clemenza di Tito* and enchanted near-contemporary *Zauberflöte* are close to the late mood represented respectively by *Henry VIII* and *The Tempest*. As for *Così fan tutte*, while resisting the temptation to equate it with *Troilus and Cressida*, one may legitimately compare its ironic bitter-sweet mood to that of *All's Well that Ends Well*, a play which is normally agreed to be later than *Hamlet*, and of course precedes the group of late plays. Mozart compressed into a decade Shakespeare's development over some seventeen years, but then his was a much shorter life-span. And by 1790, Mozart himself must have been growing aware that his health, no less than Constanze's, had been badly shaken.

At least once earlier in Vienna he had narrowly escaped death, probably from some sort of severe chill. All the way back into his childhood there are records of colds and allied pains, caused apparently by rheumatism. In April 1790 he was suffering considerably from rheumatic pains; they affected his head and caused acute toothache – a sinister omen of the burning pains he was to feel in his head during the last stages of his fatal illness in the following year. In 1790 the chill was not easily shaken off, or Mozart caught another one when the summer came; by August he described his state to Puchberg as '*Krank und voll kummer und Sorge*'.*

Even before *Così fan tutte* was produced, he had had to borrow money from Puchberg against the payment it would earn. In late December 1789 Puchberg had responded with 300 gulden. In the following January he sent a further 100 gulden. The opera was comparatively well paid for, but the amount was just half what Puchberg had lent him in this brief period.

Mozart's hopes included finishing the six quartets for the King of Prussia and gaining a place at the new Austrian Emperor's court. He drafted a petition to the Archduke Franz, the Emperor's son, although the surviving draft breaks off uncompleted. However, he must have sent in some petition, for in May he believed it was a good sign that Leopold II had not so far rejected or accepted his application – though this delay was probably, in fact, without any significance. Whatever he asked was not granted. Illness and money troubles, which had probably now reached almost inextricable complications with borrowings from moneylenders as well as from Puchberg, accumulated as the year advanced. Constanze's health required her to spend part of the summer once again

---

* 'Ill and full of worries and cares.'

at Baden. One weary, short letter to her from this dreary time asks if she could not manage occasionally to write on her own initiative: *'muss es denn nur Antwort seyn?'* For a period Mozart joined her at Baden, because this arrangement was cheaper, but probably it was not easy to compose there. The first performance of *Così* since Joseph II's death brought him into Vienna again, still desperate for money, and apparently intending to write some piano sonatas.

But the *'Verzeichnüss aller meiner Werke'* had never had fewer entries than it had in 1790. By September Mozart had written two more Prussian quartets (K.589 and 590) and arranged some more of Handel's music for Van Swieten. Apart from completing *Così*, this was all he recorded in the nine months – an astonishing, significantly empty lapse of time that charts almost better than any words his state of mind. His position had returned to what it was when he first got himself dismissed from the Prince-Archbishop's service. Count Arco had indeed warned him: *'hier dauert der Ruhm eines Menschen sehr kurz.'** How bravely Mozart had riposted: *'Glauben sie denn, das ich in Wienn bleibe?'*† Yet he had remained in Vienna; and just as he had done in 1781, so in 1790 he looked round for some pupils: the last and least satisfying way of earning some money.

Probably one of the only two pupils he managed to find in 1790 (while willing to take up to eight) was Franz Xaver Süssmayr, then aged twenty-four. Mozart became fond of Süssmayr; he paid him the compliment of a nickname, 'Snai', and was soon to be making affectionate fun of him. Süssmayr took lessons in composition and theory; and Mozart on his deathbed gave him one final lesson, and a solemn charge, in entrusting to him completion of the Requiem.

Another pupil – possibly the other one of 1790 – who took a few piano lessons from Mozart around this time was Josef Frank, later a famous doctor. He recalled being received rather coldly by Mozart; and cold emptiness was Mozart's own description of his feelings in 1790. Temporarily, and only temporarily, his creative urge had congealed. With some hope perhaps of awakening it, as well as of making money and escaping from Vienna, he planned a new journey in the autumn: to Frankfurt, where Leopold II was due to be crowned as Holy Roman Emperor.

He recognized that he still possessed, even if it was no longer appre-

---

* 'A man's fame is very short-lived here.'

† 'Did you think I'm going to stay in Vienna?'

ciated in Vienna, his virtuoso talent as a performer. How little it was appreciated there was confirmed at the triple Habsburg wedding festivities on 19 September; three of the new Emperor's children were being married, and the musical celebrations entirely excluded Mozart and his work. But elsewhere it was a return to his boyhood role that seemed to offer the best chance of success. The very city of Frankfurt, which he had visited in 1763, had been the site of five concerts, one of which had been attended by the young Goethe. The journey led back largely through the past. Mozart was to see on his travels in 1790 so many people and places to stir the various, usually happier, associations of childhood and early manhood. It was like a farewell appearance. His father must often have come to mind; but probably he did not remember how at Frankfurt Leopold had scratched on a window-pane (still in existence) '*Mozart Maitre de la Musique de la Chapelle de Salzbourg avec Sa Famile, le 12 Aout 1763*'. Before that evocative memorial twenty-seven years later, Mozart's frozen state of mind might have melted into weeping.

In his fresh travels, accompanied by his brother-in-law Hofer, he was very much Leopold's son, crossing Germany with an eighteenth-century eye for architecture which was soon to be judged old-fashioned. Gothic Nuremberg he found hideous; but Neumann's Würzburg was a '*schöne, prachtige stadt*'.* About imperial Frankfurt itself, crowded for the coronation, he had little to say except concerning the people he met. He had barely settled in before he encountered Madame Porsch, who turned out to be a girl he and Constanze used to play hide-and-seek with at Madame Weber's house when he was first in Vienna. Acquaintances from Munich, Mannheim, even Salzburg, kept on appearing. The ex-court castrato from Salzburg, Ceccarelli, sang at a concert Mozart organized. Dorothea Wendling, the Ilia of the happy Munich première of *Idomeneo*, was another person from his past who had come to Frankfurt.

Yet, though Mozart probably seemed cheerful, even confident, he shrank from the need to be in company – another sign of unusual disturbance. '*Es ist alles kalt für mich*,' he wrote to Constanze ' – *eiskalt*.'† Absence from her, he assured her, was the cause of such feelings. So, perhaps, it was: she may have appeared a symbol of life and love, gleaming prospect of a distant, better future which he saw now only through tears. Their present separation warned him perhaps of

* 'Beautiful, splendid town.'
† 'Everything is cold as far as I am concerned – cold as ice.'

irreparable separation. As it continued, the strain grew greater: '*Als ich die vorige Seite schrieb; fiel mir auch manche Thräne aufs Papier* . . .'*

His letters were full of money problems and possible solutions. Constanze was instructed in detail about managing such affairs. Meanwhile, she and Karl moved to the last apartment they would occupy with Mozart: in the Rauhensteingasse, close to St Stephen's Cathedral and quite near to the house where she and Mozart had first had lodgings after their marriage. To return quickly, settle to work, take pupils: that seemed to him the best plan for the future. On the other hand, a temptation existed to travel 'even further', so as to try and bring back a large sum of money. Yet, even apart from separation, there was the aching uncertainty about whether further travels would achieve this. Frankfurt, filled with court officials, guests and visitors, applauded Mozart's concert – which included the 'Coronation' piano concerto (K.537) – but proved financially no more generous than Vienna. And 'Coronation' seems a bitterly ironic name to have got attached to a piano concerto played by a performer-composer who had no part in the celebrations. In travelling to Frankfurt, the Emperor had brought Salieri in his train. For the day after his ceremonial entry into the city, a performance of *Don Giovanni* was planned; it was cancelled and replaced by one of Dittersdorf's operas. On the coronation day itself, the mass was by the court composer at Mainz, Righini. Even on the morning of Mozart's privately-sponsored concert, competing attractions underlined his bad luck: some Prince gave '*ein gros Dejeuné*' and there were manoeuvres by the Hessian troops.

Mozart retreated. At Mainz – where a local newspaper with cruel carelessness announced him as in the service of Archduke Franz – the Elector asked him to play. At Mannheim, where he had first met Aloysia Weber, and indeed Constanze, the theatre put on *Figaro*; and an amusing incident paid tribute to Mozart's ordinary, commonplace appearance. An actor attempted to turn him away from listening to a rehearsal, supposing him an idle spectator. Surely you will allow *Kapellmeister* Mozart to listen, Mozart asked – and the actor later recorded his acute embarrassment at realizing the composer's identity. Reluctantly leaving Mannheim, Mozart sped through Augsburg and on 29 October reached Munich.

Karl Theodor was still the reigning Elector and was then engaged in entertaining the King of the Two Sicilies, a music-lover and father of

* 'While I was writing the last page, many tears fell onto the paper . . .'

two of the brides at whose wedding festivities in Vienna Mozart had not been required. Mozart was particularly asked by the Elector to remain in Munich to play for the king, and he commented sarcastically on the fine honour this did the Viennese court, '*dass mich der König in fremden Landen hören muss*'.* Several of Mozart's earlier Mannheim friends, including the Cannabich family, were still living at Munich. And there he met also a newly-married Frau Danzi, who was in fact an old pupil of Leopold's, Margarete Marchand, who had been at Salzburg in the summer of 1783 when Mozart and Constanze at last paid their wedding-visit.

Salzburg was near enough, if Mozart had cared to go on there after his pleasant, civilized interlude in Munich; and outside Salzburg, at St Gilgen, lived Nannerl. He passed by and stopped instead at Linz, with its rather more agreeable memories. Early in November he was back in Vienna, installed in the Rauhensteingasse apartment.

In a year when so much had stirred boyhood associations, it was suitable that England should suddenly reappear as a possible country to visit. Mozart may well have found waiting for him in Vienna on his return a letter from London, written in French by Robert O'Reilly, manager of an Italian opera season. O'Reilly asked him to consider a visit to London from December 1790 until June 1791, during which period he would compose '*au moins deux opéras, ou sérieux ou comiques*',† for three hundred pounds. The letter was to serve as a contract; Mozart had only to accept it.

An English music publisher, John Bland, had possibly visited him during the previous year, for in his catalogue of 1790 Bland claimed to have personally settled a connection with Mozart, as well as with Haydn, Vanhal and others. Earlier in 1790 the *Public Advertiser* (which in 1765 had once referred to the 'little German Boy' as the 'greatest prodigy' of Europe) mentioned a comic opera *mélange* performed at the King's Theatre, some of the music being by 'Hogart'. In this way was signalled Nancy Storace's singing of Susanna's 'Deh vieni' from *Figaro* and Zerlina's 'Batti, batti' from *Don Giovanni*: probably only the second English public performance of any music from Mozart's operas. In 1789 Nancy Storace had sung at the same theatre the Susanna-Count duet 'Crudel! perchè finora', with Benucci (the first Figaro) as the Count.

* 'That the King has to hear me in a foreign land.'
† 'At least two operas, either serious or comic ones.'

Mozart probably replied to O'Reilly, but if so the letter is lost. Perhaps he declined totally; perhaps he put off the opportunity for another year which never came. Since English musicians were not to forget Nannerl in poverty and illness at the end of her life, and were to send the dying Beethoven a hundred pounds 'to be applied to his comforts and necessities during his illness', it is natural to think that in London Mozart might at least have died in less penury than he suffered in Vienna. Or, possibly, he might have lived much longer. Certainly it is not fanciful to suppose that he too might have been able to write home that his arrival had caused a great sensation in London, just as Haydn could record, modestly but unmistakably, in January 1791.

In December 1790 a dinner was held in Vienna to say farewell to Haydn who, at the age of fifty-eight, was travelling to London for the first time. The German-born impresario Salomon had managed to tempt him with this prospect, after the death of his patron Prince Nicolaus 1 Esterházy. Salomon is said to have invited Mozart at the same time, to come in the following year. The parting between Haydn and Mozart is likely to have been painful. At that moment Mozart must have passionately wished he had accepted O'Reilly's offer, for the two composers could then easily have travelled together. Haydn's symphonies written in London might have been paralleled by Mozart's London operas. And yet, Mozart was to write two more operas, regardless of London. He chose to remain at Vienna; and if he wept at saying goodbye to Haydn, believing they would never meet again, it was probably of Haydn's death he thought, not of his own.

It is true that when they parted Mozart had less than a year to live. But the few months which remained were of such rich creativity – producing great operas and slight, delightful German dances, religious work like the *Ave Verum* as well as the *Requiem*, and the clarinet concerto as well as his last piano concerto – that they represent years by any ordinary standards. It was as if the frozen surface of 1790 had only increased the force of the energy which finally broke through. Never had Mozart's mind been more intensely vital than in the period that his body failed.

5

The Europe Mozart had known was dying. A few months before Leopold 11 travelled to Frankfurt for his imperial coronation, his brother-in-law, Louis XVI of France, attended another sort of ceremony on the Champ-de-Mars, celebrating the overthrow of the Bastille in the previous year. And there, before his people, Louis swore a new style of oath: to maintain the constitution decreed by a new body, the National Assembly. It was a very different event from the traditional ritual of a Holy Roman Emperor's coronation; it may have seemed something very distant too, at that time, to the new Emperor, and not totally displeasing. Though his sister was the Queen of France, he and his government were by no means sorry to see France weakened internally.

Gradually, however, the French democratic contagion spread. It became clear that not even emperors were safe. References to 'French principles, so fraught with danger at the present time . . .' Leopold personally soon specified as needing to be censored in Austrian newspapers. The futile flight of the French royal family to Varennes, and their capture, in June 1791 seriously alarmed him. Maria Theresia's old minister, Kaunitz, shrewdly indicated the threat that democracy in France could bring to every European sovereign: never again might each be able to bequeath 'an undamaged crown'. Mozart's patron, Frederick William II of Prussia, united with the Austrian Emperor to issue the Declaration of Pillnitz on 27 August 1791, a monarchic counterblast to democracy which, however, declared more than it meant to perform.

The Emperor certainly recognized that he must make some voluntary concessions to preserve his own sovereignty. Bohemia's future was particularly under review at the time he was in Prague in the autumn of 1791, when Mozart's coronation opera, *La Clemenza di Tito*, was performed in his presence for the first time; it may indeed have had some relevance, in its flattering references to a clement ruler, to Bohemia's hopes of benefits from Leopold. But the Emperor never lived to decide his policy for the country. He died three months after Mozart, while the imperial exchequer was still considering Constanze's application for a pension, granted after the Archduke Franz had succeeded to the throne.

Under the new emperor, Austria, joined by Prussia, at last went to war against France, only to be beaten at Valmy. The abolition of the French monarchy speedily followed. In January 1793 Louis XVI was guillotined. England and Holland and Spain turned on France. All Europe was at war. And places as far apart as Mainz, Mantua, Amsterdam, even Vienna, where the boy Mozart had demonstrated his wonderful virtuosity, now heard the gunfire which accompanied the birth of a new century, a new world and the arrival of Napoleon. The Holy Roman Empire was dismembered. Hieronymus Colloredo proved to be the last Prince-Archbishop of Salzburg. Europe faced a totally unexpected Emperor, with no lineage but ability, self-elected, self-crowned, who was also largely its conqueror. And it was the daughter of the one-time Archduke Franz, the great-granddaughter of Maria Theresia, who had to be handed over to Napoleon to become his Empress.

Mozart's last year of life was spent in the first floor apartment on the Rauhensteingasse. 'It was not without strange sensations that I ascended the identical stairs which he had so often passed,' Vincent Novello wrote in 1829, 'and down which he was at last brought down as a corpse.' The four-roomed apartment, to which Novello could not gain access, can be furnished retrospectively from the inventory made at Mozart's death. His few belongings, his own manuscripts, the music and books he still owned, provide perhaps the clearest, as well as the very last, view of his personal environment. Among his books alone could be traced something of a long, peripatetic career: Kirkby's *Automathes* (published in London, 1761) which Leopold had probably bought on the spot; a 1765 local guide-book to Venice; one part of the set of Molière which Fridolin Weber had given to Mozart at Mannheim in 1778, before he set out for Paris. A few volumes of the *Kleine Kinderbibliothek* (1783) were probably bought for Karl's benefit. A complete run of Cramer's *Magazin der Musik* (published at Hamburg up to 1789) provided a few printed references to Mozart, recognized as a composer whose music was at once great and yet difficult.

Such bare pebbles of fact are the more welcome amid the clouds of uncertainty which began to gather about Mozart in his last year and which still obscure the exact facts of his death, funeral and burial. Even harder to distinguish are the true facts about the genesis of his two last operas, not to mention the aura of mystery which was for long wrapped round the *Requiem*. What might have scarcely seemed significant had he lived took on a somewhat dangerous, faintly legendary, quality because he died. From that moment history and memory replaced actuality; and the possibly awkward shape of real recollection was slowly softened under the growing awareness that Mozart had been a tremendous genius, one of the very greatest of European artists, for all he had seemed just a pale, harrassed little man who died in debt and was buried virtually as a pauper.

A new role began for Constanze, relict of a genius, owner of his manuscripts and herself destined to become almost a venerated cult figure. In 1827 a visitor to a concert at Munich described how singers and audience – he became increasingly aware – were focusing on an ordinary-looking, plainly-dressed, middle-aged lady: 'She was *Mozart's widow!*' Two years later, Mary and Vincent Novello met her in Salzburg with such a shock of various emotions that Mary Novello at least 'could do nothing but weep and embrace her'.

By then the widow must have been well used to her own importance, but commonplace touches of Constanze Weber still showed through. Of her two husbands she remarked contentedly that 'she could not say which had been most kind to her, she could have wished to live for both . . .'. And Mozart might have smiled to hear her solemnly pronounce that she did not admire the plot of *Così fan tutte*. Trite sentiments dripped from her pen, just as they had done when she addressed her fiancé's sister some forty years earlier. It is difficult to believe that it was actually on the day of Mozart's death that she made the entry which appears in his album, lamenting his loss and protesting that he would never be forgotten by her or by the whole of Europe – for in 1791 'the whole of Europe' was little occupied with Mozart. If she did, still an unhappy stiltedness in writing (at which Mozart had often hinted) makes the entry more embarrassing than poignant; it would remain a disconcerting effusion for someone who was supposed on that day to be utterly prostrate with grief. But she dated it 5 December 1791.

Yet it was not apparently until 1808 that she bothered to go out to the cemetery of St Marx to try and find Mozart's grave. Neither she nor several of those who were supposed to be Mozart's close friends accompanied the coffin on its way to burial, although it is now known that the weather at the time was not the traditional storm of snow and rain once supposed, but positively mild. Mozart received the cheapest of all funerals. His coffin was placed in a common grave, unmarked and unrecorded. Constanze's tardy visit was hopelessly too late for the place to be located, but little has been lost as a result, except possibly the pious memorial she might have felt it decent by then to set up. As it was, her failure to provide any monument continued to scandalize Mozart's friends.

Privately, she probably never quite forgave her first husband for dying prematurely and leaving her with debts to face. In 1810 her second husband, Nissen, was pointing out to Karl Mozart that his father's personal estate had yielded less than Constanze had been promised in their marriage contract. And although only traditional, there seems something convincing in the flash of irritation revealed by her remark supposedly made when accidentally smashing Mozart's death-mask: she was glad the ugly old thing was broken.

That was a drastic disposal of the past. Mozart's real features no doubt began receding in Constanze's mind under the gentle pressure of flattering engravings, prettifying in Romantic fashion the appearance of the man, while she herself tinted his character with little water-colour dabs of early nineteenth-century sentiment. Her Mozart was so fond of picturesque scenery and flowers – perhaps he had been, but the claims sound remarkably uncharacteristic. Constanze seems nearer the truth when she said that Mozart had had no particular fondness for the '*plaisirs de la table*'; but then there can have been little opportunity for such things in a household Leopold Mozart had found 'highly economical' long before the extreme indigence of the last years.

Mozart's possessions at death might have served to furnish some pictures by Chardin: one tin teapot, three brass candlesticks, one lacquered despatch box, one old wardrobe and a small quantity of kitchen equipment. That is only a selection of the items which sparsely filled a few rooms, but simplicity and practicality are so totally the tenor of a fairly short inventory that the mention of a billiard table 'with 5 balls, 12 cues' comes as an unexpected luxury. Mozart's fondness for billiards was something Constanze did admit; and Mozart himself jokingly documents playing a lonely game two months before his death, while *Die Zauberflöte* was becoming a success, and just after Constanze had left Vienna for yet another period of convalescence at Baden: '*Spielte ich mit Hr. von Mozart (der die Oper beim Schikaneder geschrieben hat) 2 Parthien Billiard.*'* Apart from the billiard table, there was not much to value or cherish: one mirror, a papier mâché screen, one clock, one roll-top writing desk and, as well as the forte-piano with pedal, his viola. Equally plain and workaday were his clothes. There was no mention of Baroness Waldstätten's crimson great-coat, but his finest suit – of brown satin, silk-embroidered – is the very costume in which he had

* 'I played with Herr von Mozart (who wrote the opera at Schikaneder's) two games of billiards.'

appeared in the previous year at his 'Coronation' concert in Frankfurt.

Perhaps he wore it for what proved his last concert appearance
altogether, on 4 March 1791. This concert was organized across the road
from Mozart's apartment, by a clarinettist, Josef Bähr, who advertised
among the attractions singing by Aloysia Lange and a piano concerto by
Mozart. On 5 January Mozart had noted in his *Verzeichnüss* the completion of a new concerto (K.595), that serenely beautiful, remote work
which seems created with total indifference to public effect. An audience
mostly of connoisseurs attended, the *Wiener Zeitung* reported of Bähr's
concert, remarking that Mozart's composition, as well as his performance, was admired. If this is more than polite cliché, it hints at a
comprehension which had arrived too late; perhaps, however, it means
merely that the audience was small.

Whatever it meant, Mozart had probably decided to risk no more
energy by offering himself to the public as a concert-performer. From
Frankfurt in October 1790 he had assured Constanze of his new plans
for their happy existence: he would take pupils and also he would settle
to working intensely (*'wenn ich in Wienn fleissig arbeite . . .'*). Perhaps he
vowed to refuse no commission – however humble it might be. He was a
composer with unusual gifts of fertility, versatility and seemingly in-
exhaustible vitality. All he asked was to be employed.

In his willingness to take any opportunity that was offered he had
already begun at Frankfurt composing a piece for mechanical organ
(K.594), commissioned by Count Josef Deym, a military man turned
modeller in wax. Deym had a gallery at Vienna in which he exhibited
clocks and automata of a kind much loved by the eighteenth century.
Topically, he was putting on display a mausoleum, which was shared by
Joseph II, to the Austrian hero and victor at Belgrade, Count Lodon.
Suitable funeral music was to be played (possibly from within the monument) and it was this that Mozart struggled to supply, struggling because
the mechanical instrument was too high-pitched and childish for his
taste, and the task very odious ('. . . *es eine mir sehr verhasste Arbeit ist*'.)
But in 1791 he went on to write some further comparable work, very
probably also for Count Deym (who, before the year was over, was to be
responsible for taking Mozart's death-mask). Perhaps intended for one
of Deym's art-clocks was the organ fantasia (K.608), though it is more
severe and in parts closer to Bach than seems quite suitable for Deym's
purposes. The gallery exhibits included a mechanical canary, an appa-

ratus representing Pan with his pipes and another of a lady who appeared to play the piano, as well as 'the Bedroom of the Graces' where flutes and other instruments were heard.

The organ fantasia (K.608), if for Deym, is yet one more instance of Mozart transfiguring a trivial or routine commission into art. Other composers might well have written suitably cheerful tinkling music for what was scarcely more than a glorified musical-box; and probably most of the Count's public was anyway attracted by what there was to see, not to hear. Mozart takes his task quite seriously, so seriously that perhaps this music was intended to alternate with his earlier piece (K.594) for the Lodon monument. After an almost pungently forceful opening, it becomes mysterious; the organ seems to throb before passing briefly into a more mechanical, musical-box mood, itself replaced by such a glittering wealth of sound that one feels Mozart is once again himself seated at a real organ. In the power and invention, Count Deym and his wax-works are forgotten; it becomes more relevant to recollect Mozart improvising on the organ of St Thomas's at Leipzig, while Bach's one-time pupil watched admiringly.

Writing for Count Deym was only one aspect of Mozart's determination to make – as well as take – opportunities. The year 1791 had hardly begun before he had produced three children's songs (K.596–8) for an album of 'Spring Songs' which was dedicated to the Archduke Franz and his wife. By the time this album was published Mozart was working on some sets of German dances, a return and also a farewell to eighteenth-century occasional music: almost noisily hilarious but unfailingly tuneful, never too countrified not to be touched by that courtly gracefulness which was soon to seem insipid and out-of-date.

Mozart, the creator of divertimenti as well as dances, never forgot – even while never pandering to – the social purpose of music in his century. Before he was born his father had written that 'musical sledgeride' which took rather a long journey in making its joke; Mozart dealt with the theme more crisply in 1791, introducing ringing sleigh bells into the third of the German dances (K.605). And Count Deym's mechanical canary comes to mind in the fifth dance of another set (K.600), nicknamed 'the canary' and obviously imitating bird noises. There is, too, an echo of the peasant toys made near Salzburg, which Leopold Mozart had amusingly utilized in his 'Toy Symphony'. In such slight ways, Mozart might seem to be summing up a lifetime of music, even while preparing to make new use of birds, bells, Pan pipes, and a flute, in the opera which by the spring of 1791 was probably under discussion: *Die Zauberflöte*.

The instigator of this was Emanuel Schikaneder, another figure originally associated with Mozart's days at Salzburg. His travelling company of actors had been wandering all over Germany and Austria before they settled in Salzburg in the autumn of 1780 for some six months. There Schikaneder became friendly with the Mozart family, who were among the most regular attenders at the theatre. Soon they had free passes to all his productions, and he was invited to join their air-gun diversions; he bought a specially fine gun for the purpose. Mozart had also promised to write an aria for him, just at the time of preparing *Idomeneo*. He managed to get this done, and Leopold was able to report Schikaneder's delight with it and its successful reception when sung. Schikaneder had turned up in Vienna, after Mozart's marriage, and had been in charge for a period of the Kärntnertor Theatre, where his first season opened with *Die Entführung aus dem Serail*. His was the company forbidden by the Emperor to act *Le Mariage de Figaro* in 1785. He moved from Vienna to organize the theatre at Regensburg, his native city, but returned in early 1789 and took over the Theater auf der Wieden in the suburbs. For a fairly humble, essentially popular theatre and its public, he put on comic or 'heroic-comic' operas, the latter pantomime-style works which mingled magic, spectacle and clowning – often taking a prominent role himself.

Like Mozart, Schikaneder was a mason, though he did not, it seems, join a lodge at Vienna; and so was Bauernfeld, Schikaneder's financial backer, who contributed an entry to Mozart's album. Before 1791 Mozart never mentions Schikaneder in his letters during the years in Vienna, but they had presumably remained friendly. Constanze's sister, Josefa Hofer, had joined the company at the Theater auf der Wieden just before Schikaneder took over, and this may have increased Mozart's interest in performances there. He went to see quite a few of Schikaneder's productions, and must have immediately understood the sort of opera Schikaneder was now proposing he should write. Magic was a popular word in Viennese opera titles at the time; one of Schikaneder's ventures of the previous year had been sub-titled *Die Zauberinsel*, and another suburban theatre in 1791 offered an opera sub-titled *Die Zauberzither*.

Die Zauberflöte was entered by Mozart in his *Verzeichnüss* in July 1791, but it was then not entirely finished (it lacked, for example, its overture).

It was not performed until 30 September. And for Mozart it was, emotionally, perhaps never finished. He quoted from it, went regularly to see it and took others to see it; he played Papageno's magic glockenspiel behind the scenes, purposely trying to disconcert Schikaneder, acting Papageno, whose deft ad-libbing set the audience laughing. It was probably the last opera that he ever attended; and he is traditionally said to have followed performances mentally during his last illness. Very likely he did, though in fact Schikaneder put on a new opera, *Helena und Paris*, a few days after Mozart became bedridden. A highly mendacious Viennese newspaper had previously announced that this would far surpass *Die Zauberflöte*, but that is perhaps merely another indication of how successful Mozart's opera was proving. *Die Zauberflöte* was a success. Even Salieri came, saw and praised it. At its core burned Mozart's belief in the vital power and importance of love. His last, perhaps his greatest, certainly his most solemn affirmation that '*Mann und Weib, und Weib und Mann*'* can reach divine heights would not easily recede from the mind of someone who had little else to sustain him as he himself faced the ordeal of death.

But in the spring Schikaneder's proposal was merely another project to be seized. Probably Mozart did not expect to make much from the commission, however hard he worked, and perhaps it was from a very modest, barely sketched plan that there slowly arose the opera's edifice. To the problem of daily existence no single solution appeared, and so Mozart continued to take on work – and to seek more. Constanze was again pregnant, and again needed to spend part of the early summer recuperating at Baden. At least once Mozart was driven to borrow from Puchberg, but the amount was small. If not desperate poverty, at least desperate, frustrating misery seems to have lessened relatively during 1791. Mozart was intensely busy, not only composing but – in so far as can be gathered from his letters – making what were probably business arrangements, possibly connected with raising money. After taking good care of herself at Baden, Constanze gave birth on 26 July to a son, baptized Franz Xaver, who lived to become a professional pianist, always inhibited by the great name he bore, and who predeceased his elder brother Karl.

Looking to the future, Mozart applied to the city council of Vienna to be appointed unpaid assistant to the ailing sixty-year-old *Kapellmeister*

* 'Man and woman, and woman and man.'

Leopold Hoffmann (who served St Stephen's Cathedral) with the hope of gaining the paid position when Hoffmann died. So many of Mozart's petitions had not succeeded. This one was agreed to; and Mozart's succession, providing he would be satisfied with the current salary, was virtually promised. Hoffmann, however, survived Mozart. Yet the council's approval possibly redirected Mozart's attention to church music – the category for which he had had least opportunity at Vienna. In this way, too, he was strangely drawn back to youth and early manhood at Salzburg. His 'Coronation' mass (K.317) was performed in the parish church at Baden, and he appears to have been particularly anxious to recover the parts quickly, perhaps with a view to performance in St Stephen's. For the choirmaster at Baden too, he wrote in June the motet *'Ave verum corpus'* (K.618), a miniature choral work for a small church, though it is no building as such which governs the ethereal quality of this lightly breathed hymn, which has something of the remote beauty of the last piano concerto, written a few months earlier. The soft opening of gentle greeting, as the voices begin their *'Ave'*, is paralleled by the soft closing bars of music. Short but not slight, the work seems to float like a cloud of incense on the air. Its joy is spiritual and unemphatic, perfectly sure, perfectly controlled and perfectly peaceful.

More agitated feelings and earlier associations were probably stirred from the first by another, quite unexpected and large-scale religious task: the *Requiem*. Mozart never knew that the commission for this came from a Count Walsegg, the owner of the house where Puchberg lodged. Walsegg's wife had died on 14 February 1791 and the widower conceived the idea of having performed on his country estate at Wiener Neustadt a requiem mass which he would – and did – pass off as his own composition. To preserve secrecy, Walsegg used as a go-between his estate-manager, called Leitgeb. The true circumstances were odd enough and the mystery of the commission may have begun to prey on Mozart's mind, though there is no proof of this; that he died with the *Requiem* unfinished was a striking fact which in itself doubtless fostered legends. That he increasingly felt he was writing a requiem for his own death seems, however, a rather consciously Romantic exegesis. It is really more subtle, and certainly no less moving, to reflect that the joyful masonic cantata, *'Laut verkünde unsre Freude'* (K.623) – confession of a different faith – was finished within three weeks of his death; in that may be heard musical proof of the belief Mozart had expressed to

Leopold, when he had been dying, of death as '*diesem wahren, besten freunde des Menschen*'.*

The *Requiem* is more likely to have prompted thoughts of life: much earlier life at Salzburg, as a boy in church again, hearing the services, as a boy at home practising the clavier to his father's satisfaction. Accompanying his father to Italy in 1770 he had listened at Milan to the requiem mass for Marchese Litta; the *Dies irae* alone, Leopold reported, lasted for about three-quarters of an hour. A requiem mass became something piercingly relevant when Mozart saw his mother die in Paris, and he was left with the even more dreadful task of getting the news broken to Leopold. Guilt, fear, damnation: these are the emotions which the sequence *Dies irae* especially makes so vivid, as it conjures up the coming of the Judge before whom all mankind is guilty, and the Last Day arrives as inexorably as the Commendatore for Don Giovanni.

If Mozart thought back to childhood, and inevitably then to his father, the *Requiem* might seem perhaps a catharsis more shattering to undergo than writing *Don Giovanni*. Death could be near or not, but it was something deserved by someone who still failed his father in 1791 as he had done in 1787. Leopold had once furiously sketched in words Mozart's deathbed – sketching, almost like Hogarth, a virtuous end and a vicious one. You can choose to die, he had said, a famous *Kapellmeister* 'about whom posterity will read in books', leaving the world after a Christian life of honour and fame, with a family well-provided for. Or, 'caught by some trollop with a room full of children suffering want, on a strawsack' ('*von einem Weibsbild etwas eingeschäfert mit einer Stube voll nothleidenden Kindern auf einen Strohsack . . .*'). Of Leopold's hectic pair of pictures, the latter might well seem to Mozart the more prophetically true.

Something made it hard for him to complete the *Requiem*, just as it had never been possible for him to complete the C Minor mass. That both were masses was probably no coincidence. A childhood world, a world of Roman Catholic belief and ritual, awoke buried emotions in which his father perhaps figured as both judge and someone betrayed, suffering from the son who should have filled his old age with pride and prosperity. And yet there must have been times when the figures of Leopold and Hieronymus Colloredo, the commissioner of much of Mozart's church music, coalesced, to represent everything from which Mozart had violently rebelled.

There also existed, or Mozart found, external reasons for not con-

* 'This best and true friend of mankind.'

centrating on the *Requiem*. Opportunities of writing for novel instruments continued to attract him. Another piece for small organ (K.616), completed in early May, was probably a commission from Deym, but it was at his own initiative that he wrote the Adagio and Rondo featuring a glass harmonica (K.617) for the blind girl Marianne Kirchgessner, who had made herself a virtuoso on this odd instrument, one already familiar to Mozart. When he wrote K.617 (entering it in his *Verzeichnüss* on 23 May) he was engaged in composing *Die Zauberflöte*; and it is from just such an enchanted, ideal world, where sublime and comic blend, that this music seems to come. The serious, uncannily grave Adagio is followed by a magically tuneful yet almost plaintively ethereal Rondo, the liquid plaintiveness of which is increased by use of a true glass harmonica instead of modern celesta. Remoteness and unearthliness shadow this music just as they do the *Ave Verum* of some three weeks later.

New effects, as much as new instruments, interested him. He was moving, possibly without totally realizing it, from the luxury of maturity into a period of simpler, more fundamentally serene if less overtly rich and 'human' music: the sort of late last style associated often with aged artists, achieved by Mozart at thirty-five. But he was old as a creator, profoundly experienced and probably increasingly, physically, exhausted. During the lonely final summer of 1791, spent by Constanze largely at Baden, the weariness and the emptiness and the lack of pleasure even in his work began to overwhelm Mozart. Writing to Constanze, sending nonsense messages to Süssmayr (who was at Baden with her) he only briefly banished what he could not quite describe: '*Es ist ein gewisses Leere – die mir halt wehe thut – ein gewisses Sehnen, welches nie befriediget wird, folglich nie aufhört – immer fortdauert, ja von Tag zu Tag wächst.*'* No longer did he speak of sexual excitement; love lay just in seeing Constanze again, exchanging a few words with her, urging her – and himself – to patience.

For so long his life had consisted of haste: to finish commissions, to gain or borrow some money, to snatch some food. For several years he had been assuring Constanze that things would improve: only a little more time was needed. When he looked suddenly at the life he was leading in that summer, he gave it a devastatingly terse epitaph: '*Das ist ein nicht gar angenehmes leben.*'†

---

* 'It's a certain sort of emptiness – which really pains me – a certain longing which is never satisfied and therefore never ceases – always continuing, indeed growing from day to day.'

† 'It isn't exactly a pleasant life.'

A few days afterwards he received a third major commission, the most urgent, socially the most important and, it might almost have seemed, some recompense for the neglect he had endured in the previous year at Frankfurt. Leopold II was to be crowned in Prague as King of Bohemia early in September. An opera was among the celebrations ordered. The impresario Guardasoni, the commissioner of *Don Giovanni*, was required to deal with this matter and, on his way down to Italy to collect singers, he presumably passed through Vienna and got in touch again with Mozart.

A year which had opened with a few, slight tasks had thus by July advanced for Mozart into an unexpectedly complicated position. He had not entirely finished *Die Zauberflöte*, which Schikaneder perhaps planned for production in the autumn. He had by no means finished the *Requiem*, though Count Walsegg very probably required this to be ready only by the anniversary of his wife's death. Nevertheless, these remained two preoccupations. Guardasoni introduced a third, which was perhaps a revival of the hopes Mozart had had in 1789 to write an opera again for Prague. Already in that year the subject of Metastasio's often-set libretto *La Clemenza di Tito* had possibly been agreed between them. Mozart may even have begun to write some of the music about that time; but Guardasoni moved to Warsaw. Back in Prague in 1791, he may well have contrived to hint that if *La Clemenza di Tito* was chosen as the subject to celebrate the Emperor's coronation he knew a composer who would certainly be able to deliver the music in the six weeks or so which were all that remained when discussions about the nature of the festivities closed.

The strongest reason for thinking Mozart had begun *Tito* before any commission for the Coronation was settled is that on 26 April 1791 Madame Duschek sang at a public concert a Mozart rondo with basset-horn obbligato which he never itemized in his *Verzeichnüss* and which can be identified most convincingly with an aria, 'Non più di fiori', which occurs in *Tito*. It is also remarkable that the words of this aria are not found in Metastasio's libretto and seem to be a contribution by da Ponte's friend Mazzolà, the court-poet at Dresden, who was the editor and emender of the version of *La Clemenza di Tito* ('*ridotta á vera opera dal Sigre Mazzolá*' [sic],* is noted in Mozart's *Verzeichnüss*) which was conducted, in the presence of the Emperor and Empress on 6 September 1791 at Prague by the composer himself. Mozart had just under three months more to live.

* 'adapted to a true opera by Signor Mazzolà.'

La Clemenza di Tito had an imperial origin. It had been written by Metastasio in honour of Maria Theresia's father, the Emperor Charles VI, and in the merciful behaviour of the Roman emperor was to be seen conscious reference to the modern one. '*E colpa mia che tu somigli a lui?*'* Metastasio asks in a *licenza* at the end, dropped from Mazzolà's version which, however, retains the shape of the story closely and should have seemed still suitably flattering to celebrate the coronation of Charles VI's grandson. 'Cut short my days, eternal gods,' Mazzolà's Tito sings at the end of the opera, 'when the good of Rome ceases to be my care.' For Rome, we might read Bohemia, quietly reminding the monarch – as does the opera throughout – that the highest rank brings the highest responsibilities.

Inevitably, the solemnity of the occasion required an *opera seria*, though the Emperor and Empress had on a previous evening attended, conceivably even enjoyed, a performance of *Don Giovanni*. Count Zinzendorf was in Prague, of course, for the coronation festivities and attended the first night of *Tito*. 'Most tedious' was his verdict, one shared probably by the court circle – as distinct from the inhabitants of Prague. The Emperor's rapture seems to have been restricted to the chief female singer, who has the basset-horn aria, and the Empress, Maria Luisa of Naples, set a fashion for later Italian denigration of Mozart by apparently stigmatizing the opera as '*una porcheria tedesca*'.†

The first performance was very probably under-rehearsed. Mozart had finished the opera in haste, having been interrupted by illness; some of the plain recitatives are said (on not very good evidence) to be the work of Süssmayr, who accompanied Mozart and Constanze to Prague on this occasion. The category of *opera seria* was rapidly falling from fashion. Metastasio's libretto, even when made more flexible by Mazzolà with duets and terzets in place of single arias, might seem rather out-of-date *ancien régime* propaganda, even to *ancien régime* rulers.

Yet later performances of the opera at Prague appear to have been enthusiastically received by a city which had applauded *Don Giovanni* and previously gone wild over *Figaro*. On the last night of *Tito* – the first night, as it happened, of *Die Zauberflöte* – it was given 'to tremendous applause' ('*mit ausserordentlichen beifall*'), Mozart heard in a letter he had from the clarinettist Stadler, who played the basset-horn accompaniment to the aria 'Non più di fiori'. Cries of 'Bravo!' greeted Stadler's

* 'Is it my fault that you resemble him?'
† 'A piece of German filth.'

playing; and the proud, rather silly and not totally reputable virtuoso exclaimed to Mozart, '*O böhmisches wunder!*'* And Bohemia was right in its attitude to the opera, recognizing that in its genre *Tito* was as great as anything Mozart had previously written. The challenge for him lay in exactly that.

Although he had written several *opere serie* – supremely *Idomeneo* – never since *Lucio Silla* (nineteen years earlier) had he been confronted by a Roman ethos. *Tito* is not only magnificent, but severe. Its grand political world, a world where men predominate, finds place for friendship but not much for love. Its plot concerns, in fact, a terrible betrayal of friendship, and this is illustrated by types of people, not by 'characters' in the sense of Susanna, Figaro or Don Giovanni. Shakespeare's late plays partly provide a parallel (e.g. the people of *Pericles* or *Cymbeline*), but plays like *Coriolanus* may also be compared because the importance of Rome, and the good of the citizens, add serious weight to the argument in both Shakespeare's and Mozart's eyes. Such responses are tentative in *Lucio Silla* (an opera which does not, however, deserve its neglect). In *Idomeneo* they are much more patent; the actuality of his suffering people compels Idomeneo to carry out the vow he has tried to avoid. *Tito* constantly declines the people's praise, even while always referring his conduct to the standards of Rome. And Rome is steadily audible in the marches and great choruses which greet his public appearances. He is almost a divine figure, human enough to feel loneliness but otherwise equipped with god-like attributes:

> *Sia noto a Roma*
> *ch'io son lo stesso, e ch'io*
> *tutto so, tutti assolvo, e tutto obblio.*†

Those proud words, delivered amid musical flourishes, unleash the opera's tremendous imperial C Major finale in which the main characters in turn, and then the chorus of Roman citizens, hail and counter-hail their Emperor, himself having to raise his tenor voice again and again and again amid this thrillingly dense, trumpet-punctuated hymn of praise.

Mozart's monarch must be benign, forgiving even when most grossly betrayed and supreme through qualities of character, not through

---

* 'O Bohemian prodigy!'
† 'Let Rome take note
  That I remain the same, and that I
  Know all, forgive all, and forget all.'

power. Tito becomes, in effect, Sarastro and also therefore the fore-runner of Beethoven's Don Fernando, liberator and object of another vast choral tide of praise, at the end of *Fidelio*. If there is any implied praise of the real Leopold II, this follows only on his recognition of a ruler's need to rule himself. Metastasio offered praise to a ruler for already being like his ancient Roman counterpart; Mozart gives Enlightenment guidance for how a ruler ought to behave. Tito is seen in a masonic rather than *ancien régime* perspective; and it would be obtuse to think the situation did not interest Mozart, or should not interest us, because Tito does not 'suffer the results of his clemency' (as it is some-what cryptically expressed in the booklet accompanying the Decca recording of the opera).

But Mozart may have had another, more personal interest in the pivot of the story of *La Clemenza di Tito*. Tito's clemency is the fixed principle, revealed by the opera's very title. The central character, however, is the Emperor's intimate friend, Sesto, who is led by love for Vitellia, herself an enemy of the Emperor and his family, to attempt Tito's assassination at her bidding. Vitellia's love for Sesto is feigned, while her professed hatred of Tito is largely revenge for his not having married her. When he abruptly declares her to be his future Empress, she has almost ludicrously to try and prevent Sesto's assassination attempt. Vitellia is a sort of Electra from *Idomeneo*, more monstrous and man-eating. A true anti-heroine, she is also the only female in the opera, apart from the sweet but shadowy Servilia, Sesto's sister, who happily loves and is loved by Sesto's friend Annio. Except for Tito's loyal com-mander of the Praetorian Guard, there are no other characters.

Thus it is on Sesto that the emotional burden of the action falls. Shown publicly honoured by the Emperor, steadily befriended by Annio, he allows his feelings for Vitellia to lead him to fire the Capitol and in the confusion stab a figure he believes to be the Emperor himself. The agonizing guilt he endures while keying himself up to the act ('*O dei, che smania è questa*')* is conveyed in a long, shuddering, accompanied recitative. A brief storm bursts from the orchestra at his realization that Tito has raised up the very man who now becomes '*il carnefice suo*', his own executioner. Against a background of the blazing Capitol and groans from the terrified populace, the other characters gather per-turbed and puzzled to witness the return of Sesto: to announce the mur-der of Tito and to define – in doom-laden, deep tones – the murderer as

---

* 'O Gods, what frenzy is this!'

'*l'uom più scellerato/l'orror della natura*'.* Though Vitellia silences him before he can accuse himself, guilt and grief invest the whole stage as the scene slowly, almost frozenly, comes to an end with funeral music and cries of '*tradimento*' from the uncomprehending Annio and the self-accusing Sesto.

This great, and dramatic, finale to the first half of the opera (entirely the work of Mazzolà and Mozart) isolates Sesto from the rest of the characters. In one way, he is Don Giovanni with a conscience; in another, he is any guilty soul, '*Culpa rubet vultus meus*', awaiting the judgment of the *Dies irae*. Sesto's act is virtually parricide. That it did not in fact succeed does not absolve him, as he fully realizes, and even when, after the ordeal of the second half, he is forgiven by Tito, he rightly sings '*Ma non m'assolve il core*'.†

The second half of the opera makes him suffer remorse, and worse than remorse, when he is at last confronted by Tito. The Emperor too suffers, even in assuming his inquisitor-like role, and it is in tragic antique fashion that the two one-time friends (though never equals) meet to discover each so changed in aspect. '*Quello di Tito è il volto?*'‡ Sesto questions, seeing the Emperor's grim face, while Tito realizes sadly how crime has transformed the appearance of Sesto. Since Sesto will not reveal the reason for his murderous attempt, Tito's instinct to forgive him is checked. He summons the guards to remove him and becomes again his judge: '*Or tuo giudice son io*'.

Those words are not in Metastasio, nor has he Mazzolà's tender touch in the moving aria for Sesto which follows, the opening words of which Mozart set to such a nostalgic adagio:

> *Deh, per questo istante solo*
> *ti ricorda il primo amor.*§

It might almost be Fiordiligi begging for forgiveness; and Sesto is indeed in something of her wracked position. Though he deserves, and willingly faces, death, yet he longs to be able before dying to assure Tito of his affection (while keeping Vitellia uninvolved). Mazzolà created a couplet which neatly goes to the root of the situation, as Sesto sings:

* 'The most wicked man/abhorred of nature.'
† 'But my heart does not absolve me.'
‡ 'Is that the face of Tito?'
§ 'Ah, for this moment alone
  Remember our first love.'

pur saresti men severo
*se vedesti questo cor.**

This is Sesto's true agony of mind. When his thoughts shift to death itself, the music shifts, agitated, defiant and almost exultant (*'ma il morir non mi spaventa'*),† before passing into wilder grief at the continuing pain which seems unbearable and which yet does not kill one (*'nè si more di dolor'*).‡ That Tito eventually preserves his life is, from one point of view, the most cruel of punishments; for Sesto must live on, never forgetting – *'finchè memoria avrà'* – the appalling betrayal of friendship into which love led him.

It would be too simple to say that Mozart is Sesto, but he certainly understands, and responds to, the character's dilemma. Two women, Aloysia and Constanze Weber, had led him into acts which Leopold Mozart might gladly have called parricide; and how often must Mozart have felt that Leopold would be less severe if only he could see into his heart? Having married Constanze, Mozart had taken a long time girding himself to encounter his father again, obviously dreading the reproaches. He had no more really killed his father than Sesto really kills Tito, but such a wish is vividly enough shown in the opera to bring its burden of ineffaceable guilt. The arguments of recent scholarship that *La Clemenza di Tito* was not so much an imposed commission as an earlier, deliberate, choice of subject make the fact of Mozart's sympathy all the firmer.

To him the libretto was not a sterile story of wooden people but – as his music reveals throughout – a poignant and terrible story of betrayal. The grandeur of the opera's framework is declared in the triumphant triple chords of the overture – as if speedily conjuring up two pillars and a pediment – and then something of the personal emotions involved in the very tender wind section which follows. The combination of cosmic stage and small-scale, suffering creatures, whose affections must give way before reasons of state, is something Mozart had hardly attempted before, and it gives a resigned, Racinian tone to the whole opera, reminding one that the story itself continues history directly from the events of *Bérénice* (who is mentioned in the opera). It is strange to reflect that the career so soon to close after *La Clemenza di Tito* had opened with the setting of the Racine-derived *Mitridate*.

* 'Yet you would be less harsh
  If you were to see into this heart.'
† 'But death does not frighten me.'
‡ 'People do not die of grief.'

Tito was a deliberate essay in severe, punishing classicism, an opera where nobody gets what they want (including the Emperor; he hoped at first to marry Servilia, who declares her prior love for Annio, and then Vitellia, who turns out to be the monster-plotter of his murder). That aspect of existence was one Mozart in certain moods felt profoundly; and the *Requiem* is an unfinished but baroque monument to perhaps the same belief.

'*Tod und Verzweiflung war sein Lohn!*'* The words were quoted – quite cheerfully – by Mozart as a message to Constanze during the previous June, quoting from *Die Zauberflöte*, on which he was then working. The joke – not one that Constanze would appreciate – is that 'death and despair' are said in the opera to be the reward of those who are deceived by women's intrigues. But death and despair are not jokes in *Die Zauberflöte*; they are challenges to be overcome, and they are indeed overcome by the lovers Pamina and Tamino. Together, given courage by love, and protected by playing the magic flute of the opera's title, they pass through ordeals of fire and water and receive consecration, virtually coronation, in a wonderful sun-filled final chorus, a triumphal tide which streams round then like the bright, white light of eternity. They are raised above mere human happiness, transfigured and absorbed into some divine sphere where neither despair nor death can reach them.

Such is the vision with which *Die Zauberflöte* closes. It is the alternative view, in alternative style, to that expressed by *Tito*, and it was aptly introduced into the world on 30 September, with Mozart conducting (out of respect for the public 'and friendship for the author of the piece', the playbill stated), on the same evening that *Tito* was heard for the last time in the season at Prague. Each opera represented something new and distinct in Mozart's career. Beside the high, antique, triumphal arch of *Tito* stands the spangled booth or striped tent in which the clowns, lovers, animals, star-flaming Queen of Night and rival magician, Sarastro, assemble to perform their amusing, spectacular and ultimately sublime opera.

That it will be sublime is made impressively clear by its overture (finished only two days before the first night). Three solemn chords in the orchestra at once prepare the listener for something more than funny pantomime – even without any realization of masonic significance in the triple effect. Slow, suspenseful strings rise only very gradually to a pounding crescendo and then again there sound three solemn horn calls

* 'Death and despair were his reward.'

before the fierily blazing power with which the overture races to a conclusion. Its excitement spills into the music – and action – that directly follow: a man rushes on calling for help, pursued by a huge serpent; he falls in total exhaustion and at his last desperate cry three veiled women with spears abruptly appear, to kill the reptile.

Die Zauberflöte has hardly begun, yet already something both vividly dramatic and serious has happened. Any audience may feel piqued to know, after such an opening, what will happen next. The first-night audience, even more than the first-night audience of *Così fan tutte*, can have had no idea of how the plot would unfold – and something of their uncertainty may have been shared earlier by the authors of the libretto. Although Schikaneder put his name alone on the title-page of the text, it is very probable that one or more members of his company collaborated with him on it; and Mozart himself may have contributed at least some phrases. He often wrote verse, and fragments of a play by him survive. Libretto and playbill described as '*eine grosse Oper*' ('a grand opera') what was in category a *Singspiel*, spoken dialogue alternating with arias, just as funny scenes alternated with serious ones. Much of the writing is scarcely more than doggerel – though effective doggerel – and for once it is possible to understand Count Zinzendorf's comment: 'an incredible farce' (though he found the music and sets pretty).

Schikaneder, instigator if not literally author, began perhaps by an idea for just a typical 'rescue' opera with magic-oriental elements. A wicked enchanter might have carried off the beautiful daughter of some queen; a wandering prince, perhaps saved by the queen from one danger, offers in gratitude to brave another and rescue her daughter. He succeeds and they marry. On the way to the rescue, he might have some adventures – to keep the opera going – and certainly be accompanied by some sort of comic servant. Probably from the first, Schikaneder cast himself in the latter role, and was therefore the more eager to write this part, or at least think up the jokes it would contain.

Either he or Mozart, or perhaps a young member of the company, Gieseke (who had previously written the libretto for one of Schikaneder's productions and who was possibly involved in *Die Zauberflöte*'s text) may suddenly have seen how such a story contained allegorically the elements of masonic ordeal: a man overcomes the fear of death and is united to truth. Masonic elements, of a kind Gebler had intended in his play *König Thamos*, for which Mozart had long before written incidental music, could be introduced to emphasize this aspect. Brotherhood of men, initiation, types of ordeal (by silence, for instance), temples to equal masonic lodges: the possibilities of analogy were endless, and to Mozart – who had written a good deal of masonic music already – must have been particularly inspiring. The prince's adventures would symbolize initiation. He would triumph not only through love and constancy but also through the power of music: another, happier Orpheus ('*Wann Orpheus Zauberlaute klingt*',* one admirer had begun his verse in Mozart's album) he might pass safely through some frightening underworld and win his bride.

Mozart, one may reasonably guess, would amend this journey so that '*Mann und Weib*' passed through such an ordeal together. For whatever the original project or projects, a most important aspect of the opera which finally emerged is that a woman who does not fear death is worthy and will also be initiated: '*Ein Weib, das Nacht und Tod nicht scheut/Ist würdig und wird eingeweiht.*' Those words consecrate Pamina at the most stirring moment of the opera. They are sung by two armed men as Tamino stands facing the *Schreckenspforten* ('fearful gates') through which he must successfully pass, by fire and water, if he is to be worthy of initiation. Pamina, previously a maiden-object, a passive reward dangled before the hero, now erupts onto the scene transfigured into an emancipated, dominant heroine: '*Ich selbsten führe dich,*'† she declares to Tamino. She commands him to play the magic flute: '*Spiel' du die Zauberflöte an.*' And thus, thanks to her guidance, a hero comes through his ordeal. The chorus that greets their triumph is really hailing the heroine of the century, whose suffering and bravery and true love ('*die Liebe leitet mich*') make her the most moving of Mozart's death-defying women and the artistic mother of Beethoven's Leonore.

However, Tamino's need to be ordered to play the magic flute during the ordeals is something which is particularly understandable when the plot of the opera is considered. Tamino is the man who was fleeing from the huge serpent when the opera began. The three ladies who killed it serve someone they start by referring to simply as 'our princess', '*unserer Fürstin*'. When the birdcatcher Papageno (Schikaneder's role) enters he explains that they and he are in the service of the 'star-blazing Queen', '*Sternflammende Königin*'. Her daughter is Pamina, with whose portrait Tamino straightaway falls in love. No sooner have the three ladies returned to say that Pamina was captured by an evil demon and that

---

* 'Whenever Orpheus' magic lute sounds . . .'
† 'It is I myself who leads you.'

their ruler hopes Tamino will rescue her than – to the sound of thunder – the Queen herself appears, a sorrowing mother but also a sovereign. Her first wonderful aria begins as a lament and then shifts into commanding coloratura exhortation to Tamino: '*Du, du, du sollst sie zu befreien gehen.*'* Her gift to Tamino on his magic quest is the magic flute, handed over by her ladies who, with Tamino and Papageno, then sing a ravishing quintet in praise of the instrument: it is worth more than gold or crowns, for through it will Mankind's happiness and contentment increase. (This seems a clear hint that the flute itself – an instrument Mozart personally disliked – has masonic significance.)

The ladies have moreover shown their moral tendency by punishing Papageno for a boastful lie that he killed the serpent; that leads them to the reflection that if all liars were punished there would be, instead of hatred and slander, love and brotherhood, '*Lieb' und Bruderbund*'. Finally, to guide Tamino and the coerced Papageno on their way to rescue Pamina – located, it is now revealed, in Sarastro's castle – the ladies promise the aid of another trio, of boys, '*Drei Knäbchen, jung, schön, hold und weise*'.† (Like the flute, these boys later prove indubitably 'good'; they save Pamina from despair and encourage her impulse to join Tamino before his ordeals.)

So far, the opera unfolds consistently. But when Tamino reaches Sarastro's territory (having inexplicably lost Papageno), he – and the spectators – learn with surprise that Sarastro is a noble, wise ruler who took Pamina away from her wicked mother for her own good. Women are anyway not to be trusted, a priest-like Speaker informs Tamino. Sarastro soon makes his appearance, with even stronger statements about the Queen's pride and the need for a man to have charge of Pamina.

Thence onwards, the opera rather jerkily adopts Sarastro's standards. All the ritual of priests, ordeals and sacred halls (of masonry) is in his hands. Pamina alone manages to make nonsense of his efforts to subordinate her part in the proceedings. The Queen is next seen as a glittering, hate-filled figure who orders her daughter to kill him. The three ladies try to make Tamino break a vow of silence. Eventually, Queen and ladies attack the temple of Sarastro and are destroyed.

Yet although this makes an effective culmination it fails to explain the provenance of the flute and the boys. If the Queen was always intended to be evil, it is odd that she should possess such 'good' magic properties.

---

* 'It is thou, thou, thou who shouldst go to free her.'
† 'Three boys, young, handsome, charming and wise.'

And for her wicked ladies to sing, without any apparent irony, of the need for love and brotherhood is to confuse any audience, however sophisticated. Even if it were presumed that the sentiments are typical hypocrisy, it would still have to be explained either why the three boys, 'charming and wise', do not prove equally misleading, or else why they originate in her kingdom when they are so patently beneficent.

Such things seem not so much subtleties as unresolved contradictions in the plot. Those who have argued otherwise have glided silently over the laudable moral sentiments of the three ladies and not even bothered to note that, while equations of night and falseness may be very well, the Queen is actually called bright, 'star-blazing', in the first part of the first act. This epithet brings her, incidentally, close to the uncontestedly good fairy, Perifirime, '*die strahlende Fee*'*, who appeared in a fairy story by a certain Liebeskind, *Lulu oder Die Zauberflöte* (one of a collection published by Wieland and others in 1786). Not only does the sub-title alone of this seem highly relevant, but the story was utilized in the summer of 1791 for an opera put on at Vienna by one of Schikaneder's rivals, *Der Fagottist, oder die Zauberzither*. Mozart went to a performance and reported it a feeble work.

It used sometimes to be thought that the production of this actual opera in the summer was the cause of Schikaneder's altering the plot of *Die Zauberflöte*, but the reason seems unconvincing and now probably finds little support. Brigid Brophy (in *Mozart the Dramatist*) has suggested other better reasons: that any final triumph of the Queen in an opera so full of masonic allusions might seem contradictory of Masonry's anti-feminist tendencies and also that possibly the first version of the plot came too near revealing some secret of masonic ritual (perhaps a vision of the goddess Isis). Whatever the exact reasons, and whatever reserves may legitimately exist about the nature of a presumed earlier version of the plot, one of the most striking facts is that, as it stands, Tamino does *not* rescue Pamina, though the beginning of the opera and the tradition of the rescue-plot would lead us to expect this. Yet the Queen's promise to him at the close of her first aria comes, almost ironically, true: 'When I see you as victor, she shall be thine for ever' ('*ewig*', 'for ever', glimpsed for a brief moment high in the empyrean as the Queen rises beyond normal compass to a top F on the first syllable).

And whatever the inconsistencies, or at least the oddities, of a patch-work libretto, Mozart took it and dipped it into such a marvellous

* 'The brilliant fairy.'

musical dye that the work of art which emerged had its own unity. *Tito* is cosmic because a great empire extends behind the clutch of inter-related characters, whose personal actions can affect it. But *Die Zauber-flöte* is, as it were, cosmic in depth, not width: what opens exotically ends sublimely, though only after emotional ordeals which have served to temper the characters of that 'noble pair', Pamina and Tamino. She especially grows in stature during the course of the opera. In other senses, too, *Die Zauberflöte* is cosmic. Its range extends from the high, rococo brilliance of the star-flaming Queen, all fire and air, to the pro-found depths of Sarastro's bass which positively evokes a solid earth on which men may, with friendly aid, reach a 'better land'. Between such extreme elements walk Tamino and Pamina, sustained in moments of great stress by the urgent, unearthly music of the trio of boy-genii, whose crystal voices suggest their inspirational nature. In a wonderful scena they win Pamina back from the brink of suicide; more briefly, still inspirationally, they intervene when Papageno contemplates suicide, reminding him that he has a magic glockenspiel (plebeian equivalent of the magic flute) which will bring him his heart's desire. For it is part of the opera's cosmic view that Papageno has his place no less than Tamino, despite, even because of, his feathered, flawed nature; and certainly no less than the hero does he believe: '*Wir leben durch die Lieb' allein.*'* So for him too there is found a mate, Papagena. Much more remarkable, it is Papageno who discovers and virtually rescues Pamina; their encounter leads to a duet-hymn in praise of love (from which the words just above are quoted) which is at once simple and touching, all the more so since the two characters are not in love with each other.

Although Papageno is comic, he never becomes a Leporello-style buffoon. Because he is the audience's persona, Everyman as well as clown, he has moments of sadness and of feeling incongruous among princes and high priests. Indeed, even among ordinary human beings he is a touch incongruous. After Papageno first dances in, singing that he is a bird-catcher, Tamino begins to wonder – looking at his feathers – if he really is a man. (The engraving of Schikaneder in the role, reproduced in the first edition of the libretto, shows how completely he assumed bird-like costume.) Papageno has no idea who his parents were and, as he tells Pamina sadly, he could pull out all his feathers when he reflects that he has no Papagena. That this figure, at that moment, shares with the heroine a duet about the power of love may have been arranged simply

* 'We live through love alone.'

to suit Schikaneder, but the result is poignantly symbolic: music fuses, as their voices mingle and soar, the half-grotesque creature who is the Queen's servant and the pure maiden who is the Queen's daughter. To them is given the lyrically solemn asserveration that man and woman, and woman and man, 'achieve divinity' '*reichen an die Gottheit an*'.

Perhaps because so many ingredients go to make up *Die Zauberflöte*, it yields at each nudge, like a kaleidoscope, a fresh pattern. Schikaneder had his requirements. Mozart also had his; writing music for Count Deym had probably given him some ideas for magic instruments and mechanical-bird effects. The rococo *Mater Dolorosa* guise of the star-flaming Queen's first appearance is replaced at her second, equally dramatic arrival ('comes amid thunder out of the middle trapdoor' is the stage direction) by boiling, bird-like rage which sends her voice up into an uncanny, quite inhuman height almost ceasing to be singing. And possibly one visual hint for the opera came from Count Deym's Lodon mausoleum, because an engraving of it shows that the structure was flanked by two armed men (comparable to those who guard the 'fearful gates' behind which lies the threat of death).

In one way, the opera seems concerned with the power of love to triumph over fears of death – at all levels of humanity. In another, it could have made a suitable celebration, like *The Tempest*, for a royal marriage. Tamino and Pamina prove themselves as worthy to rule as did Idamante and Ilia in *Idomeneo*; and instead of *La Clemenza di Tito*, a Habsburg couple might well have been greeted with *Die Zauberflöte*, which no less preaches that a prince must practise self-control and virtue if he is to be worthy of reigning.

Above all, however, the opera pays tribute openly to the power of music. The flute and the glockenspiel in themselves symbolize this power: they need no Orpheus to perform on them, because the power resides in music, not in the musician. When Tamino first plays on the flute 'all sorts of wild animals' come to hear him, but his flute is also answered by Papageno's glockenspiel announcing that he and Pamina have equally been drawn by its music. Then the glockenspiel in turn proves music's charm. Sarastro's black-hearted Moorish servant Monostatos and his band of slaves seize Pamina and Papageno but are set dancing to the glockenspiel's tune; when they have danced out harmlessly, Pamina and Papageno sing of the need for everyone to have such a magic instrument: a man's enemies would then disappear and he would live in perfect harmony, ('*in der beste Harmonie*').

To Mozart this was more than allegory. Perhaps he was, unconsciously, teaching Schikaneder a lesson on the evening he went behind the scenes and played the glockenspiel himself. When Schikaneder had a pause in his glockenspiel aria, Mozart mischievously played an arpeggio. Startled, Schikaneder looked into the wings and saw Mozart. At the next pause, Schikaneder waited and so did Mozart. After an interval Mozart again played an arpeggio, whereupon Schikaneder struck the fake glockenspiel he held on stage, saying: 'Shut up.' Everybody laughed, but as Mozart pointed out (describing the incident to Constanze) it was probably the first time that the audience realized that he did not strike it himself (*'dass er das Instrument nicht selbst schlägt'*).

'Prima la musica e poi le parole';* but of course it was one of Mozart's greatest gifts as an opera composer that he illuminated the words with his music, not subordinating but clothing them with such sounds that by the time he has finished the result is of Shakespearean richness and force. In *Die Zauberflöte* the music is everywhere – despite the patches of spoken dialogue, spoken largely when Papageno is present – and is for everyone. If it has less obvious 'character' than the music for Mozart's other operas, that is simply because of its variety. Its idiom becomes entirely its own: a *Zauberflöte* style, *'in der beste Harmonie'*. A few of the most banal words – *'Lebet wohl, auf Wiedersehn'* – are sufficient to stretch over the ravishing close of the quintet in which Tamino and Papageno part from the three Ladies, the music seeming at once to bless the parting and just hint at reluctance on both sides. It is extraordinary to realize that this quintet began with Papageno's humming noises, his mouth having been padlocked as a punishment for lying about killing the serpent, and has included the gift of the flute, Papageno's refusal to accompany Tamino on his quest, which is reversed by the present of the glockenspiel, and a first, apparently firm, farewell sung straightforwardly by all five voices; the quintet continues with Tamino and Papageno stopping the Ladies' departure by asking how to find Sarastro's city, and then hearing the mysterious pizzicati and sotto voce singing which introduces the promise of their guidance by the three boys. Only after that does the true farewell begin, the first Lady uttering her own last *'Auf Wiedersehn'*, echoed by the second Lady and completed by an answering last *'Auf Wiedersehn'* from the two men.

For all its shimmering beauty, such music is steadily advancing the action. And music becomes the action, in what amounts to nearly one

* 'First the music and then the words.'

half of the first act, the finale marked as beginning when Tamino is led in by the boy-genii to the temples of Sarastro's territory. Thence onwards for the rest of the act there is no unaccompanied spoken dialogue. The power of flute and glockenspiel are displayed, but the triumphant duet of Pamina and Papageno seems short-lived because they have hardly defeated Monostatos before a stirring sound of trumpets and drums with an unseen chorus proclaim the arrival of Sarastro. Vividly, music catches Papageno's collapse and Pamina's emergence as a true heroine who answers his shivering question of what they shall say with a ringing twice-sung 'Die Wahrheit!' ('The Truth'). And now a chorus of alternating thunder and swift pianissimi leads on Sarastro himself, who steps from his chariot silently to confront Pamina and Papageno; the pause before Pamina sings her confession allows one to appreciate the choral force before which she must bravely declare herself, and Sarastro's kindly but majestic bass response emphasizes her candour and youth. This moment of tension is hardly resolved before the chattering allegro of Monostatos thrusts him and his new prisoner, Tamino, onto the stage. In the exultant meeting of the two lovers – face to face for the first time – Sarastro, Monostatos and the whole dignified atmosphere are temporarily blotted out: a few hectic bars and ecstatic cries throw them into each other's arms. The chorus immediately thunders for an explanation and Monostatos jabbers for his reward which Sarastro ironically rapidly pronounces: to be bastinadoed. Sotto voce murmurs of praise come from the chorus, and then Sarastro in slow solemn tones orders Tamino and Papageno to be prepared for the ordeal of initiation. A colossal, brilliant chorus thereupon salutes, while it creates a cosmos of virtue and justice which can turn earth to a heavenly state; and even when the voices finally cease their huge hymn to the future, the orchestra with every instrument at its disposal still radiantly, martially, magnificently, sustains the fabric of this bright vision before the curtain falls.

Without Handel, not even Mozart perhaps could have ended his long finale with a chorus yet more thrilling than the series of musical denouements which have preceded it. And a comparable chain of excitement is never so firmly established in the second half of the opera, where the action becomes rather jerky, for all the musical power of certain scenes. Yet it is there that Pamina not only grows to heroic stature but suffers the agony of thinking Tamino does not love her (since he will not speak to her – bound by a vow during initiation). Sarastro a little too patly allows her to suffer; and the tragic extent of what she undergoes is revealed in the plangent grief of her stark aria '*Ach, ich fühl's –*' a wild lament which is far removed musically from the grief of Countess Almaviva or Elvira. Its almost expressionist freedom is part of the freedom of *Die Zauberflöte*, perhaps to Mozart's own taste the most perfect of his operas. Certainly it is one which he patently loved, and which he lived to see – in a very few weeks – become a patent success.

In October Constanze was again enjoying convalescence at Baden and Mozart was eating lonely meals in the Rauhensteingasse – something he much disliked. After an enjoyable visit to *Die Zauberflöte* on the evening of Friday the seventh, he sat down to supper with a fresh snowdrop-white tablecloth and a double candlestick with wax candles: it seemed to him a luxury worth reporting to Constanze, while reflecting on the applause which the opera was increasingly receiving. On Saturday he went to it again when he played his trick on Schikaneder and heard the rest of the opera from a box close to the orchestra. On Sunday he took old Frau Weber to it, remarking beforehand sardonically that probably she would *see* but not *hear* it: '*Die schaut die Oper, aber nicht die hört die Oper.*' Her other musician son-in-law, Hofer, had previously given her the libretto to read, and perhaps she liked the opera sufficiently for Mozart to take her again the following week, when he took his son Karl to see it; Karl was certainly delighted by the performance.

With this visit, presumably Karl's first to any opera of his father's, another aspect of *Die Zauberflöte* comes movingly to mind: its sense of a new generation, to be born from the marriage of Tamino and Pamina and also from that of Papageno and Papagena: '. . . *unsrer Liebe Kinder schenken.*'* This was the aspect Goethe seized on in his attempted sequel telling the story of the son of Tamino and Pamina. The vision of a better, brighter future which *Die Zauberflöte* promises must lie with a new generation; and Mozart was taking practical steps about Karl and his education at the same time as he offered him the evening at the opera.

Worried by the poor standards of the countrified school Karl was then attending ('*einen guten Bauern mögen sie wohl der Welt erziehen!*'),† he planned for him to attend a school in a suburb of Vienna, run by the Piarists, a specifically teaching order founded by St Joseph Calasanctius, and concerned with secondary education. Perhaps nothing came of these

* 'To send children to reward our love.'
† 'They're concerned with giving the world good peasants.'

plans because Mozart died. In October he thought that a month or so, perhaps with Constanze at Baden, could hardly affect Karl's education one way or another. Choice of school was one more problem which needed attention, like the unfinished *Requiem*, the orchestrating of a clarinet concerto he had written for Stadler and a sorting out of which clothes exactly Constanze had sent to the laundry.

Mozart's last surviving letters touch on such points (except for the Requiem which he never mentions) in basically optimistic mood. They give no support to the later, widely disseminated belief that he had by then become depressed and obsessed by premonitions of death. Letters in earlier years, like those of 1788, are truly depressed, desperate and nearly hopeless in tone. But the success of *Die Zauberflöte*, which continued throughout the autumn of 1791, was steadily encouraging. Praise for it from for instance Salieri – his one-time rival – was something to be treasured, as recognition of its basically serious nature; there was, Mozart could report to Constanze, no piece in the opera which did not draw a '*bravo*' or '*bello*' from him. At the end he and Madame Cavalieri pronounced it '*würdig bey der grössten festivität von dem grössten Monarchen aufzuführen*'.* In the absence of Haydn in London, Salieri probably represented the musical opinion Mozart most respected. And all the time, the general public reception of the opera remained warmly favourable. When Zinzendorf went to hear it in November he noted it was the twenty-fourth performance and that there was 'a huge audience'.

Such a success was greater than Mozart had ever before experienced in Vienna. As an omen for the brightening future, nothing could be more encouraging. He may well have begun to concentrate on the Requiem only at this very time, with *Die Zauberflöte* established and Stadler's clarinet concerto (K.622) finished. The new work for Stadler was completed just at the time of the opera's first night, but it had originally been begun, with a basset horn as the solo instrument, three years before. Although Mozart could, and often did, work with superb speed, he also drafted, brooded over, modified or rejected sketches for a great deal of his music – working in this way much more than used to be realized. The clarinet concerto probably passed through a number of stages, with change of instrument and change of key (from G to A), and ironically the version in which it now survives is itself partly adapted and partly altered, it seems, from what Mozart intended. Nevertheless, it remains

---

* 'Worthy of being performed at the greatest festivity held by the greatest monarch.'

worthy, and even at times reminiscent, of the clarinet quintet, though the instrument seems more patently the hero of the concerto, which at its brightest yet remains strangely shadowed. The first movement unfolds like a bale of shot silk, soothingly smooth and sensuously delightful, rippling as if drawn so rapidly through some ring that the very material turns liquid as it flows. Then it runs more slowly, and a different, darker hue is seen, still sensuous but sensuously rich. The clarinet which had bubbled brightly among the strings now blows like a mournful elfin horn in a landscape from which twilight is gradually sucking the colour. More ambiguous than a slow movement, this first movement is wonderfully woven to display the clarinet's affecting power, with its tendency to return from even the most rollicking excursion and touch the listener to tears.

Shot silk becomes, in the adagio, the deepest, heaviest of velvets, unfolded with almost painful slowness as the clarinet begins, and the orchestra joins in, a stately threnody. What was liquid grows thickly viscous, scarcely oozing, and appearing rather to accumulate sweetness as it is stored up, half-honey, half-amber, a precious substance mellowing in a late summer which it seems will never end. Such inspired slowness excludes time, and the long note on which the movement closes serves to seal it off in a poignant dimension. Briskly, the last movement dances away – dancing almost a hornpipe, and yet it too flags and grows oddly broken in effect before making obligatory and here pecking-fowl-like nods towards a cheerful finale which cannot efface the impression of the garnered richness of the slow movement, that adagio beyond sadness which seems to say that 'ripeness is all'.

In some ways, there is more sense of Mozart taking farewell of life in the clarinet concerto than in the Requiem. Though Constanze later encouraged the idea that he more and more associated the Requiem with his own death, it remains hard to accept her very simple equation. Doubtless the commission disturbed him, but many of the emotions it caused were probably always incomprehensible to her, even if she was aware of them. Death is gazed at and overcome in *Die Zauberflöte*, and something of the same battle between light and darkness is central to the liturgical drama of the requiem mass; it is present too in Mozart's *Requiem*, a work which unfortunately is textually and traditionally also a considerable conflict between the light of a few facts and a large area of obscurity.

How close in time work on the Requiem was to that on *Die Zauberflöte* became apparent when a sheet of sketches for passages in both turned up recently. And probably the Requiem advanced gradually under revision, from many such sheets, out of which was built the final form of the great choral prayers of the Introit and the Kyrie, and most of the Dies Irae sequence. Yet the mass is, in some senses, now for ever under revision. It is a baroque monument flawed by never being finished, never polished to that marble firmness which Mozart would have required. Instead, it is patched. The dutiful Süssmayr worked as well as he could, guided by Mozart's sketches and verbal instructions, but the instructions at least were dictated by dreadful, fatal, urgency. For Constanze's sake perhaps almost as much as his own, Mozart must have wished at the end to die feeling that the work could be handed over to the patron as complete. A battle against time is only one of the battles to have marked the Requiem, leaving it uneasy, uneven, opening in dark majesty but wandering after the stunningly vivid word-painting of the unorchestrated (by Mozart) Offertory into a mixture of barrenness and Mozartean pastiche. Yet Süssmayr achieved a strangely effective touch in having the mass close almost as it had begun. Borrowing a beautiful melody from the second part of the Introit, a soprano pleads in angelic tones – the last of Mozart's high, almost disembodied, spiritual voices – for eternal light: '*Lux aeterna luceat eis, Domine.*'

The sombre orchestral opening is contrastingly black: a huge pall of sound rapidly slashed with silver sobs from the strings amid the choir's rising shout for eternal peace and perpetual light. Mozart seems to be turning back to earlier ecclesiastical music, himself turning uneasily between heavy, traditional Baroque tomb-sculpture and the almost Romantic idiom of his charting of the soul's progress through the Dies Irae. That sequence offered him the greatest challenge, for it had never been set by him before and, combined with the force of its words, its onomatopoeia was already overwhelming. Mozart carried that even further, sending huge shudders through voices and strings at the words '*Quantus tremor*', calling the trombone sepulchrally to sound before the measured bass delivery of '*Tuba mirum spargens sonum*', letting a triple salute of '*Rex*' reverberate before trumpets and chorus hail the '*Rex tremendae majestatis*' and making hauntingly distant the barely voiced appeal of '*Voca me cum benedictis*'. The Last Judgement, the flames of hell, the crushed soul weeping in penitence and terror: each in turn is pictured, but the anguished uncertainty is never resolved – and perhaps it could not be.

The more intensely Mozart conjured up this eschatology, the more he must have hesitated over his own commitment to it. Death is here no friend and the individual's bravery ('*Ho fermo il core in petto*', as Don Giovanni declaimed before the prospect of damnation) is no aid to salvation. The close of the Dies Irae finds the soul like a cinder, needing to be watered by tears of repentance and revived by the mercy of God. Where every man is guilty there is no place for '*Lieb*' und *Bruderbund*'.

The failure to finish the Requiem seems to indicate emotional, and perhaps also asrtistic, doubt. No requiem mass was to be held in Vienna at Mozart's own death; as usual, it was reserved for Prague to pay him due homage, and there a requiem was celebrated with muffled drums and trumpets and Madame Duschek as soloist, attended by a vast congregation. But at Vienna his own masonic lodge commemorated him by a circular letter (unfortunately lost) and by an oration on his death which does survive. The two types of memorial symbolize the two aspects of Mozart's nature, fused in the finished, triumphant temple which by the end *Die Zauberflöte* has become, but riven in the Requiem which is fissured, not only perhaps by doubt but by fear. The emotions excavated are too cavernous for the edifice – at least when this is being built by someone whose physical strength is failing and whose best hope of survival lies in creating positive, affirmatory statements. Mozart might turn back to Handel, but it has well been said of him (by Brigid Brophy in *Mozart the Dramatist*) that he could not achieve in the Requiem the supreme confidence of asserting: 'I *know* that my redeemer liveth.'

It was in an actual masonic temple, the one where a few months later the oration on him was to be delivered, that Mozart appeared for the last time in public. He was conducting his last piece of music, the cantata '*Laut verkünde unsre Freude*' (K.623), celebrating the inauguration of the new premises of his own lodge. On 15 November he listed the work in his *Verzeichnüss*; on 18 November he conducted it. Radiance and jubilation stream from the music – free from weariness or shadow, and the more moving for its apparent energy at a time when Mozart had scarcely three weeks to live.

The cheerful yet hymn-like chorus which opens and closes the cantata suggests not recollection of Handel but anticipation of Beethoven, while in other passages *Die Zauberflöte* comes to mind. Schikaneder possibly, or Gieseke more probably, wrote the words; and '*Weisheit*' and '*Tugend*' and '*Arbeit*'* still retain their power to inspire Mozart. A long tenor

* 'wisdom' ... 'virtue' ... 'labour'.

recitative leads into an ardent, Tamino-style aria, followed by a solemn duet for a second tenor and bass, all celebrating the festal day and virtually consecrating the new temple. This is religious music, elevated, universal and irresistibly joyful.

Where can we find ways to conquer the enemy of nature, death? a fellow-mason was to ask rhetorically in the oration delivered after Mozart's death. He answered – as Mozart too would have done – that the means lie in 'our masonic temple', built in order to form good men. That is the belief which radiates from the cantata which celebrates inauguration of the new temple of the ideally-named 'New-Crowned Hope' lodge, and which also becomes quite solemnly Mozart's parting musical message to mankind. After all his experiences, illnesses and penury, with his genius broken at last by years of over-exertion and discouragement, he roused himself to express once again that fundamental belief which had burned at the heart of *Figaro* no less than at the heart of *Die Zauberflöte*: a hope for mankind coming eventually to live *'in der beste Harmonie'*.

On the evening of conducting his cantata, Mozart had perhaps already felt the symptoms of an approaching chill. As a child, and probably also during adulthood, he had often fallen ill quite suddenly. By 20 November he had taken to his bed. From the first, this chill seemed unusually serious, and possibly already at this stage he appeared so alarmingly ill that a doctor was sent for in the night.

That it was more than an ordinary chill became obvious as his joints swelled. What had begun as a chill was turning into a fever, rheumatic fever probably, of the kind he had suffered from dreadfully when a small boy at The Hague, and from a severe bout of which Dr Barisani had probably cured him in Vienna. The Mozarts' new doctor, Dr Closset, was only two years older than Mozart and was a celebrated, popular physician, earning a salary of a thousand gulden from his appointment alone as personal doctor to Kaunitz. He had written learnedly on putrid fever a few years before, and seems rapidly to have recognized that Mozart's case was very grave indeed – perhaps hopeless.

He had been Mozart's doctor long enough to know that natural physical frailty was overcome in Mozart only by incredible nervous energy. Closset had been attending him in the black summer of 1789, when Mozart's creative ability had temporarily been swallowed up in physical weakness and total misery. In the November of 1791, it was perhaps physical weakness that was more to be feared, especially as Mozart's state fluctuated without really improving. He took medicine, and the chemists' bills mounted up. Yet he did not recover.

St Cecilia's day, 22 November, was Frau Weber's name-day. Mozart was much too ill to go and congratulate her, but when Sophie Weber came to see him on what must have been the following Saturday he claimed that he should be well enough to congratulate his mother-in-law in person on the octave of her feast day, Tuesday 29 November. Yet Sophie may have doubted, if she saw how swollen Mozart's body had grown – for all the bravery of his claim, made at a moment when he was perhaps feeling less feverish. It was becoming painful for him to move in the bed and privately he had probably begun to wonder if he would ever get up again. Possibly on this visit Sophie brought the dressing-gown she and Frau Weber had made as a convalescent present; it was not mentioned among Mozart's possessions in the inventory of four days after his death, presumably because – unlike the itemized two nightgowns, four white cravats, one nightcap and eighteen pocket handkerchiefs – it had never been used.

Before the octave of St Cecilia was over, Dr Closset summoned a younger colleague and friend, Dr Matthias von Sallaba, to a consultation at Mozart's bedside. Still in his twenties, Sallaba – a native of Mozart's beloved Prague – had published earlier in the year a *Historia Naturalis Morborum*, dedicated to Closset. The book contains a detailed account of '*inflammatio rheumatica*', and reports one case when Sallaba had called in Closset and they had argued about the significance of the patient's symptoms. Closset had proved correct, not least over the likely termination of the illness: a fortnight after the consultation the patient died.

About Mozart's symptoms there must have been little argument by Monday 28 November, when the two respected but powerless experts met. Mozart retained complete consciousness, and this meeting can only have confirmed for him that he had no more than a short time to live. One task remained unfinished – the Requiem – and perhaps this loomed more prominently to the dying man than all the work he had accomplished. There had often been times when he delayed, when he had been creatively blocked until the last moment, but nearly always he had managed to emerge triumphant. It was true that he had never completed the commissions from the King of Prussia, but of scarcely any other major commission, the Requiem apart, could that be said. And of finished works, a very approximate count indeed would have established more than six hundred, carrying him back to what Leopold had proudly entitled 'Opus No. 1', published at Paris in 1764 by '*J. G. Wolfgang Mozart de Salzbourg, Agé de Sept Ans*'. Leopold dated the beginning of Mozart's actual composing to two years earlier: a career of thirty years, if Mozart had survived a little longer and reached his thirty-sixth birthday on 27 January 1792.

In fact, he had a bare week to live. Only three or possibly four people were present in the room when he died, and of them only Sophie Weber left any account. She wrote it years later; she muddled a few, unimportant, things and doubtless she often told the story before she set it down for Constanze's second husband's biography of her first husband. But Sophie Weber had been present; and the agony she experienced during the day and night which culminated in Mozart's death is still so fresh in her narrative as to give it artless but harrowing authenticity. She claims no dramatic last words and no great death-scene but conveys a numbness alternating with fluster in the living, and in Mozart resignation combined with final thoughtfulness for Constanze. Her words are the best, least lurid light provided to take us back into the room where Mozart lay.

Mozart continued to retain consciousness, but physically he was weakening. From childhood his sensibility had been acute; he would weep if told he was not loved, Schachtner, the Salzburg court-trumpeter, remembered. As an adult, he remained easily moved to tears by parting and absence, those tokens of death. And now his sensibility was exacerbated unbearably, and the song of his pet canary (which had replaced the dead starling) was too great a strain on his emotions. It had to be removed out of earshot. The starling had been nearly able to whistle the theme of the rondo from his then most recent piano concerto (K.453), and the unbearableness of the canary's song lay perhaps in its ability to catch some tune from *Die Zauberflöte*, possibly Papageno's opening '*Der Vogelfänger bin ich ja*'. Six years later Constanze was to give a concert in Prague and to offer little Franz Xaver Wolfgang Mozart, making his first public appearance, singing this very song.

Thoughts of *Die Zauberflöte* and the *Requiem* seem to have pressed alternately on the dying man: the achieved success which he could follow now only in imagination, and the quite unfinished work which it seemed he would never hear. Another week was ending, the fever no doubt taking its course, and it might appear remarkable that Mozart still lived. A new month had come. It was Saturday 3 December, and Mozart had been in bed for very nearly a fortnight. That evening the fever flared so violently that Constanze was convinced he would not survive the night. He did, however; but by the Sunday there could no longer be any illusion about the imminence of death.

When Sophie Weber came in the morning to enquire, Constanze met her and told her of the dreadful previous night, begging her to stay. Constanze could not bear even to go into the room at that moment; she sent Sophie in to see how Mozart was. He was fully conscious, and totally aware. In turn, he too begged Sophie to stay the night, saying: '*Sie müssen mich sterben sehen.*'* She attempted reassurance, but he pleaded with her to remain to comfort Constanze. For himself, he already had – he told her – the taste of death on his tongue.

Sophie agreed to stay, but had first to return home and explain the position to Frau Weber. Constanze took her to the door and asked her to go also to one of the local churches, St Peter's, to try to get a priest to come. St Peter's was probably chosen because this had been the parish church of Frau Weber and her daughters when they first moved to Vienna, and it was there that two of Mozart's children had been baptized. Sophie set off on both tasks, probably going first to the church, where she had some difficulty in persuading a priest – conceivably because Mozart was well known to be a mason, or because he was living outside the parish. She had then to go back outside the main city, to the Wieden district, close to Schikaneder's theatre, where she and her mother lived. All this took time, more probably than she quite recollected. Frau Weber, shocked by the news, was persuaded not to spend the night alone but to stay with her other daughter, Josepha Hofer, '*die Königin der Nacht*'.

In the afternoon, while Sophie was absent, Hofer and the Tamino of the production, Benedikt Schack, were among the small group who came to Mozart's bedside for a rehearsal of the *Requiem*. Schack took the soprano part; Hofer was the tenor; the bass was sung by the current Sarastro; and Mozart himself was the alto. The audience probably consisted of Constanze and Süssmayr. Schack was a good friend of Mozart's, recognized as such long afterwards by Constanze, acknowledging how intimately he had known her husband. Schack is the authority for the scene which Sophie, as she hurried in and out of Vienna, did not witness. The rehearsal began. The four singers reached

* 'You must see me die.'

the Dies irae, but got no further than the verse '*Lacrymosa dies illa*'. The force of those words had become too terrible to be endured. Mozart laid the score aside, and started to weep bitterly.

Sophie saw the score, lying on the quilt, when she returned to the apartment. Schack and the other singers had gone. Mozart had recovered sufficiently to be explaining to Süssmayr how the *Requiem* should be completed. Süssmayr probably stayed, alone with the two women and the sinking man. At some point a priest came. Mozart did not take communion, as his mother had in her last illness, but he was annointed and received the sacrament of extreme unction.

Even while Sophie had been hastening back through the streets, it had been growing dark. It was now Sunday night. *Die Zauberflöte* had often been played on a Sunday, and perhaps was again that evening; the theatres were certainly open. The Rauhensteingasse was probably quite quiet, and the first-floor apartment overlooking the street even quieter. Mozart lay, presumably in what was so soon to be itemized as the 'matrimonial bed', dying by degrees yet still conscious: swollen in body, suffering more and more from a burning head, suffering so intensely that the two frightened women felt they must send for Dr Closset.

Closset was eventually located at the theatre and there he stayed until the end of the performance. It was perhaps his duty, if he was some sort of theatre-physician; or perhaps it was impossible to get a message to him until the play was over. He came to the apartment, but there was little he could suggest for relief except the application of cold compresses. Afterwards, Sophie said she had ventured to question the wisdom of this. However, she put the cold compresses round Mozart's fevered head, with its profusion of fine pale hair of which he had once been proud. Such a violent shock at once convulsed the body into unconsciousness.

Midnight merged into the first hour of the new day, Monday 5 December. Mozart had noted the clock striking when writing to Constanze a few months earlier, but he heard nothing now because he had slipped into a coma. Some sort of painful movement, however, continued to be made by his lips – perhaps, as Sophie believed, some fragment of music somewhere forced itself onto his breath, possibly indeed a last recollection of the Requiem.

Then even the movement of the lips ceased. It was five minutes to one o'clock in the morning. Mozart was dead.

Afterword

THIS book, as will be clear to anyone who has read it, is the work of a Mozart-lover who is no musicologist. I have not pretended to what I do not possess in the way of knowledge; nor can I claim to have carried out any original research. I happily, gratefully, acknowledge debts to the classic biographies and studies of Mozart, from Nissen and Jahn onwards, including the Wyzewa and Saint-Foix volumes, Alfred Einstein's work and the many contributions of Otto Deutsch, culminating in his *Documentary Biography*, which has been beside me throughout writing. On that and the Bauer-Deutsch edition of Mozart's *Briefe und Aufzeichnungen* my biographical framework has been based. I should also mention Dr Ludwig Alois Friedrich, Ritter von Köchel, whose often revised, corrected and expanded catalogue of Mozart's work still remains 'Köchel'; *Der kleine Köchel*, in the 1968 edition, has been another desk-side companion.

What I append as bibliography is no more than a few books which are accessible, often in English; some of them are referred to in the text. There is no need for a display of bibliographical erudition, for up to 1962 at least the *Mozart-Handbuch*, edited by O. Schneider and A. Algatzy, will provide references to reading matter for the seriously interested which should occupy them for about a decade.

At the same time, I should like to acknowledge a more general debt to all those people in recent years, in various countries, who have revived – and often recorded – so much eighteenth-century music, including many operas. That one may now write and speak, however amateurishly, as having heard the music of Wagenseil, Stamitz, Boyce, Avison and Sammartini, to name only a few, is an advantage for which I feel truly grateful. I realize my great good fortune, too, in having seen several of Mozart's earliest operas, as well as some of those by once famous composers like Piccini and Grétry; and it was nice that the path to writing this book led via such places as Wexford and Drottningholm.

I owe a specific debt of gratitude to Mr Eric Hughes of the British Institute of Recorded Sound, through whose great kindness I have been able to hear, and thus admire, *Mitridate*. Mr David Williams, of the Central Library at Grimsby, was most courteously co-operative in arranging for me to have access to the now rare 1956 Philips recording of *La Finta Semplice*. I am very grateful to Robert Cook, who in a crisis period typed a part of this book, made many useful enquiries in connection with it and who perhaps stimulated the whole project when a few years ago he gave me for Christmas the Hachette *Génies et Réalités* volume on Mozart. For much generous comment on the work in progress I must thank Christopher White. And I should gratefully record the kindly reception by my publishers of both the project and the performance; I feel fortunate to have met there such enthusiasm for Mozart.

There remains one long-standing debt, of which I am very conscious. Over several years I have depended on the skill of Mrs Grace Ginnis for the typing of my work. This book in particular owes much to her ability and interest, and offers a suitable occasion for stating my warm gratitude.

M. L.

Some Books for Further Reading

Abert, H., *W.A.Mozart. Neuarbeitete und erweiterte Ausgabe von Otto Jahns Mozart*, 1923–4

Anderson, E., *The Letters of Mozart and his Family*, 1938; (2nd ed.) with additions etc., ed. A.Hyatt King and M.Carolan, 1966

Bär, C., *Mozart: Krankheit-Tod-Begräbnis*, 1966

Batley, E.M., *A Preface to the Magic Flute*, 1969

Bauer, W.A. and Deutsch, O.E., *Mozart: Briefe und Aufzeichnungen*, 1962

Benn, C., *Mozart on the Stage*, 1946

Brophy, B., *Mozart the Dramatist*, 1964

Dent, E.J., *Mozart's Operas*, 1949

Deutsch, O.E., *Mozart und seiner Welt in zeitgenössischen Bilder*, 1961

Deutsch, O.E., *Mozart, A Documentary Biography* (transl. E.Blom, P.Branscombe and J. Noble), 1965

Einstein, A., *Mozart, his character, his work*, 1965

Farmer, H.G. and Smith, H., *New Mozartiana*, 1935

Fitzlyon, A., *The Libertine Librettist* (Da Ponte), 1955

Greither, A., *Mozart*, 1970

Holmes, E., *The Life of Mozart*, 1st ed., 1845, Everyman ed., n.d.

Jahn, O., *Wolfgang Amadeus Mozart*, 1856–9 (transl. P.Townsend, 1882)

Jouve, P.J., *Mozart's Don Juan* (transl. E.Earnshaw Smith) 1957

Kelly, M., *Reminiscences* (ed. T.Hook), 1826

King, A.Hyatt, *Mozart in Retrospect*, 1955

King, A.Hyatt, *Mozart Chamber Music* (BBC Music Guide), 1968

Komorzynski, E.von, *Emanuel Schikaneder*, 1951

Lang, P.H. (ed.), *The Creative World of Mozart*, 1963

Levarie, S., *Mozart's Le Nozze di Figaro*, 1952

Medici, N. and Hughes, R., *A Mozart Pilgrimage* (Novello travel diaries), 1955

Mueller von Asow, H. and E.H., *Collected Correspondence and Papers of Christoph Willibald Gluck* (transl. S. Thomson), 1962

Nettl, P., *Mozart and Masonry*, 1957

Pusch, E. (ed.), *Letters of an Empress* (Maria Theresia to her children and friends), (transl. E.R. Taylor), 1939

Robbins Landon, H.C. and Mitchell, D., *The Mozart Companion*, 1956

Robbins Landon, H.C., *Collected Correspondence and London Notebooks of Joseph Haydn*, 1959

Robinson, M.F., *Opera before Mozart*, 1966

Russo, L., *Metastasio*, 1921

SOME BOOKS FOR FURTHER READING

Saint-Foix, G. de, *The Symphonies of Mozart* (transl. L. Orrey), 1947

Schenk, E., *Mozart and his Times* (ed. and transl. R. and C.Winston), 1960

Sheppard, L.A. (ed. and transl.), *Memoirs of Lorenzo da Ponte*, 1929

Terry, C.S., *Johann Christian Bach* (foreword by H.C.Robbins Landon), 1967

Valentin, E., *Der früheste Mozart*, 1956

Valentin, E., *Mozart, a Pictorial Biography*, 1962

Wangermann, E., *From Joseph II to the Jacobin Trials*, 1959

Wyzewa, T.von and Saint-Foix, G.de, *Wolfgang Amédée Mozart. Sa vie musicale et son œuvre*, 1912–46

Index

Index of Persons

Index of Works

Note: K. stands for the number of the work as per Köchel's (revised) catalogue.